HOW TO SURVIVE

MIDDLE SCHOOL

U.S.
HISTORY

Visit us on the Web! rhcbooks.com

Educators and librarians, for a variety of teaching tools, visit us at RHTeachersLibrarians.com

Library of Congress Cataloging-in-Publication Data is available upon request.

ISBN 978-0-525-57144-5 (trade)

ISBN: 978-0-525-57149-0 (ebook)

Printed in the United States of America

10 9 8 7 6 5 4 3 2 1

First Edition

Random House Children's Books supports the First Amendment and celebrates the right to read.

Writers: Rebecca Ascher-Walsh, Annie Scavelli, Elizabeth Fee, Greg Brooking
Curriculum and Equity Consultant: Sonja Cherry-Paul
U.S. History Consultant: Greg Brooking
Sideshow Media Editorial and Production Team: Dan Tucker, Julia DeVarti
Penguin Random House Publishing Team: Tom Russell, Alison Stoltzfus, Brett Wright, Emily Harburg, Eugenia Lo, Katy Miller

Produced by Sideshow Media LLC
Illustration and Design by Carpenter Collective

HOW TO SURVIVE
MIDDLE SCHOOL

A DO-IT-YOURSELF STUDY GUIDE

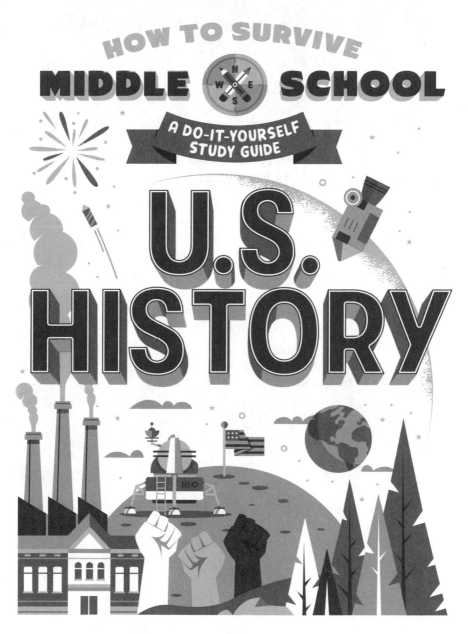

U.S. HISTORY

REBECCA ASCHER-WALSH, ANNIE SCAVELLI

BRIGHT
MATTER
BOOKS
NEW YORK

TABLE OF CONTENTS

INTRODUCTION
HISTORY: A FACT-FINDING MISSION WITH THRILLING NEW DISCOVERIES!   1

CHAPTER 1   13
BEFORE AND AFTER THE EUROPEANS ARRIVED

1. Studying U.S. History: Where Do We Start?   14

2. Original American Populations   18

3. Europeans Enter the Picture   25

4. European Colonization of North America   28

CHAPTER 2   39
HOW THE UNITED STATES CAME TO BE

1. An Irresistible Opportunity   40

2. The French and Indian War (1754–1763)   46

3. The Rise, and Rising Up, of the Colonies   49

4. The Founding Fathers and One Founding Mother   54

5. The Declaration of Independence   57

6. Battling It Out   59

7. The Constitution: A Tale of Two Houses   65

8. A New President for a New Country   72

CHAPTER 3   77
WESTWARD EXPANSION

1. Double or Nothing: The Louisiana Purchase   78

2. Lewis and Clark Expedition   84

3. *Marbury v. Madison* and Judicial Review   88

4. The War of 1812   94

5. From Homespun to Factory: The First Industrial Revolution   97

6. Andrew Jackson and Jacksonian Democracy   100

7. A New President and an Economic Depression   105

8. The Mexican-American War   106

CHAPTER 4   111
A WAR IS BREWING

1. The Excuse for Enslavement   112

2. The Abolitionist Movement   117

3. The Underground Railroad   124

4. The Nat Turner Rebellion   128

5. The Government Tries to Keep the Country Together   131

6. A Turning Point Toward War   137

7. The Election of 1860   139

CHAPTER 5   145

THE CIVIL WAR AND ITS AFTERMATH

1. Southern Uprising   146

2. The Emancipation Proclamation   151

3. Black Soldiers in the Union Army   153

4. War Rages On   158

5. The Gettysburg Address   164

6. Reconstruction   167

7. A Country Now Connected, Literally   173

8. The End of Reconstruction   175

CHAPTER 6   181

THE GILDED AGE AND THE PROGRESSIVE ERA

1. Big Change Rides the Rails   182

2. What Was the Gilded Age?   187

3. The Second Industrial Revolution and Immigration   191

4. Factory Work   197

5. The Rise of Big Business   203

6. The Jim Crow South   206

7. The Progressive Era and the Social Gospel   209

CHAPTER 7 — 221

THE UNITED STATES ENTERS A WORLD WAR

1. America's New International Influence — 222

2. Theodore Roosevelt Steps into the Presidency — 225

3. The Women's Movement Gains Momentum — 236

4. The United States Enters World War I — 241

5. The War Ends — 253

CHAPTER 8 — 259

FROM ROARING TO WARRING: THE '20S, '30S, AND '40S

1. The Roaring Twenties — 260

2. The Stock Market Crashes — 269

3. FDR: A New President and a New Deal — 275

4. The Seeds of World War II — 281

5. Two Victories for the Allies — 288

CHAPTER 9 — 295

FROM THE COLD WAR TO CIVIL RIGHTS

1. America after World War II — 296

2. A Cold War Sets In — 299

3. The Cold War in the United States — 306

4. The Civil Rights Movement — 313

CHAPTER 10   329
WAR AND DISILLUSIONMENT

1. The Vietnam War   330

2. The War at Home   335

3. Growing Distrust and Activism   343

4. The Equal Rights Amendment   346

5. Big-Time Money Troubles   348

6. The Presidency of Jimmy Carter   351

7. The Reagan Era   354

8. The AIDS Crisis Begins   359

9. President George H. W. Bush   361

CHAPTER 11   369
PROSPERITY AND CONFLICT

1. The Presidency of Bill Clinton   370

2. A War Against Crime, on U.S. Soil   377

3. Scandal and Impeachment   379

4. The George W. Bush Era   383

5. The War on Terror   387

6. The Second Term of the Bush Presidency   392

CHAPTER 12   399

A FIRST DRAFT OF THE HISTORY OF TODAY

1. The 2008 Presidential Election   400

2. The Obama Era   402

3. The 2016 Presidential Election   408

4. The Trump Presidency   409

5. Pandemic   412

6. Gun Control   415

7. The #MeToo Movement   417

8. Climate Change   419

9. A Racial Divide Continues   421

10. New Leaders Promise "A Time of Healing"   424

CHAPTER 13   429

HOW TO THINK LIKE A HISTORIAN OUT IN THE REAL WORLD OF RESEARCH, NEWS, AND SOCIAL MEDIA

1. Important Things to Know (and Emulate) about Historians   431

2. Detecting Bias   436

3. Evaluating Internet Sources   444

4. Fake News   452

BONUS SECTION 462

1. The Declaration of Independence, Translated into Plain English   462

2. U.S. Presidents   478

TEXT CREDITS 481

ABOUT THE CREATORS 482

In CONGRESS, July 4, 1776.
DECLARATION,
By the REPRESENTATIVES of the
UNITED STATES OF AMERICA,
In GENERAL CONGRESS Assembled.
W

HISTORY: A FACT-FINDING MISSION FILLED WITH THRILLING NEW DISCOVERIES!

CHAPTER CONTENTS

JOINING THE ADVENTURE

KEEPING THINGS REAL

GETTING RESOURCEFUL

PACKING UP
(OR... HOW TO USE THIS BOOK)

JOINING THE ADVENTURE

It's understandable to think that what is happening right now is the most interesting thing in the world, especially if it's about us. And it's true that history is about the past. But what's amazing is that the more we learn about the past, the more we have a chance to understand what's happening in the present. And that gives us a kind of superpower: by understanding how human beings have acted before, we can change the future!

That's especially vital when it comes to our relatively new country. In its short time of existence, it has had a history that is thrilling, inspiring, violent, shameful, hopeful, and above all, complicated.

IT'S OK TO ASK QUESTIONS AND TO THINK CRITICALLY

First and foremost, we have to throw away the idea that asking questions about our nation's history is somehow disrespectful or unpatriotic. How else will we solve problems and injustices that every country faces? We can look critically at some of the actions our country has taken, while still loving it deeply and believing in its ideals.

OUR FOUNDING DOCUMENTS

Just consider the Declaration of Independence and the Constitution—documents written by the Founding Fathers that declared the United States separate from Britain and then set up how our country would run. The Enlightenment movement in Europe inspired the Founding Fathers.

Enlightenment thinkers believed in the power of human reason and the ability to change things. You can see those ideas in the documents. No longer would human beings be the voiceless subjects of a monarch, who was answerable only to God. Now, human beings would be governed by people of their own choosing, and there would be elections from time to time to hold leaders accountable. The leaders would have to follow the same laws as everyone else.

AN IDEAL... BUT AN IMPERFECT ONE

Think about our right to free speech, or to practice whatever religion we want. These documents are filled with ideals that have helped make the United States a beacon for people drawn by the promise to have a say in how they were governed. Americans would keep individual freedoms that would guarantee them the same right to "life, liberty, and the pursuit of happiness" as every other person.

But... the United States is a complicated place and has always been so. We don't need to look further than the Declaration of Independence as an example. This document truly is extraordinary. But because *people* wrote and interpreted it—and people aren't perfect—it has its faults.

WAIT, *WHO* IS CREATED EQUAL?

Take the statement "All men are created equal," which was a stunning idea back in 1776. For the Founding Fathers, those "men" didn't include women, or either gender of Blacks and Native Americans, who certainly weren't considered equal by most people. It's been up to activists throughout history to try to make that statement more inclusive, and we are a country still struggling to right those wrongs. Consider racism in courts and businesses, or the way immigrants at the Mexican border have suffered. As you read about U.S. history, you will see ongoing conflicts between people who interpret the Declaration of Independence and Constitution in different ways.

It is all of these people who make our history so fascinating. They're people just like you and the people you know. Some made decisions you will agree with, and others made decisions you will think are terrible. But even the people who made huge, wonderful, world-changing decisions were flawed. And those flaws make them even more fascinating once we dig in and study them.

For instance: George Washington was an extraordinary general and our first president. He did so many great things to get the country up and running. He also benefited from the labor of enslaved people who "belonged" to him and his wife, Martha.

People are filled with contradictions, and history is as well. And that means that if you dig deep enough, history can be as thrilling a story as anything you've read or seen and loved.

KEEPING THINGS REAL

One of the reasons U.S. history gets a bad reputation when it comes to the excitement factor is because it's boring to read on and on about (supposedly) "perfect" people who always knew the right thing to do. And why *is* U.S. history, and Western history in general, so filled with "perfect" *white* guys? Well, it's not; it's just been told that way for a long time. As the Nigerian author Chinua Achebe once said in an interview, "Until the lions have their own historians, the history of the hunt will always glorify the hunter."

Textbooks tend to portray their nation's history in as positive a light as possible. But, in reality, history is messy. History can show us the beautiful achievements of humankind. But it also shows us the ugly side of humanity, and that can be unpleasant to face. It's so much *nicer* if it becomes a happy story, right? And plenty of educators in the past have wanted to do just that, erasing the nastier side of what humans have done. That's how history can go off the rails from fact to fiction.

GETTING RESOURCEFUL

Being a good historian, as you're learning to be, means that you don't rely just on one story before you decide what might have happened.

Here's an example: During Thomas Jefferson's first term as president, rumors began circulating that he was involved with Sally Hemings, an enslaved woman in his household. For two centuries, historians argued whether this was true. Some believed he fathered at least six of her children, while others said there was no proof. Historians have now looked at oral, written, and scientific evidence, including DNA tests. Most people accept that Jefferson fathered Hemings's children. As historians, we study the evidence, keep an open mind, and form our best conclusions.

PRIMARY AND SECONDARY SOURCES

So, what are the sources that are considered evidence? Historians rely on two kinds. The first are primary sources. This means documents of whatever variety that were created at or near the time of the event. The second is—you guessed it—secondary sources. These analyze the primary sources and explain them to help you understand them better. In this book, you'll see a combination of both.

For instance, a photograph of a Civil War battlefield taken during the war is a primary source. It shows what the battlefield looked like at the time of the battle. Another example of a primary source is a soldier's letter home to a family member. It's a firsthand account. A secondary source would be a book about the Civil War written by someone who had looked at these photographs, read the letters, and tried to make sense of it all.

You can find more information about using primary sources and secondary sources on page 432.

TEXT CHECK

Which sources can you trust online? The internet can be a big help when it comes to researching history. It can also be misleading, biased, and just plain wrong. So how do you learn the difference?

When you are reading about history online, you'll want to read at least two sources. Look for sites and studies that come from universities, newspapers, or historical societies. You'll learn much more about researching on the internet in Chapter 13, "How to Think Like a Historian."

WHO CAN YOU TRUST?

Yourself! You are learning to be an investigator of history, and that means not only learning about history, but also learning what to take in and what to question.

Keep in mind when you are reading about history that many voices have been silenced. For instance, if you can't write, your story may be omitted. If you aren't allowed to speak freely, your narrative is silenced. And if you're killed, your experience may die with you.

So what voices might be left out of U.S. history? Some important examples include poor people, Black people, Native Americans, immigrants, and women, many of whom have had their stories silenced or ignored. So while you're reading about American history, think about the voices that might be missing. Let's get quiet enough to imagine the points of view of those who couldn't speak for themselves, and what they might say if they had the chance.

Why do we capitalize the "B" when we are writing about Black people but not the "w" when we write about white people? When we use the word "Black," it speaks to a sense of identity and community. Historians have acknowledged this by capitalizing the names of other ethnic groups, such as Asians or Native Americans. It also returns some of the power that was stripped from Black people when they were enslaved and forced to come to this country. White people have less shared history and culture, and for the most part they haven't experienced discrimination based on skin color. In 2020, the Associated Press, an important global media organization, announced it would make this change in its articles.

FINALLY, REMEMBER HISTORY IS ALWAYS BREAKING NEWS!

Every day, through the work of historians, archaeologists, and other academics, we learn more about what happened in the past. That means the narrative of history is always changing, and we are always learning more. History isn't about dusty old papers; it's a living, breathing thing. You might be the one to discover something new.

History isn't "his" story, or the stories of other random people that have nothing to do with us. History is *our* story, and about how we came to be who we are today. So let's do some digging!

PACKING UP (OR. . . HOW TO USE THIS BOOK)

Before you get going on this exciting adventure, here are some presents for you: tools to help you navigate. You'll see them pop up in the pages ahead as guideposts, along with some questions and ways to think about what you're reading. Check them out:

SYMBOL/ TOOL	WHAT IT IS	HOW TO USE IT WHILE YOU READ
	People use a GPS so they don't get lost. It helps them figure out where they are, get directions, or explore a new area.	When you see the GPS, stop and pay attention to the big picture. You might… • Ask yourself some big picture questions before you read. • Preview the text by skimming the headings, timelines, charts, and illustrations.
	Boots give hikers sure footing, even on rocky paths. All serious hikers pull on their boots before setting out.	Think of boots as knowledge you already have that supports new knowledge. When you see the boots, it's time to: • Think back on what you already know about the topic. • Recall something you've already read about.
	A pickaxe is a digging tool. Notice how it has a sharp point to get into small places!	Your pickaxe will help you dig deeply for meaning. Take it out when you need to… • Dig out important words or phrases that help you understand the text. • Find evidence and important details.

	People use binoculars to see things that are far away. But people in different places will see the same thing differently.	Binoculars will remind you to consider point of view in a text. You will need to think about things like… • Who is telling the story? • Whose story is *not* told? • How would someone else see this? • Who wrote this text, when, and why?
	People use a magnifying glass to examine something up close.	The magnifying glass will remind you to stop and focus on one thing. You can magnify your understanding by… • Thinking about how one part is important to the whole. • Paying attention to new vocabulary.
	Stop and pay attention.	• Beware of a common misconception or a common error.

You'll notice that vocabulary terms appear throughout the book in yellow boxes like these. Definitions for these terms are also collected for you at the end of each chapter.

SO WHAT'S IN IT FOR YOU?

First and foremost—and you'll have to trust us on this—fun. Because when you realize that you're stopping to think about these people and their ideas, and not just memorizing dates and names, you'll suddenly feel it all click. When you learn more about the past, it's easier to understand where and how you live right now. And when that happens, you'll want to learn much more.

Once you understand the past, you haven't just gained knowledge. You've accessed your superpower to change the future. So grab your backpack and get to it!

1 BEFORE AND AFTER THE EUROPEANS ARRIVED

"American" history began long before the first European colonists arrived. In fact, people had lived and thrived on the land for thousands of years before Europeans got here. The cultures of these Native peoples inform some of the ways we live today, as well as who we are. Let's uncover who they were and why they matter.

CHAPTER CONTENTS

STUDYING U.S. HISTORY: WHERE DO WE START?

ORIGINAL AMERICAN POPULATIONS

EUROPEANS ENTER THE PICTURE

EUROPEAN COLONIZATION OF NORTH AMERICA

STUDYING U.S. HISTORY: WHERE DO WE START?

It can be difficult to imagine the world without you in it, right? That's how many historians have felt as well. Historians are expert at recognizing bias in their sources, but many have written or talked about U.S. history without recognizing their own biases. Until recently, most historians have been white people—white men, by and large. This means that sometimes it can seem as if America began when Christopher Columbus set foot here, or when the first colonizers arrived. In fact, people have been living in North America for tens of thousands of years.

How can we possibly know anything from that time? Historians work alongside archaeologists, who discover and study physical remains (such as pottery) from ancient cultures. Historians also work with anthropologists, who look at how human beings used to live. And they work with linguists, who study language. In the next sections, you'll learn some of what they found out.

archaeologist: a scientist who studies human history by digging up and excavating sites and analyzing the artifacts they found there. It's a lot of digging in the dirt and learning secrets about ancient societies!

anthropologist: someone who studies how human beings used to live. Anthropology is a bit of a combination of history and science.

linguist: someone who studies speech and language.

A WORD ABOUT DATES

When you're reading about ancient history, you're going to run into abbreviations before or after the date. Let's take a look at some of those:

BC: Before the birth of Jesus Christ

AD: Anno Domini (Latin for "the year of our Lord")

BCE: Before the Common Era

CE: In the Common Era

You'll often see "BC," or before the birth of Jesus. That's because the Romans, who controlled much of the world in ancient times, became Christian. The Roman calendar was popular throughout Europe and Asia. The Common Era came along later to unify many of the world's calendars and remove any religious associations. So "10 BC" and "10 BCE" are different ways of referring to the same year.

50 BCE	25 BCE	1 CE	25 CE	50 CE	75 CE
-50	-25	0+1	+25	+50	+75

Looking at the timeline can help you understand how this works. (Notice that there's no year zero on the timeline, because there never was a year "0.")

When you see "BC" or "BCE" before something, the bigger the number, the longer ago it was. For example, 50 BC is 25 years longer ago than 25 BC. And when it comes to centuries, the century refers to what we think of as 100 years before that. So the first century refers to the years 1 to 100, the twentieth century refers to the 1900s, the twenty-first century refers to the century beginning in 2001, and so on.

A GREAT MIGRATION

The first humans lived in southern Africa some 200,000 years ago. At some point, groups of them made their way to what is now Europe and Asia, and then on to North, South, and Central America.

How did they get from Europe and Asia to North America? Nobody knows for sure. For a long time, people thought that 13,000 years ago, people moved from Siberia into Alaska by traveling on a land bridge that connected the two places at the time. From Alaska, they moved throughout North America. But that theory got kicked to the curb when archaeologists found sites that showed people had been on the continent for as long as 2,000 years before then.

The next theory to be tossed around was that as the ice sheets covering North America melted, people traveled down the Pacific shore by boat on something called the Kelp Highway (*kelp* is a kind of seaweed). If this is right, people first arrived in North America at least 22,000 years ago.

land bridge: just what it sounds like: a connecting piece of land. Since the continents have shifted over time, land bridges allowed travel between places that are now separated by oceans.

DISCOVERY AT COOPER'S FERRY

Archaeologists discovered the oldest human artifacts (human-made objects) in North America at a site in Cooper's Ferry, Idaho in 2019. Archaeologists found stemmed points, which include blades, spears, and knives. In a blow to the land bridge theory, tests called carbon dating showed that the artifacts may be 16,000 years old. Interestingly, they observed that the artifacts were similar in form to those found in Japan from the same period.

 Why do you think it could be important that the stem points scientists found in Idaho are similar to the ones found in Japan?

_____

_____

_____

_____

_____

LAND OR LANGUAGE?

Historians group some Indigenous American populations based on where those groups lived. For instance, the Plains Native Americans is a category that includes many nations whose members lived in the middle of North America. Historians group others based on what language they spoke. More than 100 nations, including the Cheyenne, Mohicans, and Ottawa, have lived all over the country. But many historians call them Algonquians for the language these peoples share.

ORIGINAL AMERICAN POPULATIONS

INDIGENOUS CULTURAL AREAS IN NORTH AMERICA AROUND 1600

Here are some of the major **prehistoric** regions that were home to loosely allied Indigenous nations.

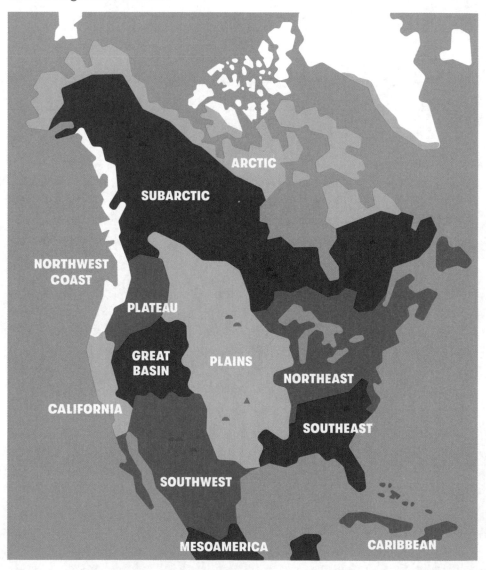

ARCTIC

SUBARCTIC

NORTHWEST COAST

PLATEAU

GREAT BASIN

PLAINS

NORTHEAST

CALIFORNIA

SOUTHEAST

SOUTHWEST

MESOAMERICA

CARIBBEAN

The ancient Puebloans, who have been traced to 7000 BCE, lived on the Colorado Plateau. People today call this the Four Corners because it is near where the corners of four state borders meet in the Southwest: Arizona, Colorado, Utah, and New Mexico. It is still home to nations that include the Navajo, Apache, and Pueblo.

THE SOUTHWEST

THE ANCESTRAL PUEBLOANS

The Ancestral Puebloans (that's the term used by most modern Pueblo) developed sophisticated irrigation systems to water their crops of corn and squash. They built villages and cities. One city, Chaco Canyon, had almost 12,000 people and 400 miles of roads, allowing trade with neighboring regions. That city flourished between about A.D. 800 and 1200. You can visit Chaco Culture National Historical Park in New Mexico.

Pueblo architecture

The architecture of the Ancestral Puebloans was so durable that some is still standing today. They used adobe bricks, mud, and stone to create multistory structures. These were built out in the open but also on the sides of cliffs. To keep homes safe from animals and intruders, the ancient Pueblo made some accessible by ladders only.

prehistoric: the word used to describe the time before humans began writing down history.

THE APACHE

The Apache arrived in the areas that now include Texas, Arizona, New Mexico, and Oklahoma between 1000 and 1400 CE. They lived in **wickiups**, also called **wigwams**, and **tepees**. Wickiups were more permanent, domed homes made from young trees. Tepees, which were easy to move, were made from long poles covered with buffalo skins and shaped like upside-down ice cream cones.

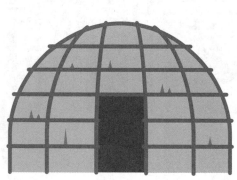

Wickiup

Tepee

wigwam: a domed home made from young trees. Also called a **wickiup**.

tepee: a shelter made from long poles covered with buffalo skins and shaped like an upside-down ice cream cone.

THE SOUTHEAST

Prior to the arrival of European colonizers, nations including the Cherokee, Chickasaw, Choctaw, Seminole, and Natchez lived in the Mississippi Valley. According to the Chickasaw migration story, they and the Choctaw were once a single nation. The Chickasaw, who were both hunters and farmers, were great warriors. They are also famous for playing stickball, or "Itti' kapochcha to'li'," which was the origin of what we know as lacrosse. Most of their villages had stickball fields.

AN ANCIENT CITY IN ILLINOIS

Cahokia, in what is now Illinois, was a thriving city from about 700 CE to 1400 CE. With as many as 20,000 residents and taking up about six square miles, it rivaled the size of Europe's greatest cities. This massive trading depot had not only homes but large structures, pottery, tools, and enormous earthen mounds. It is likely that members of the Chickasaw nation came from Cahokia. You can visit the Cahokia site today.

THE NORTHEAST

The Northeast was home to the Haudenosaunee (Iroquois), the Delaware, and the Shawnee, among others. French colonists called the Haudenosaunee the Iroquois. This is not how they refer to themselves, and today, more historians and journalists are using "Haudenosaunee."

They were a group of six nations, and "Haudenosaunee" means "people who build a house."

Haudenosaunee (Iroquois) longhouse

They lived in structures called longhouses, which generally measured 80 to 100 feet. The homes didn't have windows, but they had a door at each end and holes in the roof so that smoke from fires could escape. Often many families would share a single longhouse.

The Haudenosaunee were farmers as well as hunters. Villages would move every two decades or so to find the best arable land for growing crops and hunting. Their confederacy, which began sometime between 1100 and 1400 CE, is the oldest continuous democracy in the world.

WOMEN'S ROLES

Women had social equality in Haudenosaunee society. They had an important role in government. Female representatives went to Great Council meetings, where chiefs from each tribe gathered to make decisions. Women owned the land on which the nation grew crops.

Haudenosaunee society was matrilineal. After a man and a woman got married, the man would move into the woman's family's longhouse. Women also participated in traditional men's activities such as gambling, and belonged to Medicine Societies, which were spiritual groups.

THE NORTHWEST COAST

Nations including the Chinook, Tillamook, and Makah lived in the Pacific Northwest. They made totem poles and built their houses from planks of cedar, a type of sweet-smelling wood. Totem poles were specific to this region and typically represented ancestors or events.

THE NEZ PERCE

The Pacific Northwest was also home to the Nez Perce, which was a name given to them by French trappers and means "pierced nose." However, they did not typically pierce their noses, and their real name was the Nimiipuu, meaning "the walking people." They were skilled riders and created the Appaloosa horse breed.

Does knowing about the renaming of Indigenous nations change your understanding of them? What does it tell you about the relationship between European colonizers and the Indigenous nations?

_____

_____

_____

_____

_____

_____

A COMPLICATING FACTOR

Because of migration and a lack of written records, it can be difficult to know which current nations are direct descendants of any one specific prehistoric group.

longhouses: structures that the Iroquois peoples lived in. They were literally long homes, and generally measured 80 to 100 feet. They had no windows, but they had a door at each end and holes in the roof so that smoke from fires could escape.

arable land: any land that is able to produce crops and is good for farming.

totem poles: very large carvings usually made from trees that typically represented ancestors or important events. Some common crests found on totem poles include the eagle, killer whale, salmon, and grizzly bear.

matrilineal: the practice of tracing one's relatives and assigning inheritance based on the mother's side of the family.

TRADING AMONG THE INDIGENOUS NATIONS

Indigenous nations traded with one another. The Pueblo city in Chaco Canyon mentioned on page 19, for example, drew traders from all over the region and beyond. In the Northeast, the Haudenosaunee and Algonquians built canoes and were able to travel to the West and Southeast to trade their fur pelts. For money, they used purple and white wampum beads.

wampum: small purple and white beads made from shells. Many Native American nations used them as money.

EUROPEANS ENTER THE PICTURE

Historians believe that Christopher Columbus was from Genoa, which is now part of Italy. He was a sailor who, in the fifteenth century, approached Spain's king and queen and asked them to pay him to find a trade route to Asia.

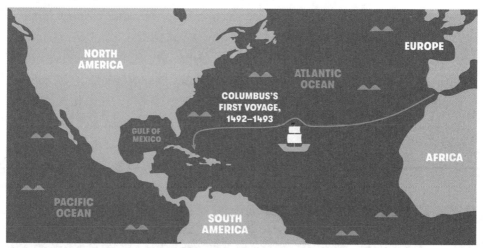

On his first journey to the Americas, Columbus landed in the Caribbean islands.

HOW'S THAT FOR A SENSE OF DIRECTION?

In 1492, Columbus guided three ships to what he thought was India. But instead of going east, in what would have been the most direct route to Asia, he headed out across the Atlantic Ocean, hoping to find a new route to Asia. (Hey, there were no accurate maps of the world yet—someone had to try it.) He arrived at a group of islands six weeks later. Positive he was near India, he called these islands the "West Indies."

The early Taíno people left various symbols and markings on caves and walls across the region. This symbol is widely understood to be the symbol for the Taíno people.

In fact, these were the Caribbean islands, which lie southeast of the United States. Columbus called the natives "Indians," but they were an Indigenous, Arawakan-speaking people called the Taíno who lived throughout the Caribbean Islands and in Southern Florida. Columbus claimed one of the islands for Spain and named it Hispaniola. We now know it as the island divided into the Dominican Republic and Haiti.

WHO WAS FIRST?

Columbus was not the first European to reach North America. An Icelandic explorer, Erik Thorvaldsson (known as "Erik the Red"), established a colony in Greenland around 985. However, Columbus became the most famous. That's because white colonizers from Europe set out for the Americas in large numbers to follow his lead.

TRUE STORY: COLUMBUS BRUTALIZED THE TAÍNO

Columbus had noticed the Taíno wearing tiny gold earrings and mistakenly thought there was gold in the area. (There turned out to be only gold flecks from the riverbed.) He left 39 men on the island to force the Taíno to help them find gold. He also enslaved 25 of the Taíno to be sold upon his return to Spain. Fewer than half survived the Atlantic journey.

When Columbus returned on his second voyage, he found that the Taíno had killed the colonizers. This time when he returned to Spain, he brought with him 400 kidnapped Taíno and enslaved them.

COLUMBUS'S CRUELTY

In the coming years, Columbus would continue to enslave the Taíno. He punished resisters by setting fire to their homes and killing them.

Columbus and his men forced the Taíno to work in dangerous gold mines and harvest cotton. When they didn't perform as well as Columbus wanted, he ordered their hands chopped off. The conditions were so awful that thousands of Taíno died by poisoning themselves.

On Columbus's third voyage to what are now called the Americas, the Spanish colonizers rebelled against his rule. He returned to Spain in chains but was released several weeks later.

In 1502, Columbus made one more trip to the Americas, funded by the Spanish monarchy. He died four years later.

Within half a century, many Taíno who hadn't been murdered by the Spanish had died from diseases the Europeans brought with them. These diseases were especially deadly because the Taíno had never encountered them before.

RENAMING A HOLIDAY

Because of Columbus's great cruelty, many states and cities have now renamed the October holiday still known in many places as Columbus Day. It is now called "Indigenous Peoples' Day."

EUROPEAN COLONIZATION OF NORTH AMERICA

We're going to investigate European colonists in greater depth in Chapter 2. But before that, let's take a brief look at what they were doing in North America in the first place.

Once Europeans got the news that there was a new place where they could make money, they began coming to North America and forming colonies. Take a look at which European nations settled where.

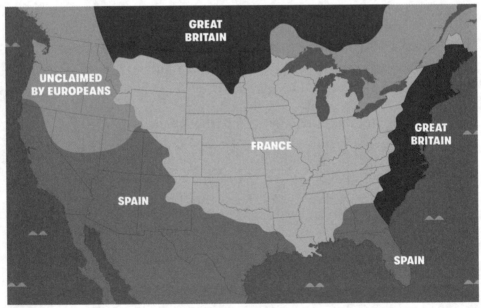

Europeans move west, circa 1700. Modern state outlines are for reference—the United States didn't exist yet, of course!

colony: a piece of land that another nation claims as its own, often using the people and land for its benefit. The process of colonization (founding new colonies) is often extremely violent.

It's not as if you could just move to, say, Spain, and set up a house on someone else's land and call it yours. What was different in the sixteenth and seventeenth centuries that allowed the colonists to do what they did?

_____

_____

_____

_____

SPANISH COLONIZATION

After exploiting Indigenous peoples in Mexico, the Caribbean, and South America, the Spanish moved farther into the North American continent. In 1513, Juan Ponce de León arrived in what the Spanish called "La Florida" ("covered with flowers.") Florida didn't provide the great wealth (or gold) Spain had hoped for. But the Spanish still fought hard to keep it, which they did until the nineteenth century. In addition to killing Native Americans, they also expelled the French, who were living near present-day Jacksonville.

At the end of the sixteenth century, Juan de Oñate led 400 people from Mexico to what is now New Mexico. The Spaniards attacked the Pueblo city of Acoma. They murdered more than half of its 1,500 inhabitants, including women and children. Oñate enslaved the surviving women and children and ordered one foot cut off of every surviving male over the age of 15.

FRENCH COLONIZATION

The French were interested in North America mainly because of the potential for trade, particularly fur pelts, with the Native Americans. In 1534, navigator Jacques Cartier decided northern America was French territory. In case anyone missed his point, he named it "New France."

Samuel de Champlain led an expedition up the St. Lawrence River. He founded Quebec in 1608. The French continued to spread out across the Great Lakes and Ohio Valley. They even traveled south along the Mississippi River to the Gulf of Mexico and as far west as the Rocky Mountains, and they moved into what is now named Newfoundland.

The French also understood the profits to be made from sugar and the labor of enslaved people in the Caribbean. By 1635 they had colonized the islands we know as Guadeloupe and Martinique.

ON A MISSION

Jesuit missionaries from France came to the Americas to try to convert Native Americans to Catholicism. Jesuits are a Catholic religious order formed in France in 1534.

A LASTING INFLUENCE

The French colonial influence is still part of American culture, including in the names of certain cities. New Orleans was named after the French city of Orléans. Des Moines means "of the monks" in French, and Detroit means "strait."

DUTCH COLONIZATION

The Dutch were skilled businesspeople and traders. The Dutch East India Company, which traded with Asia, sent an English captain named Henry Hudson to find a northwest passage to Asia. Instead, in 1609, he stumbled on what we know as the Hudson River and New York Harbor. In 1621, investors formed the Dutch West India Company to take advantage of colonization in the Americas.

When the Dutch saw the fur pelts that were available for trade, they claimed the area for themselves. They named it New Netherland.

New Netherland stretched from what is now Albany, New York, south to Delaware. One of the towns in the Dutch-claimed land was New Amsterdam. Today we call it New York City.

MANHATTAN

In 1624, thirty Dutch families established a settlement on what we now call Manhattan. In 1626, the West India Company's Director General, Peter Minuit, bought the land from Native Americans. He paid them with goods worth about 60 guilders, which would be less than $1,200 today.

A few years later, the Dutch would buy Staten Island for goods that included cloth, hoes, and axes. The Manahatta, Lenape, and Munsee Native Americans all lived in the area, but historians don't know who might have agreed to the land sale.

Native Americans and Europeans had significant cultural differences, a fact which the Europeans exploited. Native Americans often received gifts in return for safe passage through their land or for permission to temporarily stay on it. It is unlikely that they thought they were selling these lands forever.

How do you think each side saw this interaction?

SLAVERY UNDER DUTCH RULE

By 1640, one-third of New Amsterdam's population was made up of enslaved people, who had largely built the colony. The Dutch allowed those they enslaved to learn how to read. Also, enslaved people could marry under Dutch law. In some instances, they could also earn wages. By the time the English took over New Amsterdam in 1664, the city's population of around 1,500 included approximately 375 enslaved people. That's about a quarter of the total population!

Under Dutch law, women had civil, legal, and economic rights in New Netherland that their British counterparts in New England and Virginia did not. These rights included owning and inheriting property before marriage or after their husband's death.

ENGLISH COLONIZATION

The English were relatively late to the land-grab party compared to France and Spain. This was partly because for a long time, Spain was the most powerful nation in Europe. England just couldn't compete with Spain in the Americas. In the late 1600s, English pirates often raided Spanish ships returning from the Americas. That temporarily quenched the English desire for overseas colonization.

The Spanish eventually got angry enough about British piracy that in 1588, they organized an armada of 130 ships to fight the English navy in the English Channel. Led by Sir Francis Drake (see page 33), the English navy trounced the Spanish. This defeat began a shift in the power struggle between Spain and Britain. It also allowed the English to investigate what the Americas might have to offer them. If nothing else, it would put the English closer to the potential treasure to be found in New Spain's ports and boost English confidence in their pursuit of building an empire.

Sir Francis Drake, an English sea captain, raided ports in New Spain in 1577. At that time, New Spain consisted of much of the North American southwest and northern Central America, parts of South America, as well as the area known today as Florida. Knowing that the Spanish would catch and kill him if he returned by the usual routes, he instead sailed around the globe to get home. This made him the first person to circumnavigate the globe since the Portuguese explorer Ferdinand Magellan led an expedition that accomplished that feat between 1519 and 1522.

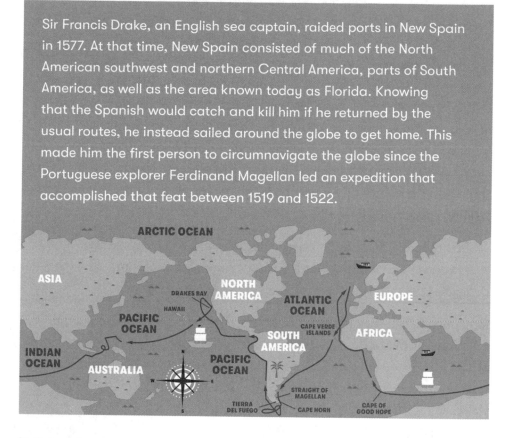

ROANOKE

In 1585, Sir Walter Raleigh and his expedition created the first British settlement in North America when they settled in Roanoke, a small island off of North Carolina. When their supplies had dwindled in a year, they returned to England, but not before murdering Wingina. He was chief of the Indigenous Secotan (an Algonquian) people.

The next year, Raleigh decided to try his luck in Roanoke again. He sent Governor John White and a group of families to live there in 1587. White then fled back to England to get reinforcements to help fight the Native Americans. When he returned three years later, the colony, which included his daughter and granddaughter, had disappeared. The word

"CROATOAN" was found carved into the fort. The disappearance of the Roanoke colony remains a mystery to this day. Many historians believe that the colonists simply went to live in the neighboring Native American settlement on Croatoan (now Hatteras) Island. According to this theory, the colonists had carved their forwarding address into the wall of the fort!

JAMESTOWN

In 1607, 144 English men and boys established the Jamestown colony, in what is now Virginia, on behalf of a group of English investors. The investors told them that they needed to generate wealth in order to receive support. So the settlers spent their time fruitlessly looking for gold rather than building homes and farming. Between starvation and a disease called malaria, only half survived the first year.

After that, colonist John Smith led with the motto "Work or starve." He required each colonist to spend four hours a day farming. Still, the colonists called the winter of 1609 to 1610 the "starving time."

Recent evidence suggests that colonists were so desperate they committed cannibalism. What (non-human) food they did have came from the Native Americans, who shared with the colonists. The colonists also went on to steal from Native American food banks.

THE KING TAKES CONTROL

The king declared the settlement bankrupt in 1624 and took over its control from the investors. Virginia became the first English royal colony in North America.

By 1630, Jamestown had become a thriving tobacco empire. It exported more than a million and a half pounds of the crop every year. It relied on the labor of enslaved people, and in 1662, slavery was officially made legal. As more people came from England to grow tobacco, the colony expanded. The search for new land on which to grow tobacco led to increased fighting with Native Americans.

THE MAYFLOWER COMPACT

The *Mayflower* was a ship that sailed from England in 1620. Among its passengers were religious pilgrims (people who go on a journey for religious reasons) heading for Jamestown in Virginia, but they got off course and ended up in Massachusetts. Jamestown already had its own rules of society, but the Pilgrims found themselves in uncharted territory. Before they even set foot on land, they signed the Mayflower Compact. This said they would rule themselves, with decisions made by the majority vote. The Mayflower Compact was a part of the foundation that led to the establishment of representative government in the English colonies. See page 42 for more about the Pilgrims.

So there you have it—the beginning of how the United States became the country it is today. The Europeans arrived hoping for a better life. Some came in good faith. Many others stole, murdered, and enslaved people to take what they wanted and then profit from it. It's not a pretty story, for sure. But we never promised pretty stories. What we did promise was gripping stories and a deeper understanding of U.S. history. And we're just getting started!

CHAPTER 1 VOCABULARY

anthropologist: someone who studies how human beings used to live. Anthropology is a bit of a combination of history and science.

arable land: any land that is able to produce crops and is good for farming.

archaeologist: a scientist who studies human history by digging up and excavating sites and analyzing the artifacts found there. It's a lot of digging in the dirt and learning secrets about ancient societies!

armada: a naval fleet of fighting ships.

colony: a piece of land that another nation claims as its own, often using the people and land for its benefit. The process of colonization (founding new colonies) is often extremely violent.

land bridge: just what it sounds like: a connecting piece of land. Since the continents have shifted over time, land bridges allowed travel between places that are now separated by oceans.

linguist: someone who studies speech and language.

longhouses: structures that the Haudenosaunee (Iroquois) peoples lived in. They were literally long homes, and generally measured 80 to 100 feet. They had no windows, but they had a door at each end and holes in the roof so that smoke from fires could escape.

matrilineal: the practice of tracing one's relatives and assigning inheritance based on the mother's side of the family.

prehistoric: the word used to describe the time before humans began writing down history.

tepee: a shelter made from long poles covered with buffalo skins and shaped like an upside-down ice cream cone. They were easy to take down, move, and put up again in a new place.

totem poles: very large carvings usually made from trees that typically represented ancestors or important events. Some common crests found on totem poles include the eagle, killer whale, salmon, and grizzly bear.

wampum: small purple and white beads made from shells. Many Native American nations used them as money.

wickiup/wigwam: a domed home made from young trees.

2 HOW THE UNITED STATES CAME TO BE

Spain, France, and the Netherlands all established colonies in North America before Britain did. Yet Britain came to dominate the territory. It outlasted its rivals and then got chucked out. How did all that happen? You're about to find out.

CHAPTER CONTENTS

AN IRRESISTIBLE OPPORTUNITY

THE FRENCH AND INDIAN WAR (1754–1763)

THE RISE, AND RISING UP, OF THE COLONIES

THE FOUNDING FATHERS AND ONE FOUNDING MOTHER

THE DECLARATION OF INDEPENDENCE

BATTLING IT OUT

THE CONSTITUTION: A TALE OF TWO HOUSES

A NEW PRESIDENT FOR A NEW COUNTRY

AN IRRESISTIBLE OPPORTUNITY

Once Spain, France, and Britain realized that having a stronghold in North America could add to their riches, each rushed to claim territory for itself. Some trade between the Europeans and Native Americans benefited both sides. (Europeans sold Native Americans firearms in exchange for animal skins, for instance.) However, from the beginning the Europeans had better weapons. And most Europeans believed that they were the superior race. Many believed that God was on their side. This allowed them to dominate Native Americans and justify (to themselves) taking their land.

BUILT FOR BUSINESS

Companies in Europe wanted employees to live in North America in order to help represent the companies' trading interests. Many Europeans and British who were too poor to own land back home jumped at the chance to start new lives. So did people who were unable to practice their religions freely. Among the first immigrants were the Puritans from England who settled in what is now Massachusetts, the Dutch Protestants in New York, and the British Quakers in Pennsylvania.

Many colonists didn't hesitate to take property long occupied by Native Americans. They not only fought with Native Americans but also enslaved some of them. They captured other Native Americans and sold them to European slave traders. The traders sent these stolen people to sugar plantations in the Caribbean, where many died of overwork and disease.

MERCANTILISM

Tensions between the colonists and Native Americans continued to build. So did those between the colonists and the European countries that had come to depend on the materials they sent back home, in a system known as mercantilism. Each country wanted to create a favorable trade balance by exporting more than it imported.

KEEPING THE FAITH

The Puritans, Quakers, and Dutch Protestants provided some of the religious traditions of the United States. Each of these groups faced oppression or persecution in their homelands. Each wanted to practice their religion freely by coming to North America. Who were they?

mercantilism: an economic idea practiced in the sixteenth through the eighteenth centuries. It was based on the idea that a nation's best chance at wealth and power was through gaining overseas territories and increasing trade with foreign nations.

persecution: the unfair and harsh treatment of a specific group of people.

QUAKERS

The Quakers, also called the Society of Friends, began in England during the seventeenth century. They believe that God is within each of us. Therefore, there is no need for a priest or minister as a go-between.

That didn't sit well with the Church of England and its leaders. They persecuted the Quakers. The Quakers were pacifists and would go on to support the antislavery movement and women's right to vote. When they arrived in North America, Quakers flocked to Rhode Island and Pennsylvania, colonies where religious freedom was allowed.

PURITANS

The Puritans came from a sixteenth-century reform movement designed to "purify" the Church of England from the Roman Catholic Church, which they believed was corrupt. They founded New England after crossing the Atlantic Ocean aboard the *Mayflower*.

Like the Quakers, the Puritans didn't think a priest was necessary when it came to their relationship with God. They also wanted to end ceremonies that weren't based directly on the Bible's teachings.

PILGRIM VS. PURITAN: WHAT'S THE DIFFERENCE?

It's principally a matter of degree. The Pilgrims were separatists, who believed the Church of England was so corrupt they had to break away from it. Puritans, a much larger group, aimed to cleanse the Church of England from within. A "pilgrim" (with a small "p") is any person who goes on a journey for religious reasons.

DUTCH PROTESTANTS

The Dutch Protestants came from the Netherlands, of course. Like the Quakers and the Puritans, they didn't believe that priests were necessary to speak for them in their relationship with God. They wanted simpler ceremonies than the Catholic Church practiced. Dutch Protestants settled mostly in New York.

 What do you think people persecuted for practicing their religions in their home countries might have been looking for in the Americas?

_____

_____

_____

_____

GIVE AND TAKE

NATIVE AMERICANS
- Fur pelts including deer, beaver, otter, mink, and bear
- Fresh meat
- Corn

EUROPEANS
- Guns
- Metal tools
- Cooking utensils
- Cloth
- Beads
- Copper
- Rum

A DEADLY TRADE

Colonists didn't just give the Native Americans objects. They also brought diseases, including influenza, smallpox, and measles. Some historians believe that as many as 90 percent of Native Americans died because of European diseases.

TRIANGULAR TRADE

The exchange between Native Americans and European colonists took place within a larger global trade—the transatlantic triangular trade. The "triangle" connected three regions: new colonies in the Americas, the European countries from which the colonists originated, and West Africa.

Europeans brought goods such as guns, cloth, and beer in exchange for people captured from Africa, who were then enslaved and taken to the new colonies for free labor. The colonies sent goods, including sugar and tobacco, back to their mother countries.

TRANSATLANTIC TRIANGULAR TRADE
(CIRCA 1500–1860S)

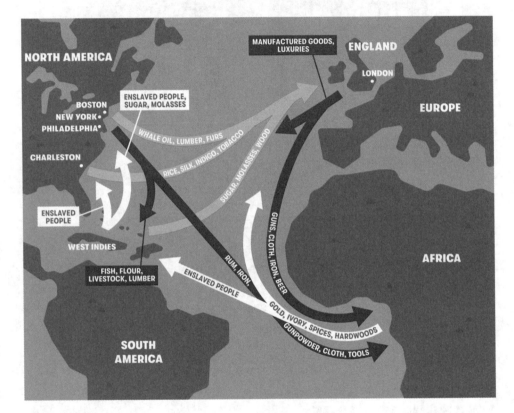

KING PHILIP'S WAR

This three-year war, which lasted from 1675–1678, included deadly conflicts between Native Americans and European colonizers. It also shows how history often reflects who is telling it.

King Philip wasn't a British king. He was a Native American named Metacom. He was a leader of the Wampanoag nation and the son of its chief, Massasoit. The colonists called Metacom "King Philip." Their name for him has gone down in history, thanks to their victory in the war.

The Wampanoag nation was literally a lifesaver for the first colonists in the area—the Pilgrims. They taught the colonists how to survive on the land during the harsh winter and how to plant crops such as corn. But conflict began as the colonists spread disease and took more land.

Then, in 1675, a Christian Native American named John Sassamon, who lived with the colonists, was murdered by Native Americans who thought he was a traitor. The colonists sought revenge by putting three Native Americans on trial and executing them. This event sparked King Philip's War.

By the end of the war, about 3,000 Native Americans (30 percent of their population) had died in the fighting. So had about 600 New England colonists (1.5 percent of the New England settlers' population).

THE FRENCH AND INDIAN WAR (1754–1763)

The colonizers who named this war left out a crucial party: Britain. This conflict began as a power struggle between France and Britain. They fought over territory in the Ohio Valley that was home to the Haudenosaunee nation (also known as the Iroquois).

What was so important about this place? The valley has a network of rivers leading to the Atlantic Ocean. Located near modern-day Pittsburgh, these rivers allowed Europeans to transport what they bought from the Native Americans without having to travel over land. It was a faster way to get animal skins and other valuables to Europe.

FRANCE AND BRITAIN DUKE IT OUT

The French considered the territory "New France." The English insisted it was part of Virginia. In 1756, Britain declared war on France in an effort to keep it for themselves. The Haudenosaunee backed Britain, which promised to protect their rights to the land. Like the Haudenosaunee, other tribes aligned with whichever nation they believed would best support their land claims.

In the last major battle between France and Britain, the British captured the Canadian city of Montréal, which had been under French control. The disputed Ohio territory, as well as nearly all of the land east of the Mississippi River, went to the British under the terms of the Treaty of Paris of 1763.

GEORGE WASHINGTON, ROOKIE?

George Washington first emerged as a military leader during the French and Indian War. Only 21 when the state of Virginia sent him to deliver an ultimatum to the French, Washington's account of his trip to the Ohio Valley was published to great fanfare. Washington had his first military engagement during this war, as well as his only surrender.

A TREATY THAT BROUGHT LITTLE PEACE

After the Treaty of Paris (1763), the French had no remaining North American land east of the Mississippi River except New Orleans and the area around it. Giving up that land was a smart move for the French! They didn't have to protect all that faraway land anymore.

It was easy for a country across the Atlantic to walk away. But the price was heavy for Native Americans who had supported the French. The British punished them by cutting off their supplies.

THE PROCLAMATION OF 1763

The Native Americans who supported the British didn't do much better. All the Native American nations east of the Mississippi came under British control. The Proclamation of 1763 stated that the land west of the Appalachian Mountains belonged to Native American nations, and British settlements were not allowed. Still, colonists continued to move onto the lands of the Shawnee (who had supported the French) in West Virginia.

The proclamation also affected colonists. They wanted access to more fertile farmland to the West. The deal Britain made didn't represent their interests. The British colonists' fight to be out from under Britain's control was about to begin.

HITTING THE COLONISTS WHERE IT HURT

War is expensive. And the French and Indian War had cost the British plenty. To help pay for the necessary ships, weapons, and supplies, Britain increased taxes on the colonists with a series of new "acts" (taxes), between 1765 and 1773. These made the colonists increasingly angry. Ultimately, they led to the colonists' desire to end British rule.

Here are the most important acts to remember:

NOVEMBER 1, 1765	THE STAMP ACT

Colonists had to buy special paper from Britain for all printed documents, including playing cards. This led to riots in Boston and Philadelphia. Britain repealed (got rid of) the act.

MARCH 18, 1766	THE DECLARATORY ACT

Britain restated its right to tax the colonies.

JUNE 5, 1767– JULY 8, 1768	THE TOWNSHEND ACTS

Britain taxed tea, glass, lead, paper, and paint. This led some colonists to boycott, or refuse to buy, British goods.

MAY 10, 1773	THE TEA ACT

Britain wanted to support its struggling British East India Tea Company. So Britain told the colonists that was the only tea they could drink. This harmed tea merchants who were already working in the colonies.

JUNE 2, 1774	THE COERCIVE ACTS (also called the Intolerable Acts)

To punish the colonists for the Boston Tea Party, the British established military rule in Boston.

 Other than making money to pay off war debts, what else might the British have wanted their tax acts to do?

THE RISE, AND RISING UP, OF THE COLONIES

By the 1760s, English colonists had been living in North America for generations. Many current colonists had been born in the New World and had never set foot on English soil. In an effort to band together, they began holding official gatherings to strengthen their position against the British. One of the first such groups to meet was the Stamp Act Congress in 1765. It was made up of members from nine of the thirteen colonies who were determined to protest the Stamp Act.

THE BOSTON MASSACRE

Five years later, the relationship between colonists and Britain became violent. Some 2,000 British soldiers—called "redcoats" for their uniforms—were stationed in Boston. It was their job to maintain Britain's laws and financial interests in the city of 16,000.

On March 5, 1770, some of these British soldiers fired into an unruly crowd of colonists. They killed five men, including Crispus Attucks (see page 50). Attucks's fellow Boston colonist Paul Revere was outraged. He published a poster called "The Bloody Massacre." The Sons of Liberty, a secret revolutionary organization, called it "the Boston Massacre." That's the name that has stuck through history.

WHO WAS CRISPUS ATTUCKS?

Crispus Attucks

Attucks, a colonist killed early on in the American Revolution, was of African and Wampanoag descent. In 1750, at about age 47, he escaped from slavery. He moved to Boston, where he worked as a ropemaker and sailor.

He and the others who died in the Boston Massacre were honored with a burial in Boston's Granary Burial Ground, which otherwise barred Black Americans.

In the mid-1800s, a Black abolitionist (see Chapter 4 for more on abolition and abolitionists) named William Nell used Attucks as an example that Black people had been part of the struggle for independence. Therefore, Nell argued, Black people should be free. In 1858, abolitionists named March 5 "Crispus Attucks Day" to remember his contributions to American independence.

WHAT WAS THE BOSTON TEA PARTY?

This was not a "party" as we know it. And nobody sipped tea! Instead, on December 16, 1773, colonists angry over the Tea Act dumped 342 chests of it into Boston Harbor.

These colonists were members of the Sons of Liberty—the secret revolutionary group of colonists mentioned on page 49. The Daughters of Liberty played an important role in protesting British rule as well. One of the Daughters' contributions was teaching women to make their own cloth so they would no longer need to import it from Britain.

The Daughters of Liberty helped make the colonies less dependent on Britain.

THE WAR IS ON

Five years after the Boston Massacre, colonial militia (called minutemen because they were expected to be ready to fight at a minute's notice) and British redcoats fought the first battle of the American Revolution. The colonists had discovered plans by the redcoats to seize guns and ammunition stored in Concord, Massachusetts. To warn the minutemen who lived throughout the countryside, riders, including Paul Revere, raced on horseback through the night.

On the morning of April 19, 1775, British soldiers reached Lexington, Massachusetts. They found about 70 minutemen waiting for them. While poet Ralph Waldo Emerson called the first shot fired "the shot heard round the world" in his 1837 poem *Concord Hymn*, no one actually knows which side was responsible for it. At least eight minutemen died.

These events became known as the "Battle of Lexington and Concord."

minutemen: soldiers in the colonial army. They're called minutemen because they had to be ready for service at a minute's notice.

Patriots: colonists who wanted independence from Britain.

Loyalists: colonists who supported continuing British rule in North America. Loyalists were also called **Tories**.

PAUL REVERE DESERVES TO BE FAMOUS. BUT NOT FOR YELLING "THE BRITISH ARE COMING!"

Paul Revere was an amateur dentist, a talented silversmith and engraver, and a spy. His information about British war plans helped the colonists begin their revolution. But his calling out, "The British are coming!" during his famed midnight ride is a myth. At this point, the colonists still considered themselves British. So shouting that would have confused people!

PATRIOTS VS. LOYALISTS

Patriots wanted separation from England. Loyalists (also called Tories) supported continuing British rule of North America.

What reasons would a colonist have for being a Patriot?
What reasons would they have for being a Loyalist?

_____

_____

_____

_____

_____

_____

WHEN DID THE FIGHTING COLONISTS BECOME THE CONTINENTAL ARMY?

A governing body called the Second Continental Congress formed the Continental Army on June 14, 1775. George Washington was named commander of the army.

NATIVE AMERICANS' ROLE IN THE REVOLUTION

Native American nations made alliances with either Britain or the colonists, much as they had during the French and Indian War. They chose the side they thought would best help them protect their lands and let them govern themselves. Most nations, including the Mohawks, Cayugas, Onondagas, and Senecas, backed the British. These nations feared that if the colonists won the war, they would continue taking over land. This fear turned out to be true.

THE FOUNDING FATHERS AND ONE FOUNDING MOTHER

The term "Founding Fathers" refers to the seven men who guided the country out of British rule and developed the beginnings of U.S. government. While they were brilliant thinkers and politicians, they were also flawed. For instance: Thomas Jefferson, James Madison, and George Washington were all "owners" of enslaved people.

ADAMS

FRANKLIN

JOHN ADAMS

A lawyer, Adams (1735–1826) was a blunt, smart politician who helped write the Declaration of Independence. He served as vice president to Washington before becoming the country's second president in 1797.

BENJAMIN FRANKLIN

An inventor, publisher, author, and skilled diplomat, Franklin (1706–1790) helped write the Declaration of Independence. He negotiated an alliance with France during the Revolution. Without that agreement, the colonies likely would have suffered defeat.

ALEXANDER HAMILTON

HAMILTON

Hamilton (1755 or 1757–1804) was born on the Caribbean island of Nevis (the year is uncertain because Hamilton might have lied about his age to seem like more of a "boy genius"). He hit the ground running when he arrived in the North American colonies. He became a leader of the American Revolution. He was the first Secretary of the Treasury (under his Revolutionary War boss, George Washington). And his ideas are largely responsible for the financial system on which the United States is built. Hamilton also founded what became the United States Coast Guard in 1790.

JAY

JEFFERSON

JOHN JAY

A leader, diplomat, and abolitionist, Jay (1745–1829) was the first chief justice of the United States. He was also New York state's second governor.

THOMAS JEFFERSON

This plantation owner, architect, writer, and lawyer (1743–1826) was secretary of state under Washington. He was also president for two terms, from 1801–1809. Jefferson was one of three Founding Fathers from Virginia.

JAMES MADISON

Madison (1751–1836) is the "father of the Constitution" for his important part in writing the document. Also, he engineered the Louisiana Purchase in 1803 (see p. 78) before going on to become the fourth president. He was a plantation owner, a lawyer, and a Virginian. He worked to expand the power of slave-holding states.

GEORGE WASHINGTON

The first president of the United States, Washington (1732–1799) was a plantation owner and military general who led the Continental Army to win the Revolution. He was the first of the three Virginians to be elected president.

ABIGAIL ADAMS

At this time, most people did not think women should be active in public life. But Abigail Adams (1744–1818) was a principled champion of women's rights and an opponent of slavery. She counseled her husband, John Adams, on all of his important political decisions. Her activism earned her the nickname "Mrs. President" when John Adams became the second president of the United States.

THE DECLARATION OF INDEPENDENCE

In 1775, the colonists continued forming a governmental body at the Continental Congress. The meeting, held in Philadelphia, included delegates (representatives) from each colony.

In June 1776, delegates chose a committee of five men, chaired by Thomas Jefferson, to draft a document that would argue for self-rule. This became the Declaration of Independence. It combined ideas about liberty and individual rights with a list of complaints about British rule. The document listed twenty-seven grievances with the King, including taxation and British occupation. It ended with a call for independence.

WHAT DOES THE DECLARATION ACTUALLY SAY?

The Declaration is based on an idea from an intellectual movement called the Enlightenment. The idea is that people have natural rights—not just rights that a king or queen allows. The Declaration states that "all men are created equal," each with the right to "life, liberty, and the pursuit of happiness." The Declaration is still one of the world's most important documents about freedom and the rights of citizens. The Declaration's language regarding "all men" being created equal excluded women. But women weren't the only people left out. Though it wasn't stated anywhere in the document, the ideas of equality and freedom in the Declaration were limited to white men.

> **Declaration of Independence:** one of the significant founding documents of the United States. It declared the colonists' intention to be self-ruling and independent from Britain.
>
> **(the) Enlightenment:** a period of philosophical and political development mostly in Europe. Enlightenment thinkers questioned the authority of monarchs (kings and queens).

On July 4, the delegates signed the document. They sent a copy to Britain's King George III. On July 8, Americans read the Declaration aloud in public across the colonies.

The Declaration did not have the force of law. However, it sent a message that the Continental Congress was determined to unite the colonies into one independent country.

 How do you think the Declaration of Independence has shaped people's beliefs about the United States? How has it influenced later events in American history?

_____

_____

_____

_____

THE PRACTICE OF SLAVERY AND THE DECLARATION OF INDEPENDENCE

Thomas Jefferson at first included a complaint about slavery in a draft of the Declaration of Independence. He blamed George III for the practice in the colonies and called it a "cruel war against human nature." Yet Jefferson himself owned hundreds of enslaved people. He never took steps to end the practice.

 What contradictions does enslavement bring to independence and democracy?

_____

_____

_____

_____

For a plain-English "translation" of the Declaration of Independence, see the Bonus Section beginning on page 464!

BATTLING IT OUT

THE FIRST KEY BATTLES IN THE REVOLUTION

 It's important to pay close attention to dates here! The colonists were preparing for self-government at the same time that they were fighting military battles. So some of these battles happened before and during the drafting of the Declaration.

THE BATTLE OF BUNKER HILL (JUNE 17, 1775)

In the first battle after the showdown at Lexington and Concord, the British attacked colonists at Bunker Hill. The British won control of the higher ground north of Boston. But the cost in human lives was brutal. In the first two hours of fighting, 2,200 redcoats died and the colonists lost more than 400 soldiers. Despite their strategic victory, the British retreated after Washington's troops fired on them with a cannon seized from their own fort in Ticonderoga, New York.

THE BATTLE OF LONG ISLAND (AUGUST 27, 1776)

Unlike Boston, New York had a large loyalist population. To secure the city, British Admiral Richard Howe and his redcoats pushed through the Continental Army's front lines in Brooklyn. The British would occupy New York City and much of Long Island until the war's end.

THE BATTLE OF TRENTON (DECEMBER 26, 1776)

Washington and 2,400 of his troops were low on supplies and feeling discouraged after being run out of New York. They crossed the Delaware River into Pennsylvania. They then made a surprise attack on Hessian soldiers in Trenton, New

Jersey. (Hessians were German soldiers-for-hire fighting for the British.)

The battle was a huge victory for Washington and the Continental Army. It's considered one of the turning points of the Revolutionary War.

THE BATTLE OF SARATOGA
(SEPTEMBER 19 AND OCTOBER 7, 1777)

In an effort to invade New England, British General John Burgoyne led the redcoats down from Canada through Saratoga, a city in upstate New York. After a successful siege on September 19, Burgoyne returned two and a half weeks later in a fight for supplies. This time, the Continental Army—led by General Horatio Gates—was victorious. Burgoyne surrendered.

The battle convinced the French that the Continental Army was the one to back. For this reason, the French became an ally of the colonists.

 What are some of the reasons you think France might have wanted the colonists out from under British rule?

_____

_____

_____

_____

_____

A CLOTHES CALL

In 1778, Washington put together the Culper Spy Ring. It was designed to keep tabs on British plans of attack in New York. One of the spies, Anna Smith Strong, used a secret code involving her clothesline. A black undergarment called a petticoat signaled to her colleagues that a fellow spy was hiding nearby so a meeting could be arranged. White handkerchiefs indicated which nearby cove they could find him in. Strong did this under the watchful eye of British troops, who were living in her home.

THE ARTICLES OF CONFEDERATION

As the fighting went on, the members of Continental Congress came up with a plan for how they would run the country. The Articles of Confederation, written in 1777 and ratified (formally approved) in 1781, was the nation's first constitution. It set up the structure of the government and defined the relationship between the states.

The founders feared the power of a king like George III. So the Articles gave most power to state governments, each of which would have their own laws and money. It also stated that alterations to the Articles would require consent from all thirteen states.

This was a flawed idea. Often, states might not see eye to eye. More than that, they were naturally distrustful of each other. And there was no executive in charge to enforce the changes.

The weaknesses of this document became clear as the war continued and, in 1787, when Shays' Rebellion erupted. The country's leaders replaced the Articles at the Constitutional Convention in 1787.

SHAYS' REBELLION

The government was made up of wealthy, educated white men, and the laws they created protected their interests. The divide between the government and poorer people showed itself during this rebellion in 1786. It happened when a Revolutionary War veteran and farmer named Daniel Shays organized a group of farmers in western Massachusetts.

A recent raise in taxes had sent some farmers to debtors' prison. Some 4,000 "Shaysites" were enraged at government tax policy, much as they had been at the British a decade earlier. They took up arms against soldiers at the Springfield Armory and temporarily took control of courts in several places. The state militia at first refused to fight the Shaysites. So wealthy Bostonians hired a private militia to help contain them.

The rebellion showed that the federal government would need more power to prevent economic crises and control future uprisings.

federal government: the national United States government, not state or local governments.

THE END OF THE WAR

These key battles would ultimately decide the war:

THE BATTLE OF MONMOUTH
(JUNE 28, 1778)

With French forces by their side, the Continental Army met the British army in Monmouth, New Jersey. The bloody battle ended in a stalemate. But the Americans proved they could stand toe-to-toe with the British.

THE BATTLES OF CHARLESTON (MARCH 29–MAY 12, 1780)
AND CAMDEN (AUGUST 16, 1780)

The British then concentrated on the Southern colonies, including two cities in South Carolina. These were two of the most thorough and humiliating defeats of the Continental Army. In Charleston, the British captured more than 3,000 Continental soldiers. During the battle of Camden, the redcoats killed or captured nearly 2,000. General Horatio Gates, the hero of Saratoga, was said to have badly mismanaged the Continental army, which outnumbered the British at Camden by two to one. He never led an army in battle again.

THE BATTLE OF KINGS MOUNTAIN (OCTOBER 7, 1780) AND THE BATTLE OF COWPENS (JANUARY 17, 1781)

The Battle of Kings Mountain, South Carolina, was the only battle fought between the Continental Army and British irregulars. These were Loyalist soldiers who were not part of the official army. Along with the Continental Army's victory at Cowpens (also in South Carolina), this battle saw the end of British control of this crucial colony. It ended British occupation of the South. The clear win also discouraged Loyalist activity throughout the colonies.

THE SIEGE OF YORKTOWN
(SEPTEMBER 28–OCTOBER 19, 1781)

George Washington led his troops, alongside French allies, against British General Charles Lord Cornwallis in Yorktown, Virginia. The Continental Army and the French Navy crushed British hopes of winning the war. It was the last major battle in the Revolutionary War.

PEACE, SIGNED AND SEALED

Britain and the United States began peace talks in Paris in April 1782. This resulted in the fourth Treaty of Paris of the century (but only the second that the United States participated in). Both sides signed on September 3, 1783, officially recognizing American independence.

THE CONSTITUTION: A TALE OF TWO HOUSES

In 1787, the Constitutional Convention took place with delegates representing every state except for Rhode Island. Led by George Washington, the Convention's members gathered to draft a new document that would fix the problems in the Articles of Confederation.

A first, important step was establishing two "houses" within Congress. The House of Representatives would have one representative for every 30,000 people. The Senate would have two representatives for each state.

The Constitution also established the process that determines how the U.S. government passes laws. First, the House of Representatives sponsors and votes on a law. If it passes, the Senate then votes on its approval. In some cases, bills may start out in the Senate. But they still need to be approved in both houses to become a law.

THE THREE BRANCHES OF GOVERNMENT

The United States has three branches of government. The House of Representatives and the Senate make up the legislative branch of government, which writes and passes the laws. The Founding Fathers also created an executive branch. Today, this includes the president, the vice president, and a president's cabinet of high-level advisers at the federal level, as well as governors and mayors at the state level. The court system is the judicial branch.

The Constitution provides for a system of checks and balances. In other words, one branch can stop the others from becoming too strong. Here are some examples of the ways the Constitution provides these safeguards.

legislative branch: the House of Representatives and Senate, which are the two houses of Congress. It is responsible for making laws, as well as overseeing tax policies and how the U.S. spends the government's money. It also has the power to declare war.

executive branch: the president, vice president, and cabinet members, who advise the president. Its main job is to enforce the laws that Congress makes.

judicial branch: The Supreme Court and federal courts fall into this branch of the federal government. The judicial branch's role is to interpret laws.

cabinet: a group of advisers and department heads appointed by the president. The Senate must approve all cabinet members—a great example of checks and balances in action!

checks and balances: the different ways in which the government branches interact with each other. They are safeguards so that no branch can become the most powerful.

Thinking about government today, which aspects of this approach have worked, and which haven't? What would be a better system?

_____

_____

_____

_____

_____

_____

_____

_____

_____

CHECKS AND BALANCES

Below is a flow chart showing how the framers of the Constitution intended for the three branches of the U.S. government to interact. No one branch has complete power. Each serves as a check on the power of the other two—the "checks and balances" you hear about so often.

The president nominates judges to federal courts.

EXECUTIVE BRANCH

The president can veto (reject) a law, but Congress can override (undo) the veto with enough votes.

Federal courts can declare executive actions as unconstitutional.

JUDICIAL BRANCH

Courts decide whether laws are constitutional. An unconstitutional law is not valid.

Congress confirms new judges appointed to federal courts.

LEGISLATIVE BRANCH

Congress can impeach and remove the President (formally accuse the president of bad behavior and vote to remove him or her from office). The Senate confirms all presidential nominations and treaties.

SLAVERY AND THE THREE-FIFTHS COMPROMISE

A state's population was the key to how much representation it got in Congress. However, Northern and Southern states disagreed on how to count their population.

Southern states, where the vast majority of enslaved people lived, wanted to include them in the population count. This would give the South more representation in the House, even though enslaved people would not be able to vote for House representatives.

Northern states including New York, Massachusetts, and Pennsylvania disagreed. They argued that enslaved people couldn't be considered both "property" and a part of the state's population.

THE THREE-FIFTHS COMPROMISE

The two sides settled on the Three-Fifths Compromise. (A compromise is an agreement in which nobody gets everything they want, but everybody gets something they want.) For every five people enslaved, the government would count three as part of a state's population.

There were conversations at the Constitutional Convention about ending slavery. But those talks stalled as the Southern states threatened disunion. The Declaration of Independence states that "all men are created equal." But members believed that continuing slavery was the only way to keep the union between the states.

The Convention did set a date to end the slave trade in 1808. But this was mainly to protect the financial "value" of the already enslaved people in the United States. While this meant people were not supposed to import more enslaved people, they continued to do so illegally, and the practice of "owning" another human being remained legal.

THE SIGNING OF THE CONSTITUTION

For the Constitution to be approved, Congress needed nine out of thirteen states to agree. Disagreements between the Federalists and the Anti-Federalists threatened this process.

Alexander Hamilton, a war hero who later became the first Secretary of the Treasury, led the Federalists. Hamilton and his allies John Jay and James Madison wrote the *Federalist Papers*. They favored a strong central government. The Anti-Federalists wanted individual states to have most of the power.

THE BILL OF RIGHTS

The Anti-Federalists proposed that the Constitution should have ten amendments known as the Bill of Rights. These limited the federal government's ability to control what people can and can't do. This is why U.S. citizens can practice the religion of their choice (or none at all). Also, they are guaranteed a trial by jury, and they are not subject to cruel and unusual punishment.

With the Anti-Federalists comfortable that individual choices would be protected, both sides shook hands. The first state to ratify the Constitution was Delaware, on December 27, 1787.

amendments: additions to the U.S. Constitution.

Bill of Rights: the first ten amendments to the U.S. Constitution. They grant rights such as freedom of speech and the right to have a trial when accused of a crime.

Federalists/Anti-Federalists: Federalists favored a strong central government. Anti-Federalists wanted individual states to have most of the power.

THE U.S. CONSTITUTION: SHORT AND SWEET

The Constitution isn't just the oldest democratic constitution in the world. It's also the shortest, at less than 5,000 words. That's about the length of one chapter in this book! Is it difficult to imagine that these men could lay out an entire system of government in only four pages? Well, you can go see the document for yourself at the National Archives Building in Washington, D.C.

PAUL CUFFE

Paul Cuffe

A free Black man of African and Native American ancestry, Paul Cuffe (1759–1817) was a Quaker and a successful businessman from Massachusetts. He spoke out strongly against slavery.

In 1780, Cuffe asked the government of Bristol County, Massachusetts, to end taxation without representation. His efforts resulted in all men— including himself—being able to vote in the state. Still, the majority of Black Americans would not be able to vote for almost another hundred years. Unfair restrictions on Black people's votes continue to this day in forms of voter suppression.

Cuffe also joined the movement to develop a colony in the African country of Sierra Leone for people formerly enslaved in America. He funded and led an expedition to bring thirty-eight free colonists to the African country in 1815.

THE POWER OF A POET

Phillis Wheatley

Phillis Wheatley (1753–1784) was the first published African American poet. This fact is as extraordinary as the life she survived to become a literary success.

Kidnapped from West Africa as a child and sold into slavery in Massachusetts, the family that "owned" Wheatley taught her to read and write. Wheatley studied the Bible, astronomy, history, and literature.

Her poetry often used Christian values to advocate the end of slavery. As she wrote in her 1773 poem *On Being Brought from Africa to America*, "Remember, Christians, Negros, black as Cain, / May be refin'd, and join th'angelic train."

In recent years, scholars have found more poems and letters that showed her determination to end slavery. At the time, her work was admired by George Washington, who praised her "great poetical Genius."

A NEW PRESIDENT FOR A NEW COUNTRY

In 1789, George Washington became the first president of the United States. He served two terms. He also set into motion Hamilton's proposal for a national bank that would assume states' debts from the war to improve the economy. In addition, he encouraged domestic spending and manufacturing to make the United States less dependent on Britain. He nominated a group of advisers who formed the first cabinet.

While he was a revered leader, Washington was also a slave owner who did no favors for Native Americans. By signing the Treaty of Greenville in August 1795, he ensured that the U.S. government received two-thirds of the land that Native Americans lived on between the Ohio River and Lake Erie. In return, the Native American peoples received—wait for it—*supplies*, such as blankets and utensils.

 How was Washington able to take advantage of the Native Americans who agreed to this treaty?

_____

_____

_____

_____

_____

_____

_____

_____

_____

WASHINGTON'S GOODBYE

The president's Farewell Address (written mainly by Alexander Hamilton and James Madison) had a lasting influence on U.S. foreign policy. Washington advised his successors to stay neutral and as removed as possible from European politics. It was wise advice for a new nation that could not yet compete with European military powers.

Washington voluntarily stepped down from power. People saw this as revolutionary in a time when kings and queens ruled most of the world. Washington also advised that Americans avoid forming factions (opposing groups) and political parties. Within the decade, however, Americans began ignoring this advice.

In offering to you, my countrymen, these counsels of an old and affectionate friend...

This line actually appeared in Washington's Farewell Address! In his speech, the outgoing president encouraged the United States to stay out of foreign affairs and to be wary of forming political factions.

CHAPTER 2 VOCABULARY

amendments: additions to the U.S. Constitution.

Anti-Federalists: Anti-Federalists wanted individual states to have most of the power.

Bill of Rights: the first ten amendments to the U.S. Constitution. They grant rights such as freedom of speech and the right to have a trial when accused of a crime.

cabinet: a group of advisers and department heads appointed by the president. The Senate must approve all cabinet members—a great example of checks and balances in action!

checks and balances: the different ways in which the government branches interact with each other. They are safeguards so that no branch can become the most powerful.

Daughters of Liberty: a secret group formed by colonial women in New England in the 1760s to oppose unfair laws and taxes imposed by the British. Their principal weapon was economic: weaving textiles so that they would not have to be imported from England.

Declaration of Independence: one of the significant founding documents of the United States. It declared the colonists' intention to be self-ruling and independent from Britain.

(the) Enlightenment: a period of philosophical and political development mostly in Europe. Enlightenment thinkers questioned the authority of monarchs (kings and queens). Their ideas influenced colonists in the Americas to question British rule as well.

executive branch: the president, vice president, and cabinet members who advise the president. Its main job is to enforce the laws that Congress makes.

federal government: the national United States government, not state or local governments.

Federalists: Federalists favored a strong central government.

judicial branch: The Supreme Court and federal courts fall into this branch of the federal government. The judicial branch's role is to interpret laws.

legislative branch: the House of Representatives and Senate, which are the two houses of Congress. It is responsible for making laws, as well as overseeing tax policies and how the U.S. spends the government's money. It also has the power to declare war.

Loyalists: colonists who supported continuing British rule in North America. Loyalists were also called Tories.

mercantilism: an economic idea practiced in the sixteenth through the eighteenth centuries. It was based on the idea that a nation's best chance at wealth and power was through gaining overseas territories and increasing trade with foreign nations.

minutemen: soldiers in the colonial army. They're called minutemen because they had to be ready for service at a minute's notice.

Patriots: colonists who wanted independence from Britain.

persecution: the unfair and harsh treatment of a specific group of people.

Sons of Liberty: a secret group formed in 1765 by shopkeepers and tradesmen in Boston to oppose the Stamp Act. Chapters of the group formed in every colony, all to oppose unfair laws and taxes imposed by the British.

3 WESTWARD EXPANSION

As Thomas Jefferson looked for ways to grow the country's economy, Americans hungered for more land. So began a push toward the West. But at what cost, and who would pay the price?

CHAPTER CONTENTS

DOUBLE OR NOTHING: THE LOUISIANA PURCHASE

LEWIS AND CLARK EXPEDITION

***MARBURY V. MADISON* AND JUDICIAL REVIEW**

THE WAR OF 1812

FROM HOMESPUN TO FACTORY: THE FIRST INDUSTRIAL REVOLUTION

ANDREW JACKSON AND JACKSONIAN DEMOCRACY

A NEW PRESIDENT AND AN ECONOMIC DEPRESSION

THE MEXICAN-AMERICAN WAR

DOUBLE OR NOTHING: THE LOUISIANA PURCHASE

Thomas Jefferson succeeded John Adams as president in 1801. Jefferson believed that economic growth hinged on two things: more land on which to grow more crops, and access to rivers and ports from which to send those goods.

Standing in his way on both counts were the French. Led by Napoleon, they took back the Louisiana territory from Spain in 1800. The Louisiana territory in question was gigantic, with excellent soil for growing crops. It was also home to the important Mississippi River port city of New Orleans. This city let Americans in settlements west of the Appalachian Mountains transport their goods to the Eastern Seaboard and Europe, as well as trade with the islands of the Caribbean. No surprise, Americans wanted guaranteed access to the port.

NAPOLEON MAKES A DEAL

Jefferson sent James Monroe, a lawyer and a diplomat (and future U.S. president), to Paris in 1803. Monroe had permission to write Napoleon a check for as much as $10 million to buy New Orleans and West Florida. Napoleon was at war with the British, so he needed cash, and fast. He made a counteroffer: for $15 million, the United States could have all of the Louisiana territory—roughly 550 million acres. With this agreement, the United States doubled its size, adding the land that would eventually become fifteen more states.

THE LOUISIANA PURCHASE

FOUR FUN FACTS ABOUT THOMAS JEFFERSON

1 You can thank him for mac and cheese, French fries, and ice cream, which grew popular in part because of his love of French cuisine and cooking.

2 He collected fossils. He even had the bones of a mastodon sent to him to display in the White House.

3 He not only had smarts but also the books to show for them. When the British raided the Library of Congress in 1814, Jefferson offered his collection to Congress—almost 6,500 volumes.

4 A brilliant architect, he designed Monticello, which has 33 rooms and took 40 years to build. He considered details down to the door handles, some of which were designed so he could close two doors with just one handle.

Monticello was a plantation that Jefferson owned and designed.

A POLITICAL SPLIT

Not everyone in the U.S. government was thrilled about the sudden expansion. The Federalists disagreed with the purchase. (Remember them? They wanted the federal government to hold more power than the individual states.) The Federalists reminded the president that according to the Constitution, he didn't have the right to buy more land for the country.

But that wasn't what the Federalists were really worried about. They believed a bigger population would mean more representation in Congress for states that supported slavery.

The Federalists weren't arguing against the potential growth of slavery on moral grounds. . . The states needed the money they got from exporting crops. They worried it would make it more difficult for northern states to compete with the South, which relied on the labor of enslaved people.

SLAVE STATES VS. FREE STATES

In 1803, there were nine states that were considered "free states," and eight "slave states." The free states still gained from the work of the enslaved. For example, most people in free states wore cotton clothes that were made using slave labor. The designations of free state and slave state show how each state was likely to vote on the matter of slavery.

A COUNTRY DIVIDED

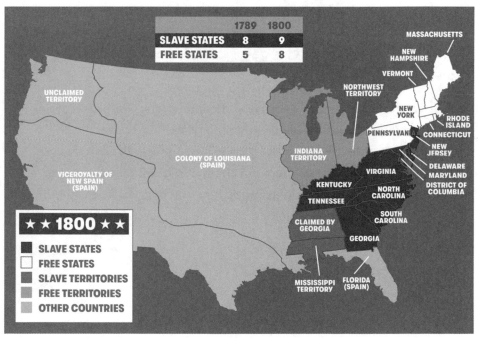

	1789	1800
SLAVE STATES	8	9
FREE STATES	5	8

In 1800, there were nine slave states (ones that allowed the enslavement of Black people), and eight free states (ones where enslavement was not legal).

Notice the tensions between slave states and free states. What problems might these tensions cause in later years?

_____

_____

_____

A DEADLY DEAL FOR SOME

 Remember from Chapter 1 that Louisiana wasn't empty land. Instead, it was home to people from many Indigenous nations who had lived there for thousands of years. But the fact that it wasn't up for sale didn't stand in the way of the white leaders, including Jefferson.

THE VIOLENCE OF ASSIMILATION

How could white people expand onto land when other people were already there? White politicians largely fell into two categories about how to get what they wanted. Native Americans could either assimilate (live by white American standards and values), or they could leave. Assimilating came at a high price. It meant that Indigenous people had to turn their backs on their own culture.

For the Americans in power, this involved encouraging—or often forcing—Native Americans to cut their hair, speak English, and convert to Christianity. But even if Native Americans made these difficult choices to survive, prejudice against them put them at a giant disadvantage. Laws designed to limit their rights made it nearly impossible for them to gain wealth and status in white society.

For the members of the nations that stood in the way of expansion, things were about to get even worse.

Why do you think white people encouraged and often forced Native Americans to assimilate?

_____

_____

_____

_____

_____

_____

_____

LEWIS AND CLARK EXPEDITION

Thanks to the Louisiana Purchase, America now owned hundreds of thousands of miles of land it knew little about. Jefferson hoped that a team of explorers might discover good trade routes throughout the country. Along the way, they could meet with Native Americans, asking them to trade furs with Americans rather than with the British and the Spanish.

In May 1804, Meriwether Lewis (1774–1809) and William Clark (1770–1838) along with a team of fifty people who ranged from scientists to adventurers, set out northwest on a paid expedition. They traveled along the Missouri River from St. Louis.

That fall, they arrived in what is now North Dakota, then home to some 5,000 Mandan Native Americans. They spent the winter there and then continued their journey with Mandan as their guides. The following winter, they reached the Pacific Ocean. By the time they returned to St. Louis in September 1806, they had spent a little more than two years traveling more than 8,000 miles.

A CROSS-COUNTRY TRIP

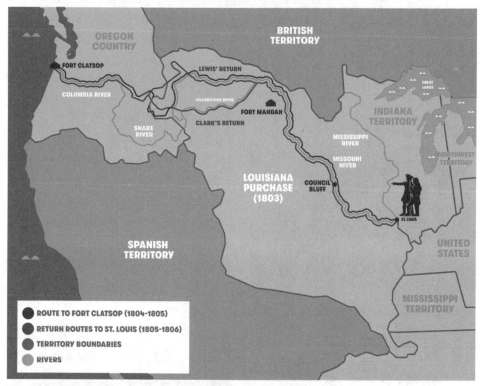

The Lewis and Clark expedition allowed the United States to gain crucial geographic information about its new territory.

THE FUR TRADE

Why was controlling the fur trade such a big deal? Today most of us are happy to wear synthetic fleece instead. So it's hard to imagine now how the animal skins the Native Americans provided would be valuable enough to cause bloodshed. Mostly, it happened because of the popularity of. . . hats.

In Europe, men and women desperately wanted fur hats. The wealthy wanted beaver hats. Poorer people wore less expensive furs, including rabbit.

KEY CONTRIBUTIONS BY PEOPLE OF COLOR

SACAGAWEA

Sacagawea

When Lewis and Clark's team lived with the Mandan, they met Sacagawea (c. 1788–Unknown). She was a 16-year-old member of the Shoshone Nation. She was forced to marry a Frenchman who was twenty years older than she was. He lived with the Nation and already had another wife. (Some tribes allowed men to be married to more than one woman at once.)

Sacagawea and her baby son joined the explorers (for no pay) as they headed west. Because there was a woman and a baby in the group, some of the fifty different Native American nations they met felt comfortable that this wasn't a war party.

Sacagawea knew Indigenous languages. She also knew, for example, which roots and berries were safe to eat. Both of these skills were vital to the explorers' survival. For her service, her husband received 320 acres of land and $500.33. Sacagawea died at about the age of 25, months after giving birth to a daughter.

YORK, AN ENSLAVED MAN

York was the only Black American on the Lewis and Clark expedition.

William Clark brought an enslaved man named York (dates unknown) on the 28-month, cross-country journey. York was a hugely important member of the team. He helped hunt buffalo, navigate trails, and handle firearms.

He was also a hero. When Clark disappeared in a storm, York risked his life to find him. Yet when the expedition was over, Clark refused to release York from enslavement for at least a decade.

THE EXPEDITION YIELDS BIG RETURNS FOR THE UNITED STATES

Thanks to the Lewis and Clark team, the U.S. government now had maps that showed how they could best move goods throughout the country. They could use connecting rivers stretching from coast to coast. The government also had a new understanding of the land and the natural resources that were available. Crucially, they had made positive connections with Native American nations who could help with trade.

NOT SO MUCH FOR NATIVE AMERICANS

Yet again, the Native Americans would face consequences because of white colonizers' desire for land, goods, and control. As an example: When Lewis and Clark arrived at the Mandan villages in 1804, the community's population was around 5,000. In 1852, Americans established Fort Clark on the land, and U.S. troops helped the Mandan fight the Lakota nation. But in doing so, U.S. soldiers introduced new diseases that killed the Mandan. By the late 1930s, the nation numbered less than 150.

 Why do you think the Mandan agreed to help the Americans?

_____

_____

_____

MARBURY V. MADISON AND JUDICIAL REVIEW

Jefferson wanted to expand the country, but he also focused on how the government should work. Jefferson's ego sometimes got the better of him. In a power move better suited to middle school than the White House, he accidentally brought about what we now know as judicial review. This established for good the idea that the Supreme Court has the final say in deciding if the laws Congress makes are constitutional.

MARBURY V. MADISON

Here's how it happened: After he became president, Jefferson had some letters from his rival, previous President John Adams. These letters gave several men the title of justice of the peace. But Jefferson decided not to send those letters (that's the middle school part). That meant the men did not become judges.

One of those men, William Marbury, was angry enough to take his case to the Supreme Court in 1801. He pointed out a law that Congress had passed in 1789. The law stated that the Supreme Court could force a person to send commissions (formally known as issuing a writ of mandamus) no matter what his personal feelings were about it.

THE SUPREME COURT'S DECISION

The Supreme Court decided that the commissions should have been sent. But they added that based on the Constitution, it wasn't their job to force someone to send commissions they did not want to send.

Today we know the case as *Marbury v. Madison*. The case not only overturned Congress's 1789 law, but it also forever established a precedent. This precedent was that the Supreme Court could overturn laws passed by Congress if the court said the laws violated the Constitution. Now, that's power!

When we talk about the importance of our government's "checks and balances," judicial review was the last crucial step in the process. Now, the judicial branch of the government helps make sure that new laws agree with the judges' understanding of the Constitution.

> **judicial review:** the principle that the Supreme Court has the power to decide if the laws Congress makes are constitutional.
>
> **precedent:** a rule or law from the past that people look to for guidance in a new decision.

HOW DO PEOPLE MAKE

SOMEONE HAS AN IDEA.
Every law begins with an idea. Anyone can have an idea for a law and submit it to their elected official—usually a member of the House of Representatives, but it can be a senator, too. If the representative or senator agrees with the idea and wants to turn it into a law, he or she writes a bill.

THE BILL GOES TO CONGRESS.
The representative or senator introduces the bill into whatever house they belong to. That member of Congress becomes the bill's main sponsor.

THE BILL GETS RECONCILED.
If the second house of Congress passes the bill, it has to go through the process of reconciliation so that both houses pass the same version of the bill before it goes to the president for signing.

THE BILL GOES TO THE OTHER HOUSE OF CONGRESS.
If the majority votes in favor of the bill, then it moves to the other house of Congress. Then the bill goes through the same process of debate, revision, and a vote.

THE PRESIDENT ACTS.
The president can sign the bill into law.

Congratulations! You've got a law!

The president can veto (reject) the bill. Then it goes back to Congress. If two-thirds of the members of both houses of Congress vote to override (cancel) the president's veto, then the bill will become law.

Better luck next time, unless two-thirds of Congress is on your side.

*If someone challenges the law, the case may enter the legal system. Because of Marbury v. Madis

LAWS, ANYWAY?

THE BILL GOES TO COMMITTEE.

A small group of representatives or senators, called a committee, researches and talks about the bill. If necessary, they make changes to it. Then they vote on whether to accept or reject it.

If the committee members agree that the bill is a good idea, they will send it to the floor of the House or the Senate for debate by the full membership. There they can suggest changes and put it to a vote.

THE BILL GOES TO THE HOUSE OR SENATE FLOOR

If the committee members agree that the bill is a good idea, they will send it to the floor of the House or the Senate for debate by the full membership. There they can suggest changes and put it to a vote.

If the committee members can't agree, or they need more information, the bill can go to a subcommittee created for that purpose.

The House or Senate can reject or table the bill. To table something means to delay it—maybe forever.

The president can choose to do nothing. Then, assuming Congress is in session, the bill becomes law ten days later.

Congratulations! You've got a law!

If Congress goes out of session during that period, the bill will not become law. This is called a pocket veto.

Better luck next time. That's why it's good to be the president!

The Supreme Court of the United States has the final say on whether a law is constitutional.

JEFFERSON AND ADAMS

John Adams and Thomas Jefferson were friends after meeting at the Continental Congress in 1775. Adams asked Jefferson to write the Constitution. Jefferson also served as vice president under Adams, even though they held vastly different political views. But during the 1800 election, the competitors threw major shade on each other.

Jefferson's supporters accused Adams of having a "hideous" character, with "neither the force and firmness of a man, nor the gentleness and sensibility of a woman." Adams's team, in turn, accused Jefferson of being a radical revolutionary who didn't believe in God. Jefferson even hired a journalist to falsely claim in the press that Adams wanted to start a war with France.

That journalist, James Callendar, was also responsible for a series of newspaper articles in 1801 in which he alleged that Jefferson had fathered children with his enslaved mistress, Sally Hemings. Modern DNA evidence and historical records show that this accusation was most likely true. Callendar, who played both sides, also wrote the quote above about Adams's hideous character.

At the end of their lives, the men renewed their friendship. They exchanged 158 letters over 14 years.

 What effects do you think this feud might have had on American politics? Can you think of modern examples of politicians behaving like this?

WHO WAS SALLY HEMINGS?

Sally Hemings (1773–1835) was an enslaved woman who, at 14, served Jefferson's daughter Maria. At the time, the family was living in Paris, where Jefferson was American Minister to France. Jefferson wrote that Blacks are "inferior to whites in the endowments both of body and mind." But his relationship with Hemings was long, and they had at least six children together.

As an enslaved person, Hemings had no legal right to refuse sexual advances. Hemings never received freedom from Jefferson. After his death in 1826, Jefferson's daughter Martha set Hemings free.

reconciliation: the process of two groups coming to an agreement or a compromise. In Congress, it involves a bill being worked on in both houses simultaneously and then combined into a single "reconciled" bill that can pass in both houses.

veto: the power held by the president to refuse to approve a bill passed by Congress, preventing it from becoming a law.

override: Congress can overrule a presidential veto if two-thirds of both houses of Congress vote to "override" it. The bill then becomes law over the president's objections.

THE WAR OF 1812

Jefferson and Adams are a great example of two people who forgave each other for past bad behavior toward each other. Britain and the United States were not yet the same success story. Britain was still hurting from the loss of territory and income. In contrast, the United States was on a quest for more power and land. The two countries returned to battle.

A MULTI-SIDED STRUGGLE

It wasn't just about these two countries—conflict is rarely that simple. Britain was feuding with France and its leader, Napoleon Bonaparte, who had crowned himself emperor in 1804. Both countries decided that the upper hand might come from blocking trade with the United States.

The United States suffered from its own embargo (an official ban) of goods going into and coming out of the country. Congress had enacted this embargo in 1807 in an attempt to force Britain and France to respect the United States' economic power. For decades, the British had been practicing impressment of American sailors. In other words, British sailors kidnapped sailors from American ships and forced them to work on British ships. (Often, the British claimed the Americans were deserters from the British Navy.) These aggressions made the situation more tense.

Then, Britain—which still controlled much of Canada—moved its attack onto land. It supported several Native American nations that were trying to protect themselves from American settlers who were moving onto their land. Americans believed that the British were encouraging the Native Americans to take up arms against the United States, pushing them to war.

> **impressment:** the practice in which British sailors kidnapped sailors from American ships and forced them to work on British ships.
>
> **embargo:** an official ban on trade with another country.

WAR BREAKS OUT

War eventually broke out in August of 1812 in Ontario, a Canadian province. British forces led by Shawnee leader Tecumseh and British general Isaac Brock defeated the United States. Brock died in the battle.

The War of 1812 turned out to be inaccurately named, since it was still going on two years later. On August 24, 1814, the British invaded Washington, D.C., and set fire to the White House and the Capitol building. The United States fought back and won the Battles of Plattsburgh, New York, and Fort McHenry, Maryland (both September 1814). The war would end at the year's end with no clear victor.

A TREATY ENDS THE WAR

After an estimated 15,000 U.S. casualties, the countries agreed to the Treaty of Ghent. It was named after the Belgian city in which both sides signed it on December 24, 1814. The treaty stated that the British would stop trying to sponsor a Native American state in the Northwest Territory. It also restored the borders between the United States and Canada.

THE BATTLE OF NEW ORLEANS

News of the Treaty of Ghent took almost two months to make its way back to the United States. In this day of constant texting and news updates, this is almost impossible to imagine. As a result of the delay, British and Americans kept fighting when they didn't have to, including the American-won Battle of New Orleans on January 8, 1815. Major Andrew Jackson led the charge, in which 2,000 British soldiers were killed within the first 30 minutes. Fewer than 100 Americans were killed. Jackson became a war hero, which paved the way for his future presidency.

NO PEACE FOR NATIVE AMERICANS

There was now peace between the United States and Britain. However, Native Americans continued to be caught in the power struggles between Europe and the United States. General Andrew Jackson immediately began attacking Seminole settlements in Florida, which Spain owned. Unable to defend its territory, Spain agreed to sell Florida to the United States in 1819. The agreement was known as the Treaty of Adams-Onis. Over the next decade, the U.S. government would force many Native Americans to move onto reservations or leave the state.

PUTTING—AND KEEPING—THE EUROPEANS IN THEIR PLACE

Americans wanted to keep the European powers out of what was now their country, as well as the area we now call Latin America. In a speech he gave to Congress in 1823, President James Monroe warned Europe about this issue. He insisted that any attempts of Europeans to interfere anywhere in the Western Hemisphere would be a potentially hostile act.

His words became known as the Monroe Doctrine. (A doctrine is a statement of rules or policy.) This one would become central to how the United States interacted with other countries in the years and decades to come.

Monroe Doctrine: a statement that European powers should stay out of conflicts in the Americas or face consequences from the United States.

 Why do you think Monroe's statement was so important?

_____

_____

_____

_____

FROM HOMESPUN TO FACTORY: THE FIRST INDUSTRIAL REVOLUTION

Americans of this period were trying to get their laws straight, taking more land, and fighting with Europe. It's hard to imagine that they would have the bandwidth for more than this. And yet. . .

Eli Whitney's cotton gin, short for cotton engine, was a device that sped up the production of cotton.

THE COTTON GIN

In 1793, Eli Whitney invented the cotton gin, a machine that removed seeds from plants. This invention made it more profitable to grow cotton. By 1860, as much as 61 percent of the world's raw cotton was coming from the southern states on land taken from Native Americans. This was mostly because of labor from enslaved Africans. Much of this cotton went to Europe to be made into cloth. But textile mills (factories that made cloth) also began opening in the northeastern United States.

cotton gin: an invention that made it easier and faster to separate cotton fibers from their seeds. It made the business of growing cotton much more profitable.

STEAMBOATS

With the growing popularity of steamboats in the early nineteenth century, it became easier to transport cotton from Southern plantations to factories up North, where workers turned it into cloth. The United States used to rely on sending raw materials to other countries for processing. Now, for the first time, it had huge amounts of its own finished product to sell.

FACTORIES

What about those women who had learned to make their own cloth thanks to the Daughters of Liberty? Forget working from home. Beginning in the 1820s, it was about working in factories.

Those factories weren't limited to producing cotton. In Connecticut, they mass-produced clocks and products made of tin. In Pennsylvania, they could melt and mold metal faster than any blacksmith. The sudden growth of factories would change American society.

HOW DID THE INDUSTRIAL REVOLUTION AFFECT WOMEN?

Factory owners wanted young women to fill the many jobs in the factories. These women could earn $3 a week, which is much more than they could make working on farms or as servants. As a result, large numbers of unmarried women moved to industrial cities like Lowell, Massachusetts, Corning, New York, and Pullman, Illinois.

Imagine what it would be like to suddenly find yourself independent for the first time. You could learn to speak up for yourself and others. Many of these women did just that. They banded together to champion reform movements.

One such organization was the Lowell Factory Girls Association. Founded in 1836, it had 2,500 members. They insisted on better working conditions for themselves. Also, they championed women's rights and prison reform and opposed slavery.

The Lowell Factory Girls Association fought hard for their rights as women and as workers.

 In what other ways do you think these new factories might have changed America?

_____

_____

_____

_____

_____

_____

_____

_____

ANDREW JACKSON AND JACKSONIAN DEMOCRACY

Americans celebrated their increasing power and their independence from European interference. Many people called the time leading up to Jackson's presidency the Era of Good Feelings. James Monroe, the author of the Monroe Doctrine (and another Virginian), was president during this period, between 1817 and 1825. Monroe's party, the Democratic-Republicans, enjoyed complete political dominance—hence the name of the era. However, those who Americans had taken land from found themselves in increasing danger.

Jackson won the election in a landslide in 1828. Jackson was a wealthy man and enslaver who owned a giant plantation, but he promised to champion the "common man." This meant ordinary white farmers and workers rather than the wealthy.

His opponents called him "King Andrew." They pointed out that he was a member of the elite class, though Jacksonian democracy did favor policies that limited the powers of the industrial and banking elite. Jacksonians wanted egalitarianism. For example, they thought a carpenter should have as much say in government as a banker did.

ENEMY OF NATIVE AMERICANS

Jackson's idea of egalitarianism had its limits, however. Only white men had power. Jackson said white Americans were entitled to land Native Americans lived on. He drew an even harsher line than Jefferson, who had supported the "assimilation" process.

Jackson signed the Indian Removal Act in 1830. Under this law, U.S. troops forcibly relocated people from the Seminole, Creek, Chickasaw, Cherokee, and Choctaw nations. The government forced Native Americans to move onto reservations. These were parcels of land that Native Americans "controlled" under the federal government's Bureau of Indian Affairs. The land parcels were isolated from the rest of the country. Only a few tribes agreed to go peacefully.

egalitarianism: the political belief that all people have equal value, and which prioritizes social equality.

Indian Removal Act: a law passed in 1830 that permitted U.S. troops to forcibly relocate people from the Seminole, Creek, Chickasaw, Cherokee, and Choctaw nations to reservations.

NATIVE AMERICAN NATIONS BEFORE THE INDIAN REMOVAL ACT OF 1830

NATIVE AMERICAN RESISTANCE

The Cherokee sought legal action to protect themselves and their land. They asked Congress for help. They found support from the Christian missionary Samuel Worcester. He had helped establish the first Native American newspaper, the *Cherokee Phoenix*.

In 1832, the Supreme Court made a ruling in the case *Worcester v. Georgia*. The court said the Cherokee were entitled to their own self-rule on their ancestral land. Therefore, they didn't have to follow state law. But Jackson upended what should have been a victory for the Cherokee. He was determined to find a way to get them off their land.

Jackson organized a small group of Cherokee men who preferred to make a deal with the U.S. government to relocate in exchange for payment. He convinced them to sign the Treaty of New Echota on behalf of the entire Cherokee nation—even though the vast majority of Cherokee opposed the treaty. This agreement paid the Cherokees $5 million for their seven million acres of land. Congress upheld the treaty, and the government forced Cherokees to leave.

NOT ALL NATIVE AMERICANS RESISTED

Elias Boudinot, who signed the treaty, was a Native American man who converted to Christianity. He and his white wife, Harriet Gold, were missionaries. Boudinot was also a newspaper editor who published editorials supporting removal. In a letter to Cherokee Chief Ross, he encouraged him to accept removal, writing the following:

> *"If the dark picture which I have here drawn is a true one,... can we see a brighter prospect ahead? In another country, and under other circumstances, there is a better prospect. Removal, then is the only remedy—the only practicable [practical] remedy. By it... our people may rise from their very ashes to become prosperous and happy, and a credit to our race."*

In 1839, Boudinot and his family moved west. Soon after, some men who opposed the treaty stabbed Boudinot to death, along with his uncle and a cousin. The men murdered them for signing the treaty.

THE TRAIL OF TEARS

The Trail of Tears refers to the deadly path that armed American soldiers forced Native Americans to travel for thousands of miles on foot. The Native Americans traveled from their homes to reservations between 1830 and 1850. The path is actually made up of multiple trails totaling more than 5,000 miles in length. It includes nine states: Alabama, Arkansas, Georgia, Illinois, Kentucky, Missouri, North Carolina, Oklahoma, and Tennessee.

The marches were agonizing and deadly. From 1838 to 1839, troops forced more than 16,000 Cherokees to leave their lands in what are now Tennessee, Alabama, North Carolina, and Georgia. They had to travel more than 1,000 miles to what is now Oklahoma. More than 4,000 of them died. It was this particular march that gave the trail its name.

> Trail of Tears: a path consisting of multiple trails that armed American soldiers forced Native Americans to travel for thousands of miles on foot from their homes to reservations.

Following the Treaty of New Echota, which most Cherokee people viewed as fake, the U.S. government violently displaced thousands of Native Americans. The brutal march westward is called the Trail of Tears.

GETTING SCHOOLED IN MISERY

Not even Native American children would be spared the brutality of "assimilation." Over the next century, white leaders built boarding schools to house children in locations across the country. To attend school, these Native American children had to leave their families. School officials did not allow students to speak their native language. They forced students to change their names, cut their hair, and otherwise ignore their culture.

In 1879, Captain Richard Henry Pratt founded the Carlisle Indian Industrial School in Pennsylvania. Pratt said that people ought to "kill the Indian, save the man." Some 10,000 students from more than 70 Native American nations attended the school before it closed in 1918. Historians estimate that only one in eight students graduated.

BLACK ENSLAVED PEOPLE AND NATIVE AMERICANS

It's not surprising that Native Americans and Black enslaved people sometimes banded together to fight their common enemy. For instance, when the Seminoles refused to leave Florida after the Indian Relocation Act in 1830, as many as 400 enslaved people escaped from plantations to fight alongside the Native Americans in the Second Seminole War. The formerly enslaved, called "Black Seminoles," helped destroy more than twenty sugar plantations.

They were not always allies, however. Some Native Americans enslaved Black people. This included Cherokee chief John Ross. Several nations relied on enslaved labor to help them rebuild when they reached their reservations. The Cherokee, Chickasaw, Choctaw, Creek, and Seminoles would also side with the South during the Civil War.

A NEW PRESIDENT AND AN ECONOMIC DEPRESSION

In 1837, Martin Van Buren (1782-1862) became the country's eighth president. Previously, he had been Jackson's secretary of state and vice president.

Three months later, the U.S. economy plummeted. This happened because in 1836, Jackson had tried to stop banks from taking advantage of people who wanted to buy land in the West. Banks were willing to lend money to almost anyone, but they charged very high interest rates for the privilege of borrowing that money. Many people bought land, couldn't pay back their loans, and lost that land. Jackson decided that the solution was that people could buy land only with gold or silver, not with paper money.

This change in the rules caused a financial panic. Banks and businesses failed, which meant many people lost their jobs and their savings. Unable to fix the economy, Van Buren failed to win a second term as president.

Why do you think banks panicked when Jackson said people could buy land with gold or silver only?

_____

_____

_____

_____

_____

THE MEXICAN-AMERICAN WAR

In 1845, newspaper editor John O'Sullivan invented the phrase "Manifest Destiny." People used this idea to say it was right for the United States to expand into new territory and to kill huge groups of Indigenous people. Manifest Destiny was the dangerous belief that God had given "racially superior" white Americans the right to triumph over "heathens," or people who were not Christian.

One such believer was President James K. Polk. He had his eye on Mexico. At first, he tried the peaceful route. He sent a diplomat to offer $25 million for territories that are now New Mexico and California. Mexico turned down this offer. So the United States attacked, beginning a war that would last from 1846 until 1848.

THE WAR'S AFTERMATH

Mexico lost half its territory. The United States gained the land that eventually became California, Nevada, Utah, Arizona, and New Mexico. The cost was high, though. About 13,200 of the 79,000 American troops lost their lives. This death rate of soldiers was higher than both World War I and World War II. Mexico may have lost as many as 25,000 people.

ABRAHAM LINCOLN SPEAKS OUT

One of the war's harshest critics was the newly elected Illinois congressman, Abraham Lincoln. Lincoln, like many other Northerners, considered the war a trick to gain more land to expand slavery. In a speech to Congress in 1848, he said of Polk, "He is a bewildered, confounded, and miserably perplexed man."

In what ways do you think the Mexican-American War led up to the
Civil War?

_____

_____

_____

JAMES K. POLK

So who was James K. Polk
(1795–1849)? He has been largely
forgotten. Part of that is his own
fault. When he ran for president,
he promised to retire after a single
term. Polk was a lawyer from North
Carolina and a slaveholder. People
call him the first "dark horse"
president, meaning his rise to the position was a big surprise. Polk died
shortly after leaving office.

SO *THAT* EXPLAINS WHY THERE WERE SO MANY PRESIDENTS

While Polk only served one term, from 1845 to 1849, that was years
more than other presidents around the same time. Zachary Taylor
(1784–1850) was a famous general in the Mexican-American War. He
succeeded Polk as president in 1849 but died of a stomach problem
16 months into his term. And William Henry Harrison (1773–1841), who
was the ninth president, died from illness only 31 days into his term in
April 1841. This makes him the shortest-serving president in history.

CHAPTER 3 VOCABULARY

cotton gin: an invention that made it easier to remove seeds from plants. It made the business of growing cotton much more profitable.

diplomat: someone who officially represents the government of a country.

egalitarianism: the political belief that all people have equal value, and which prioritizes social equality.

embargo: an official ban on trade with another country.

impressment: the practice in which British sailors kidnapped sailors from American ships and forced them to work on British ships.

Indian Removal Act: a law passed in 1830 that permitted U.S. troops to forcibly relocate people from the Seminole, Creek, Chickasaw, Cherokee, and Choctaw nations to reservations.

judicial review: the principle that the Supreme Court has the power to decide if the laws Congress makes are constitutional.

missionary: someone who tries to convince people to follow a certain religion.

Monroe Doctrine: a statement that European powers should stay out of conflicts in the Americas or face consequences from the United States.

override: Congress can overrule a presidential **veto** if two-thirds of both houses of Congress vote to "override" it. The bill then becomes law over the president's objections.

precedent: a rule or law from the past that people look to for guidance in a new decision.

reconciliation: the process of two groups coming to an agreement or a compromise. In Congress, it involves a bill being worked on in both houses simultaneously and then combined into a single reconciled bill that can pass in both houses.

Trail of Tears: a path consisting of multiple trails that armed American soldiers forced Native Americans to travel for thousands of miles on foot from their homes to reservations

veto: the power held by the president to refuse to approve a bill passed by Congress, preventing it from becoming a law.

4

A WAR IS BREWING

Abolitionists and enslavers had opposing views on slavery, and everyone else seemed to take one side or the other. On top of that, economic tensions between the North and the South were growing. Was war impossible to avoid? Let's take a look.

CHAPTER CONTENTS

THE EXCUSE FOR ENSLAVEMENT

THE ABOLITIONIST MOVEMENT

THE UNDERGROUND RAILROAD

THE NAT TURNER REBELLION

THE GOVERNMENT TRIES TO KEEP THE COUNTRY TOGETHER

A TURNING POINT TOWARD WAR

THE ELECTION OF 1860

THE EXCUSE FOR ENSLAVEMENT

Economic greed as well as racism drove the practice of slavery. White plantation owners relied on the unpaid labor of the enslaved. And so did their trading partners in Northern factories and other places all over the world. Many people believed that anyone who wasn't white—and by that they meant a white man—was not their equal.

PRIMARY SOURCES ON SLAVERY

In the case of Black Americans, enslavers didn't stop there. They even claimed that the enslaved somehow benefited from their loss of freedom. Here's what *The Staunton Spectator*, a Virginia newspaper, reported in 1859:

> "We have never [doubted] that the condition of the Southern slaves is the best and most desirable for the negroes. . . the Black man's lot as a slave is vastly preferable to that of his free [brothers] in the North. . . The intelligent, Christian slave-holder [of] the South is the best friend of the negro."

 What do you think the motive of the writer was? Do you think the writer is a believable source?

_____

_____

_____

_____

_____

Compare the words in *The Staunton Spectator* to these words from Billy Collins, who was enslaved in Alabama. He is one of the thousands of former enslaved people whose voices historians have recorded.

"My mother was sold away from me. I was so lonesome without her that I would often go about my work and look for her return… but she never came back."

Collins continued, "My master was so cruel to his slaves [he was] almost crazy at times. He would buckle us across a log and whip us until we were unable to walk for three days. On Sunday, we would go to the barn and pray for God to fix some way for us to be freed."

 What do you think of the newspaper's account after reading this?

_____

_____

_____

_____

_____

HOW ENSLAVED PEOPLE BUILT THE COUNTRY

Why was the United States financially successful? It was economically independent from Europe. Also, it had products to sell to Europe. But a huge reason the U.S. economy grew so fast was because of millions of enslaved people who were forced to work for free. And it wasn't only the unpaid labor of the enslaved that benefited slaveholders—it was their knowledge, skills, and innovations.

People in the South grew many crops. These included tobacco, sugar cane, and indigo. (A valuable blue dye comes from indigo.) These crops were important, but nothing was more crucial than cotton. It was the biggest export the United States had, making up more than half of the country's profits from everything it sold abroad. Before the Civil War, the South grew 61 percent of the world's cotton.

As the demand for cotton grew, factories in the North became an important part of the cotton industry.

BEYOND THE SOUTH

But cotton (and enslaved labor) didn't enrich the South only. Cotton exports paid for a lot of the land, buildings, and machines that became the basis of the Industrial Revolution in the United States. Now factories, mostly in the North, could process the crop even more quickly. As a result, the demand for cotton grew even more.

So did the demand for unpaid labor. From 1790 until 1860, the number of enslaved people in the United States skyrocketed from 500,000 to four million.

NOT ALL SOUTHERNERS OWNED SLAVES

The vast majority of enslaved people lived on large plantations owned by wealthy Southerners. That meant that a state could have many more enslaved people than enslavers. Take Texas in 1860. More than 182,000 people were enslaved, making up more than 30 percent of the state's population. Enslavers were only 27 percent of the population but they controlled 73 percent of the state's wealth.

LOTS OF NORTHERNERS OWNED SLAVES TOO

The divide between the North and South in terms of slavery wasn't always one of ideals. Most of the North had less fertile land than the South—in other words, the land didn't grow crops as well. So Northerners relied less on people to work on the land. Instead of huge plantations with hundreds of workers, they tended to have small family farms and more shops and factories. That doesn't mean slavery didn't exist in the North.

SLAVERY IN THE NORTHEAST

In 1740, one-fifth of New York City's population was made up of enslaved people. Connecticut allowed slavery until 1848. Rhode Island's population had the largest percentage of enslaved people compared to free people in the country. The state also played an enormous role in the slave trade. By the end of the eighteenth century, Rhode Island ships had made at least 1,000 trips from Africa to the United States.

DO A PRESIDENT'S ACTIONS SPEAK LOUDER THAN WORDS?

Enslaved people literally built the White House. They dug huge stones out of the ground, cut logs, made bricks, and worked alongside white wage workers and craftspeople. They helped rebuild the White House in 1814 after the British burned it down in the War of 1812.

So where did the presidents stand on the issue of slavery? Regardless of what they said they believed, at least nine presidents brought enslaved people to work for them at the White House. They included Thomas Jefferson, James Madison, James Monroe, John Quincy Adams, Andrew Jackson, Martin Van Buren, John Tyler, James K. Polk, and Zachary Taylor. (George Washington "owned" enslaved people, but he never lived in the White House.)

THE ABOLITIONIST MOVEMENT

Though people had spoken out against slavery in the 18th century, an organized and vocal campaign to abolish (end) slavery began in Northern states in 1830. This movement further divided a country where many Northerners wanted abolition and many white Southerners wanted to keep slavery. Both sides argued loudly—and sometimes violently. The growing intensity helped bring about the Civil War. Two government decisions made the argument burn hotter.

THE FUGITIVE SLAVE ACT

The first was the Fugitive Slave Act, which Congress passed in 1850. It said that all enslaved people who escaped must be captured and returned to their captors. The Act said that all citizens had to cooperate with slave catchers. Seven years later, in a case called *Dred Scott v. Sanford*, the Supreme Court ruled that no Black people, whether free or enslaved, were legal citizens. These two decisions together meant that enslavers also had the right to take their enslaved people with them when moving to Western territories.

abolition: to abolish something is to end it; abolitionists wanted to end slavery.

Fugitive Slave Act: an 1850 law passed by Congress that said that all enslaved people who escaped had to be captured and returned to their captors, even if they were in "free" states.

Why do you think the government was so eager to protect the rights of enslavers?

_____

_____

_____

THE RISE OF THE KNOW-NOTHINGS

The thirteenth president of the United States, Millard Fillmore (1850–1853), was elected as a member of the Whig Party. Later, he became a member of the Know-Nothing party. It was anti-immigrant and anti-Catholic. Some of its members were involved in violent rioting and assaults. The party earned its name because when outsiders asked about their beliefs, members were supposed to say, "I know nothing." The group changed its name to the American Party in 1855.

WOMEN RAISE THEIR VOICES

Thank antislavery beliefs for leading directly to the women's rights and suffrage movement, in which women fought for the right to vote. Lucretia Mott was a Quaker minister, and Elizabeth Cady Stanton was a wealthy woman who worked for equality and justice. In 1840, the men who organized the World Anti-Slavery Convention in London wouldn't let them attend.

This caused Mott and Stanton to organize a women's rights convention. In 1848, the first convention to "discuss the social, civil, and religious condition and rights of woman" took place in Seneca Falls, New York. There, Stanton presented a document she had helped write called The Declaration of Sentiments. She used the Declaration of Independence as her inspiration to put forth the argument that women were entitled to equality under the law.

BLACK WOMEN AND THE SUFFRAGE MOVEMENT

The definition of who deserved that equality seemed to be limited to white women. There is no evidence that Black activists who were involved in the suffrage movement were invited to the convention. Stanton and Susan B. Anthony also objected to the Fifteenth Amendment, which would give Black men the vote. They thought it would get in the way of women's rights to vote, or as Stanton put it, "educated, refined women." In the white suffrage fight, Black women were left out in the cold.

Despite this exclusion, Black women were still a vocal part of the fight for suffrage. Black women such as Ida B. Wells-Barnett and Frances Ellen Watkins Harper called out anti-Black violence and exclusion in the suffrage movement. In 1866, Harper gave a speech at the National Woman's Rights Convention, and stated that "We are all bound up together," demanding that the fight for women's suffrage include Black women. Later, in 1896, Wells-Barnett and Harper founded the National Association of Colored Women.

IDA B. WELLS-BARNETT   FRANCES ELLEN WATKINS HARPER

While the fight for Black freedom and women's rights sometimes went together, only Black women had to live with both forms of inequality.

suffrage: the legal right to vote.

In 1849, California became one of the first states to extend property rights to women, though this did nothing to help Black women. That meant that when a California woman got married, her property legally stayed her own. In the other states, it automatically went to her husband to do with as he wished.

THE GOLD RUSH

In 1848, a former carpenter from New Jersey named James Marshall discovered flecks of gold floating in a river in California's Sacramento Valley. What followed was a gold rush, as thousands of people made their way to California in hopes of making their fortune. So many men arrived in 1849 that they were known as "forty-niners." The non-native population of California grew by almost 100,000.

By the turn of the century, the two largest gold fields in California yielded the modern-day equivalent of more than $25 billion in gold to eager miners. Hydraulic mining, which uses powerful jets of water to blast through rock, was developed in 1853. It replaced the need to dig for gold by hand, but it damaged the environment.

A TWO-WAY STREET

Many of the most famous abolitionists supported the women's rights movement. Likewise, many of those seeking women's suffrage also fought for abolition. These included:

FREDERICK DOUGLASS

Frederick Douglass (1818–1895) was a crucial figure in the abolitionist movement. He escaped slavery and published a book called *Narrative of the Life of Frederick Douglass, an American Slave.* He spoke loudly and insistently about women's right to vote.

SUSAN B. ANTHONY

Susan B. Anthony (1820–1906) was an author and women's rights advocate as well as a Quaker. She also supported the abolitionist movement. She was one of the first women to appear on U.S. money, although that didn't happen until 1979.

HARRIET TUBMAN

Harriet Tubman (c. 1820–1913) is famous for her work freeing enslaved Black people as a leader of the Underground Railroad, which you will learn about later in this chapter. She was also an activist for women's right to vote.

SOJOURNER TRUTH

Sojourner Truth (1797–1883) escaped enslavement in New York. She delivered a speech arguing for women's rights at the women's convention in Ohio in 1851, which became famous as the "Ain't I a Woman" speech.

In 1827, New York passed an antislavery law that declared the state's enslaved people would be emancipated. When Truth's former owner illegally sold her five-year-old son Peter, she filed a lawsuit to bring Peter back. Truth was one of the first Black women to sue a white man in a United States court and win.

A decade after her "Ain't I a Woman?" speech, Abraham Lincoln invited Truth to the White House. When she was in Washington, D.C., she made a political statement by riding on whites-only streetcars.

emancipate: to free someone from captivity or bondage.

How does the misquoting affect what you learned from her speech, instead of the words she actually spoke? What does this say about how the teller of a history can shape and rewrite it?

_____

_____

_____

_____

THE COMPLICATED LEGACY OF *UNCLE TOM'S CABIN*

Harriet Beecher Stowe, an abolitionist, wrote this novel in 1852. It had a strong and lasting effect on Americans who were gearing up for a fight.

The book's main character, Uncle Tom, is enslaved and suffers greatly. The text reveals a brutal portrait of enslavement. It tries to teach the idea that Christian love can help people overcome any anger and bitterness, no matter what the cause.

It would go on to be the best-selling book of the nineteenth century, behind only the Bible. Its author intended it to be an antislavery argument. She based the book on real accounts of people who were enslaved. But the book also described Black people in stereotypical ways. It said that Black men should always forgive white people and be submissive (willing to obey).

 Stowe's book may have helped more people understand the price of slavery. But she also promoted harmful stereotypes about Black people. Despite being an abolitionist, do you think it's possible she might have had racist ideas about Black people, even if she wasn't aware of it? How do you think Stowe's own biases may have affected her writing?

_____

_____

_____

_____

_____

bias: prejudice or slant in favor of one side of an issue over another, usually in a way considered to be unfair.

This word is so important for historians that there is a whole section on bias and how to detect it beginning on page 436!

THE UNDERGROUND RAILROAD

 The Underground Railroad wasn't underground and usually didn't include a train. Instead, it was a complicated network of people who brought the enslaved to freedom.

They did this through a series of safeguarded "stations," such as homes, churches, and abandoned buildings. The "conductors" leading these missions were mostly Black. But white or Black, all conductors knew that helping runaways could bring a death sentence.

The African Methodist Episcopal Church began in 1816. It helped enslaved people escape. So did the Quakers; historians credit them as the first organized group to help the cause. (In 1786, George Washington blamed them for trying to help one of his enslaved people escape.) Quaker abolitionist Isaac T. Hopper started a network in Philadelphia to help bring people to freedom. Quakers in North Carolina helped set up safe houses and escape routes.

THE AFRICAN METHODIST EPISCOPAL CHURCH

Reverend Richard Allen (1760–1831) was born as an enslaved person in Delaware. Allen bought his freedom and became a minister. In 1787, he broke from the Methodist Church because of its restrictions on Black members. In 1805, he began leading services in the newly constructed "Roughcast Church," so called because it was built from crude brick and stone. It was the first brick church in America to be built by and for Black Americans as a place to worship without racial oppression.

In 1816, Allen banded together with numerous other Black Methodist churches to form the African Methodist Episcopal Church (AME). It included congregations in cities in free states, as well as Maryland, Kentucky, Missouri, and Louisiana. The Roughcast Church, a leading member of the AME, became a station on the Underground Railroad.

Today, the African Methodist Episcopal Church has more than 2.5 million members. Its mission is to "minister to the social, spiritual, and physical development of all people."

 History books teach us about the Quakers helping with the Underground Railroad. However, the African Methodist Episcopal Church often goes unmentioned. Why do you think this might be? Hint: it has to do with who is telling the story.

_____

_____

_____

_____

_____

_____

SEEING THE UNDERGROUND RAILROAD

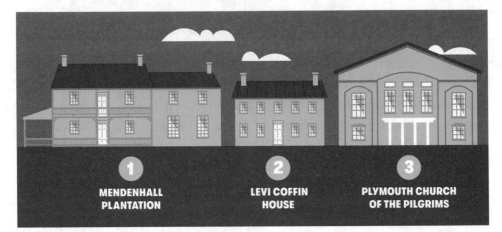

1 MENDENHALL PLANTATION	**2** LEVI COFFIN HOUSE	**3** PLYMOUTH CHURCH OF THE PILGRIMS

You don't just have to imagine it. Many states have preserved sites that were crucial stops for enslaved people on their way to freedom, and you can visit them today. These include:

1 **MENDENHALL PLANTATION IN JAMESTOWN, NORTH CAROLINA**
Richard Mendenhall, a Quaker, opened his home to those who opposed slavery.

2 **LEVI COFFIN HOUSE IN FOUNTAIN CITY, INDIANA**
More than 1,000 fugitive enslaved people found their way to freedom from this home.

3 **PLYMOUTH CHURCH OF THE PILGRIMS IN BROOKLYN, NEW YORK**
Its preacher, Henry Ward Beecher, was the brother of Harriet Beecher Stowe of *Uncle Tom's Cabin* fame. He was outspoken about his opposition to slavery. The church became known as Brooklyn's center for enslaved people, who would hide in the basement before making their way to Canada. "I opened Plymouth Church," Beecher said, "though you did not know it, to hide fugitives."

ROUTES ON THE UNDERGROUND RAILROAD

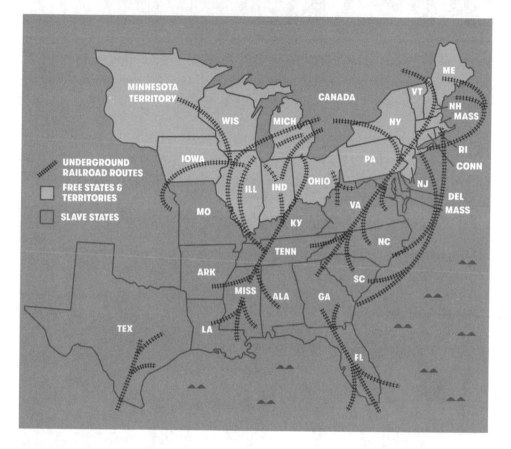

HARRIET TUBMAN, UNDERGROUND RAILROAD CONDUCTOR

Harriet Tubman was perhaps the Underground Railroad's most fearless, and famous, volunteer. After escaping enslavement in Maryland, she returned South nineteen times, rescuing more than 300 people. Tubman was a spy for the North during the Civil War. She became the first woman in the United States to lead a major armed military operation.

THE NAT TURNER REBELLION

The enslaved Nathaniel "Nat" Turner (1800–1831) led an uprising in 1831. It resulted not only in a massacre, but also in the heightening of proslavery beliefs in the South.

Turner was enslaved by Joseph Travis in Virginia. Turner was a preacher who believed God had chosen him to lead his people to freedom. He and several other enslaved men first killed the Travis family. Over the next two days, they were joined by about 75 other enslaved people and killed approximately 55 more white people.

Nat Turner and his supporters organized their rebellion of enslaved people in secret.

THE AFTERMATH OF THE REBELLION

Turner avoided capture for six weeks. Then white authorities discovered him and sixteen of his followers. The authorities put him on trial and then hanged him.

The rebellion resulted in stricter laws, such as one that said Black people were no longer allowed to preach to one another. White mobs attacked and killed enslaved people who had not been part of the uprising. It also caused an ever-deepening divide between enslavers and Free-Soilers that would lead to the Civil War.

WHO WERE THE FREE-SOILERS?

The Free-Soilers were an antislavery political group whose slogan was "free soil, free speech, free labor, and free men." The Free-Soilers didn't hold these beliefs because they thought they were morally right. Instead, they were trying to keep the South from dominating the Western territories economically. They wanted to be able to own land and work for wages without competition from the unpaid labor of the Southerners' enslaved people. The majority of the party's members were not abolitionists, and they were not interested in Black people having equal civil rights.

> **Free-Soilers:** an antislavery political group who wanted to prevent U.S. territories from becoming slave states.

PROSLAVERY LAWS GET STRONGER

The strengthening of Virginia's proslavery laws after the Nat Turner Rebellion was a warning to anyone trying to help the enslaved. An act in Virginia, passed on March 25, 1832, threatened to punish anyone who wrote, printed, or distributed any materials encouraging uprising. It read:

"Such person if a slave, free negro or mulatto, shall, on conviction before any justice of the peace, be punished for the first offence with stripes, at the discretion of the said justice, not exceeding thirty-nine lashes; and for the second offence, shall be deemed guilty of felony, and on due conviction, shall be punished with death."

In other words, a Black person who encouraged an uprising would be whipped or killed. As for a white person caught committing these crimes? He or she faced a fine of $100 to $1,000.

 What do you think about the difference between how white and Black people were punished for committing the same crime? Do you think things are different today? What are some examples that support your belief?

_____

_____

_____

_____

_____

_____

THE GOVERNMENT TRIES TO KEEP THE COUNTRY TOGETHER

Governmental arguments over slavery did not focus on the rights of the enslaved. Instead, the states focused on their economic interests. To keep the country together, Congress passed a series of compromises. Basically, for every new slave state, there would be another free state. This meant there would be a balance of power within Congress between free states and slave states.

How did people decide whether a new state would allow slavery? That depended on a line drawn by the Missouri Compromise in 1820. The line, drawn at the 36° 30′ latitude line, divided the country between the North (free states) and South (slave states).

THE MISSOURI COMPROMISE LINE

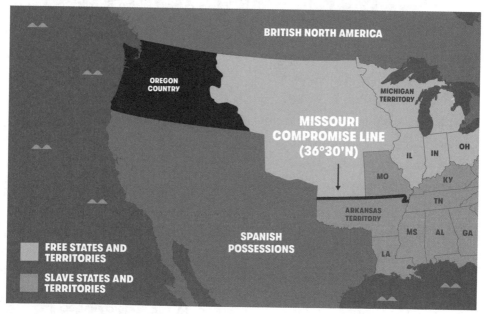

BRITISH NORTH AMERICA

OREGON COUNTRY

MICHIGAN TERRITORY

MISSOURI COMPROMISE LINE (36°30'N)

IL   IN   OH

MO   KY

ARKANSAS TERRITORY   TN

SPANISH POSSESSIONS   MS   AL   GA

LA

FREE STATES AND TERRITORIES

SLAVE STATES AND TERRITORIES

But in 1829, the country nearly came undone. That year, South Carolina threatened to secede from the Union because it believed it was being unfairly taxed. Let's take a look at what led up to that.

THE NULLIFICATION CRISIS

In 1828, Congress passed a tariff (tax) on goods imported from Europe. It did this to make the North's factories and businesses stronger. The tariffs on European goods made them more expensive for Americans to buy. Because of this extra expense, Americans were more likely to buy similar goods from U.S. businesses.

People in South Carolina were furious that the bill benefited their rivals in the North. They refused to enforce the bill, saying it was against the Constitution. South Carolina filed something called an Ordinance of Nullification. In other words, they officially said that a law they did not like was not valid.

SOUTH CAROLINA ACTS—AND SO DOES THE PRESIDENT

The South Carolinians said the law was not valid within the state. They threatened to leave the Union. But they calmed down when Andrew Jackson signed a new tariff bill in 1833. This law lowered tariffs. Taking no chances, Jackson also passed the Force Bill. It allowed officials to collect tariffs in the South with armed soldiers if necessary. The Union was saved—for a while.

THE KANSAS-NEBRASKA ACT

In 1854, Congress passed the Kansas-Nebraska Act, which basically overturned the Missouri Compromise. This bill said that the people who lived in a territory could decide for themselves if it would be a slave or free state. Historians call this popular sovereignty.

The result was a flood into Kansas and Nebraska by people who wanted to help decide whether those states would become free states or slave states. The Free-Soilers set up towns to establish residency and vote against slavery.

Proslavery Americans called Border Ruffians also rushed in. They stuffed ballot boxes with fake ballots so their side would win. They also frightened voters by showing up armed at elections. They destroyed the printing press of an abolitionist newspaper, and they looted the town of Lawrence, Kansas.

BLEEDING KANSAS

The battle between the two sides broke out in warfare in 1854. This led to a two-year period that people called Bleeding Kansas. Proslavery Missouri senator David Atchison encouraged Border Ruffians to defend slavery "with the bayonet and blood." Atchison said it might be necessary "to kill every God-d***ed abolitionist in the district."

Historians estimate that the conflicts led to between 60 and 200 deaths during this time. Perhaps more significant than the numbers was the fact that white people died over the issue of slavery.

secede: to formally withdraw from something.

popular sovereignty: the belief that government is based on the consent of the people. In the nineteenth-century United States, proslavery politicians like Stephen Douglas used the idea to say that federal territories should decide by popular vote whether they would allow slavery when they entered the Union.

The federal government officially made Kansas part of the Union in 1861. Nebraska joined six years later. Both joined as free states, with no slavery allowed.

A ONE-TERM PRESIDENT

Franklin Pierce (1804–1869), a lawyer from New England, was elected the fourteenth president in 1852. He lost support in his home region by signing the Kansas-Nebraska Act. Pierce didn't run for a second term, since the Democrats chose to nominate James Buchanan (1791–1868) as their candidate instead.

THE LINCOLN-DOUGLAS DEBATES

In 1858, a senate race in Illinois fascinated the country. The current senator was Stephen A. Douglas, and his challenger was Abraham Lincoln. They agreed to hold debates in seven cities.

The main topic was slavery. Douglas had written the Kansas-Nebraska Act. He continued to champion popular sovereignty and the right of states to decide the slavery issue for themselves. Lincoln argued that slavery should not be allowed to expand beyond where it already existed.

Tens of thousands of people stood in the audiences to watch the two men fight it out. Lincoln made a famous point about the fractured country. "A house divided against itself cannot stand," he said. In case anyone missed the point, he added, "I believe this government cannot endure, permanently half slave and half free."

A VICTORY FOR DOUGLAS

Douglas prevailed on Election Day. He won an additional term as senator. But Lincoln became a political star thanks to his brilliant debating skills. Lincoln would benefit most in the long term, and he went on to defeat Douglas and two other candidates in the 1860 presidential election.

CLASHING IDEAS: OPPOSING INJUSTICE AND EXCUSING SLAVERY

Remember the Founding Fathers? They invented a lasting system of representative government based on the idea that all men are created equal. Yet many of them were enslavers who agreed to the Three-Fifths Compromise. Even the most brilliant leaders, making the most revolutionary changes, held contradictory beliefs.

Lincoln would go on to end slavery as president of the United States. But listen to his flip-flopping on the issue of slavery during the debates.

At one debate, he said, "I have no purpose, directly or indirectly, to interfere with the institution of slavery in the States where it exists. . . . I have no purpose to introduce political and social equality between the white and black races."

At a later debate, he said, "I am. . . pledged to a belief in the right and duty of Congress to prohibit slavery in all the United States' Territories." He called slavery "a moral, social, and political evil."

 Why do you think Lincoln might have said both of those things? Do you think it's possible for the same person to believe both of them?

_____

_____

_____

THE RISE OF ABRAHAM LINCOLN

Lincoln was from Kentucky, but he wasn't a wealthy Southerner like many other men in government. Instead, he was born in a one-room log cabin. He grew up poor, and he was mostly self-educated.

Lincoln was only 25 when he won election to the Illinois state legislature in 1834. In 1847, he won election to the U.S. House of Representatives. There, he introduced a bill to end slavery in the District of Columbia. The bill didn't pass, but it was a model for future antislavery laws.

WHIG-GING OUT: A LOOK AT POLITICAL PARTIES

A political party called the Whigs formed in 1834 to oppose the policies of Democratic president Andrew Jackson. The Republican Party was founded in 1854. Its purpose was to oppose the expansion of slavery. In 1855, the Whigs dissolved. Some became Republicans and others, Democrats. In the second part of the nineteenth century, the Republicans were the more liberal party, and the Democrats were more conservative.

A TURNING POINT TOWARD WAR

For many people in the 1800s, the issue of slavery had no middle ground. This came into focus with the attack on Harpers Ferry in Virginia, which John Brown led in 1859.

Brown grew up in Ohio in an antislavery family. He failed at many business attempts and declared bankruptcy when he was 42. In 1837, he went to an abolition meeting in Cleveland. After that, he dedicated his life to ending slavery.

Though the raid on Harpers Ferry was unsuccessful, it managed to raise tensions in the increasingly polarized United States.

THE RAID ON HARPERS FERRY

Brown had the financial backing of a group of abolitionists known as the "Secret Six." He gathered his own army of twenty-two men, which included five Black men and three of Brown's sons. He made his plans: They would raid the U.S. Armory and Arsenal in Harpers Ferry, a place where the government stored weapons. Then they would start an armed revolt of enslaved people to destroy the institution of slavery.

During the raid, Brown's people took 60 hostages, including enslaved men, and killed six men. The U.S. marines, led by Robert. E. Lee, overran Brown the next morning. They killed ten of Brown's men, including two of his sons.

A GUILTY VERDICT STIRS EMOTIONS

The state of Virginia found Brown guilty of **treason**. The judgment by Southerners was just as unforgiving. In contrast, some Northerners admired Brown for his courage. On the day of his execution, many church bells rang out in the North.

Southerners were enraged. How dare the Northerners celebrate a criminal who had threatened their lives? Southern politicians also falsely claimed that Lincoln had supported Brown's plan.

> **treason:** to betray one's country, especially by trying to overthrow the government or by killing its leader or leaders.

A PREDICTION FROM THE GALLOWS

Brown's guards led him to the gallows to be hanged. Brown handed his guard a piece of paper that said, "I, John Brown, am now quite certain that the crimes of this guilty land will never be purged away [removed] but with blood."

One newspaper summed up the results of the raid. It stated: "The Harpers Ferry invasion has advanced the cause of disunion more than any other event since the formation of the government."

 In what ways do you think the raid on Harpers Ferry changed things for the country? Did it make a civil war more or less likely, in your view?

_____

_____

_____

_____

THE ELECTION OF 1860

Sectionalism resulted in increasing tensions between the North and the South. In 1860, it split the Democratic Party. A Northern group and a Southern group each named its own candidate for president.

The Northern Democrats backed Illinois senator Stephen A. Douglas. (Remember him? He won his third term by defeating Abraham Lincoln.) Douglas still believed in popular sovereignty.

The Southern Democrats threw their weight behind then-President John Buchanan's vice president, John C. Breckinridge. At 36, he was the youngest VP in history. Breckinridge, who was from Kentucky, thought that the federal government should take steps to protect slaveholders in the territories.

Still *more* unhappy Democrats joined with Unionists and former Whigs to form the Constitutional Union Party. On May 9, 1860, they put forth their presidential candidate: Tennessee slaveholder John Bell.

THE ELECTORAL COLLEGE, EXPLAINED (REALLY)

It can be mind-numbing to try to understand the electoral college. But it's important because it explains how a presidential candidate can win an election without winning a majority of individual votes (called winning the popular vote).

In the 1860 election, the Republican candidate, Lincoln, won an electoral college landslide with 180 electoral votes—compared to 72 for Breckinridge, 39 for Bell, and 12 for Douglas. But Lincoln won only 40 percent of the popular vote. That happened partly because there were so many candidates. When voters have many possibilities to choose from, a candidate can win even if he or she gains a fairly small percentage of the vote. That's called a *plurality*.

CREATING THE ELECTORAL COLLEGE

When the founders wrote the Constitution, they created the electoral college. It was supposed to be a compromise between those who wanted citizens to choose the president directly and those who wanted Congress to do so. Each state chooses its electors. Their votes count as well as those cast by ordinary people at the polls.

Here's where it gets funky: Each state gets at least three electors, who are its representatives and senators. But that number goes up depending on a state's population (and thus how many representatives they have in the House). The larger the population, the more electoral votes that state will have. Remember, a state's population count at that time included all white men and three out of every five enslaved men. A candidate can win the most votes in the country, but if she or he loses a powerful state's electoral college votes, then that candidate may be out of luck.

Like so much else in our country, the electoral college has to do with slavery. Remember the Three-Fifths Compromise (page 68)? Because of that rule, a slave state could have more political power than a free state that had the same number of voting citizens. Each voting citizen counted as a whole person. But each enslaved person—who could not vote—counted as three-fifths of a person. So the slave states would have higher numbers of representatives in Congress based on their overall populations—which they would use to expand the practice of slavery!

LINCOLN WINS!

Though he only received 40 percent of the popular vote, Lincoln won victory in the electoral college. With 180 electoral votes, he became the sixteenth president of the United States. His victory was short lived, since it came right as the country was teetering toward civil war.

A NATION CRUMBLES

The Confederate attack on Fort Sumter marked the beginning of the Civil War.

Before Lincoln could even be sworn into office, eleven Southern states seceded from the Union. People in those states were convinced that Lincoln was going to destroy the institution of slavery. Six weeks after the sixteenth president of the United States took office, the Confederate army fired on Fort Sumter in Charleston, South Carolina. The Civil War had begun.

CHAPTER 4 VOCABULARY

abolition: to abolish something is to end it; abolitionists wanted to end slavery.

bayonet: a blade that is attached to the shooting end of a rifle for hand-to-hand fighting.

bias: prejudice or slant in favor of one side of an issue over another, usually in a way considered to be unfair.

emancipate: to free someone from captivity or bondage.

Free-Soilers: an antislavery political group who wanted to prevent U.S. territories from becoming slave states.

Fugitive Slave Act: a law passed by Congress that said that all enslaved people who escaped had to be captured and returned to their captors, even if they were in "free" states.

popular sovereignty: the belief that government is based on the consent of the people. In the nineteenth-century United States, proslavery politicians like Stephen Douglas used the idea to say that federal territories should decide by popular vote whether they would allow slavery when they entered the Union.

secede: to formally withdraw from something.

sectionalism: putting more importance on the interests of the region where you live rather than on those of your country as a whole.

suffrage: the legal right to vote.

treason: to betray one's country, especially by trying to overthrow the government or by killing its leader or leaders.

NOTES

5
THE CIVIL WAR AND ITS AFTERMATH

A country went to war with itself. What did that mean, and how would it end? Read on.

CHAPTER CONTENTS

SOUTHERN UPRISING

THE EMANCIPATION PROCLAMATION

BLACK SOLDIERS IN THE UNION ARMY

WAR RAGES ON

THE GETTYSBURG ADDRESS

RECONSTRUCTION

A COUNTRY NOW CONNECTED, LITERALLY

THE END OF RECONSTRUCTION

SOUTHERN UPRISING

In December 1860, South Carolina made good on its second threat to secede from the United States. Alabama, Florida, Georgia, Louisiana, Mississippi, and Texas soon followed its example.

In February, these states created the Confederate States of America (the CSA). Their capital was originally in Montgomery, Alabama, but by May it had moved to Richmond, Virginia. The president of the CSA was Jefferson Davis, who had been a U.S. senator from Mississippi.

The Confederate States adopted a constitution that allowed individual states more decision-making power than the U.S. Constitution. This meant each state could protect its interest in slavery.

THE WAR BEGINS

To strengthen its military, the Confederacy (CSA) began seizing Southern forts, which the U.S. government controlled. On April 12, 1861, in an attempt to take Fort Sumter in South Carolina, the Confederates opened fire for the first time. This marked the official beginning of the Civil War. The conflict lasted for a day and a half before the Union backed down. Only one soldier died, and that was from an accidental explosion.

The victory convinced North Carolina, Tennessee, Arkansas, and Virginia that it was in their best interests to secede as well. Those states joined their fellow Southerners in the Confederacy.

> **Confederate States of America:** Also known as the Confederacy or the CSA, this is the collection of states that broke from the Union, prompting the Civil War.

WHICH SIDE WERE YOU LITERALLY ON?

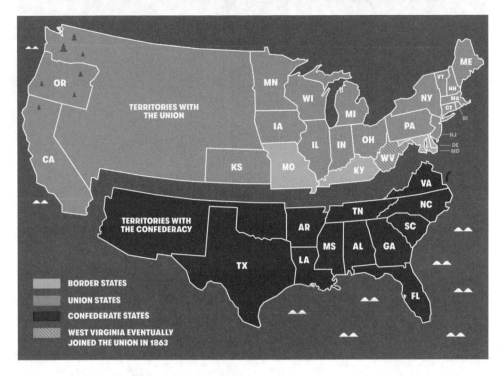

A RACIST FOUNDATION

The Confederacy's vice president, Alexander Stephens, summed up its principles in a speech he gave on March 21, 1861. He said that the CSA's "foundations are laid, its cornerstone rests, upon the great truth that the Negro is not equal to the white man; that slavery and subordination to the superior race is his natural and normal condition."

The Confederate states may have framed the war to be a fight over state's rights. But this primary source is evidence that enslavement and racism were at the heart of the conflict.

subordination: the condition of being less powerful or in a lower class or rank than someone or something else.

Why would a flag from the 1860s be a symbol for white supremacists, even today?

_____

_____

_____

_____

white supremacy: the belief that white people are superior to all other people, often connected with actions and violence to enforce that belief.

writ of habeas corpus: the constitutionally protected right of a person who is charged with a crime to appear before a judge.

LINCOLN REACTS

To strengthen the Union, Lincoln declared martial law. In other words, he had the military take over the jobs that police ordinarily do. He also suspended the writ of habeas corpus.

Lincoln's decision to suspend habeas corpus allowed military authorities to arrest anyone they believed was a threat to the Union. Because it is such an extreme measure, Lincoln's decision remains controversial to this day.

Do you think Lincoln was right to suspend habeas corpus? Why or why not?

_____

_____

_____

_____

A THREAT FROM WITHIN

Why would the president worry about a threat to the Union within the Union? Remember, the White House was in slave territory. It was only 95 miles from Richmond, Virginia, the Confederate capital. Neighboring Maryland, a slave state, was officially part of the North. But it had a strong loyalty to the Confederate side.

WHO DO YOU THINK HAD THE UPPER HAND AT THE BEGINNING OF THE WAR?

The North had a population of twenty-two million. The South was home to only nine million people, four million of whom were enslaved. The North also benefited from its profitable factories and the strength of its railroad system. But the South was fighting a war on its own turf, and that turf was vast.

FAMILIES FORCED TO FIGHT EACH OTHER

While a map during the Civil War shows strict boundaries between states and sides, families were often emotionally caught in the middle. First Lady Mary Todd Lincoln had brothers who fought for the Confederacy.

Familial fighting could lead to tragedy. In his memoir, *The Irish Brigade and Its Campaigns*, Union captain D. P. Conyngham wrote about one such event that took place during the Battle of Malvern Hill in 1862. Here are his words:

PRIMARY SOURCE

"I had a Sergeant Driscoll, a brave man, and one of the best shots in the Brigade. When charging at Malvern Hill, a company was posted in a clump of trees, who kept up a fierce fire on us and actually charged out on our advance. Their officer seemed to be a daring reckless boy, and I said to Driscoll, 'If that officer is not taken down many of us will fall before we pass that clump.'

"'Leave that to me,' said Driscoll; so he raised his rifle, and the moment the officer exposed himself again, bang went Driscoll, and over went the officer, his company at once breaking away.

"As we passed the place, I said, 'Driscoll, see if that officer is dead—he was a brave fellow.'

"I stood looking on. Driscoll turned him over on his back. He opened his eyes for a moment, and faintly murmured 'Father,' and closed them forever.

"I will forever recollect the frantic grief of Driscoll; it was harrowing [extremely painful] to witness it. The [officer he had killed] was his son, who had gone South before the war."

 When we read history, we are reading about real people.

THE EMANCIPATION PROCLAMATION

Lincoln issued the Emancipation Proclamation on January 1, 1863. In it, Lincoln declared that all people who were enslaved in Confederate states were now free. This was a big step, but it was not the same thing as declaring that all enslaved people were free.

The Proclamation applied only to states that were in rebellion against the Union. What about enslaved people in the four border states, which had not seceded from the Union—Maryland, Kentucky, Missouri, and Delaware? Those people were still legally considered the property of their enslavers.

With the signing of the Emancipation Proclamation, Lincoln declared that all enslaved people in the Confederate states were free.

A BALANCING ACT

By applying the Emancipation Proclamation only to the rebel states, Lincoln believed he could allow it as a war measure intended to hurt the Confederacy. He believed he did not have the authority to change the slavery laws of states that stayed in the Union.

But this was also a smart political calculation. Lincoln knew that if he banned slavery in any state that was not in rebellion, that state would likely join the Confederacy.

Of course, the Union had to win the war for the Emancipation Proclamation to take effect. But one important part of the Emancipation Proclamation took effect immediately. It announced that Black men could fight in the armed forces.

Previously, the Militia Act of 1862 had allowed Black men to join civilian militia groups. The Emancipation Proclamation allowed them to join the U.S. military as well. This allowed the Union army to improve its chances of winning the war by increasing its numbers.

THERE WERE ACTUALLY TWO EMANCIPATION PROCLAMATIONS!

Lincoln issued what became known as the preliminary (first) Emancipation Proclamation in September 1862. It gave the Confederacy until the end of the year to end its rebellion. If the Confederates had surrendered, slavery would have survived, at least for a time. But they didn't surrender.

Lincoln issued the second Emancipation Proclamation on New Year's Day 1863. That was the beginning of the end for slavery in the United States. But Lincoln's priority was clear. His main goal was to put the Union back together. He believed ending slavery was morally right. But he was willing to sacrifice that goal to make the country whole again.

BLACK SOLDIERS IN THE UNION ARMY

Frederick Douglass

From the first days of the Civil War, the abolitionist Frederick Douglass wanted Black men to join the war effort. Douglass saw military service as a pathway to citizenship. "Once let the black man get upon his person the brass letter, U.S., let him get an eagle on his button, and musket on his shoulder and bullets in his pocket," Douglass wrote, "there is no power on earth that can deny he has earned the right to Citizenship."

At the beginning of the war, Douglass pressured Lincoln to include Black men in the army. In August 1861, Congress passed the First Confiscation Act. It stated that all enslaved persons fighting in or working for the Confederate military were free.

Lincoln was concerned that any further action would suggest the war was about ending slavery rather than preserving the Union. That suggestion probably would have caused Maryland and other border states to secede.

BLACK MEN ANSWER THE CALL

By the following summer, it was clear that if the Union was going to win the war, it needed more soldiers. Congress passed the Second Confiscation Act. This law stated that the enslaved were "forever free."

However, this applied only to the enslaved in Union-occupied areas in the South. Congress also passed the Militia Act. This allowed Black men to serve in militias, which are groups of civilians with some military training.

Black men responded by organizing military units called regiments in Louisiana, Kansas, and South Carolina. These formed the beginning of the United States Colored Troops.

Soldiers of the United States Colored Troops

THE 54TH MASSACHUSETTS INFANTRY

It was February 1863, one month after Lincoln's Emancipation Proclamation. Abolitionist governor John A. Andrew of Massachusetts issued the Civil War's first call for Black soldiers. More than 1,000 men responded. They came from as far away as the Caribbean and Canada to form the 54th Massachusetts **Infantry**, the first Black regiment of the North. Two of Frederick Douglass's sons joined as well.

infantry: soldiers who fight on foot, not on horseback.

FACING DISCRIMINATION

While Black soldiers were central to the Union's victory, they faced discrimination. Here are a few examples of the unequal treatment Black soldiers were subject to:

- They were allowed to serve only in segregated all-Black infantries, which white officers led.

- Until Congress passed a bill in 1864 that allowed equal pay for Black and white soldiers, the government paid Black soldiers $10 a week. That was $3 less than white soldiers.

- White officers and soldiers often assigned Black soldiers the worst and most back-breaking jobs, such as digging trenches.

- Frequently, white leaders assigned inferior equipment to Black soldiers. Black soldiers often received poorer medical treatment than white soldiers.

Black soldiers wouldn't serve side by side with white soldiers for nearly another century.

By the end of the Civil War, about 179,000 Black men were soldiers. That was 10 percent of the U.S. army. Another 19,000 served in the navy. Nearly 40,000 Black soldiers died—30,000 of infection or disease.

THE BATTLE OF FORT WAGNER

The 54th became the first Black infantry to lead an assault when they attacked Charleston's Fort Wagner on July 18, 1863. The 54th lost, and 40 percent of their soldiers were killed. Northern newspapers reported on their heroism, helping turn white public opinion in favor of Black soldiers.

PRIMARY SOURCE: SAMUEL CABBLE

While white soldiers often fought for political reasons, Black soldiers were fighting for freedom. Samuel Cabble, a 21-year-old private in the 55th Massachusetts Infantry, was enslaved before joining the army.

In a letter to his wife, Cabble wrote the following:

> I have enlisted in the army I am now in the state of Massachusetts but before this letter reaches you I will be in North Carlinia and though great is the present national dificulties yet I look forward to a brighter day When I shall have the opertunity of seeing you in the full enjoyment of fredom I would like to no if you are still in slavery if you are it will not be long before we shall have crushed the system that now opreses you for in the course of three months you shall have your liberty. Great is the outpouring of the colered peopl that is now rallying with the hearts of lions against that very curse that has seperated you an me yet we shall meet again and oh what a happy time that will be when this ungodly rebellion shall be put down and the curses of our land is trampled under our feet."

Cabble and his wife both survived the war. They reunited and moved to Colorado.

 What can you learn about the life of a Black soldier from Cabble's letter that you couldn't learn from a textbook?

_____

_____

_____

_____

NATIVE AMERICANS IN THE CIVIL WAR

Some 20,000 Native Americans joined the Confederate and Union armies. In general, the Native American nations supported the side they felt would best help them retain their land. Stand Watie, a member of the Cherokee nation, was the first Native American to serve as a Confederate general. He was also the last confederate general to surrender. His older brother was Elias Boudinot, the newspaper editor and writer we read about in Chapter 4 who supported relocation.

WAR RAGES ON

Conditions for most soldiers were miserable. They did not have enough food and clothing, and they slept outside in punishing weather. They were often infested with lice. Two-thirds of soldiers who died lost their lives because of diseases, including dysentery, which killed 45,000 men. Official figures show that more than 103,000 Confederate soldiers and more than 200,000 Union soldiers deserted.

deserted: left the military without permission.

scorched-earth policy: a military strategy that involves burning land and crops in order to stop the invading enemy from using those resources.

BATTLES TO REMEMBER

The Civil War included more than 10,500 military engagements (fights between opposing sides). There were about a hundred significant battles and fifty major battles. Here are a few you should know about.

THE FIRST BATTLE OF BULL RUN ALSO KNOWN AS THE FIRST BATTLE OF MANASSAS	
WHAT HAPPENED	WHY IT MATTERS
On July 21, 1861, the Union army set out from Washington, D.C., to seize Richmond, Virginia. Only 25 miles into their march, the Confederate army met and overwhelmed them. Almost 5,000 soldiers on both sides died.	This was the first major Civil War battle.

THE BATTLE OF ANTIETAM
ALSO CALLED SHARPSBURG

WHAT HAPPENED	WHY IT MATTERS
On September 17, 1862, Robert E. Lee led the Confederacy to meet the Union Army, led by General George B. McClellan, in Maryland. While the Union claimed victory, historians consider the battle a tie.	Taking place over two days, this was the bloodiest American military fight to date, with 22,000 soldiers injured and 3,600 killed.

THE SIEGE OF VICKSBURG

WHAT HAPPENED	WHY IT MATTERS
In March 1863, Major General Ulysses S. Grant led Union forces to Vicksburg, Mississippi, near the Mississippi River. The plan was to stop Confederates from sending supplies and troops along the waterway. The siege ended on July fourth, with each side suffering enormous losses.	The Union gained control of the river. This basically split the Confederacy in half. After the surrender of the city, the town of Vicksburg would not celebrate Independence Day (often known as the Fourth of July) for 81 years.

SHERMAN'S MARCH TO THE SEA

WHAT HAPPENED	WHY IT MATTERS
Beginning on November 15, 1864, Union General William Tecumseh Sherman led 60,000 soldiers on a 285-mile march from Atlanta, which he had captured in July, to Savannah. Guided by a scorched-earth policy, they stole food and livestock and burned buildings in an effort to break Georgia's morale.	Ending with the Union capture of Savannah, Sherman's march fatally hobbled the Confederacy's ability to wage war.

WAR PATHS

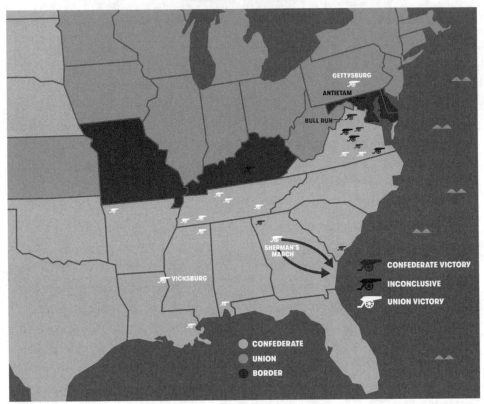

GETTYSBURG

ANTIETAM

BULL RUN

SHERMAN'S MARCH

VICKSBURG

🔫 CONFEDERATE VICTORY

🔫 INCONCLUSIVE

🔫 UNION VICTORY

⬤ CONFEDERATE

⬤ UNION

⬤ BORDER

The Union gained a new state when western counties in Virginia opposed secession. On June 20, 1863, this land was admitted to the Union as West Virginia.

NEW YORK... PRO-SLAVERY?
AND THEN SOME.

 Remember that people's beliefs during the war didn't only depend on where they lived.

In April 1861, New York City's mayor, Fernando Wood, called on the city to secede and join the Confederacy. Why? He wanted to protect the enormous profits manufacturers made by sending their goods to the South, especially those made with cotton. Wood called the South "our best customer. She pays the best prices, and pays promptly."

Wood was also proslavery. He called it a "divine institution," probably because the Bible mentions slavery. Plenty of New Yorkers agreed with his economic and political views.

AN ILLEGAL BUSINESS

New York state abolished slavery in 1827. However, New York City remained a center for people illegally selling enslaved people. The city's ship owners built slave ships, and its businesspeople financed trips to and from Africa.

The profits from trafficking human life were huge. It was possible to buy an enslaved person overseas for about $40 in goods, such as cloth or beads. That same enslaved person could sell for between $400 and $1,200 in the United States. An average cargo ship could hold as many as 800 enslaved people. Therefore, one "successful" voyage could result in what is today tens of millions of dollars. Between 1858 and 1860, New York launched nearly a hundred slave ships.

SECESSIONIST SUPPORT IN NEW YORK

A month after Lincoln's election, close to 2,000 New York businessmen banded together to support secession. Speaking on their behalf, attorney Hiram Ketchum said, "If ever a conflict arises between the races, the people of the city of New York will stand by their brethren, the white race."

In addition, antiwar politicians and newspapers encouraged rage among working-class white citizens. Many of these citizens were Irish or German immigrants. Antiwar forces insisted that the Emancipation Proclamation would mean competition for their jobs from formerly enslaved Black people heading north.

THE DRAFT

Nothing significant came of New York's secessionist and antiwar efforts. But Lincoln's Civil War Military Draft Act, signed on March 3, 1863, sparked outrage. The draft meant all males between twenty and forty-five years old had to serve in the war.

A man could pay the government $300 to avoid being drafted. But that was how much an average American earned in a year. So paying to avoid the draft was something that only the very rich did.

Draft riots broke out in Detroit and Boston. But none were as deadly as what took place in New York.

THE NEW YORK DRAFT RIOTS

On July 13, 1863, the day after the draft took place, thousands of white workers attacked government buildings and targeted Black citizens. Several thousand people, some armed with clubs and bats, stormed the Colored Orphan Asylum. This building was home to more than 200 children. The mob stole their bedding, food, and clothing, and set fire to it.

Rioters also attacked white abolitionists. But the worst violence was reserved for Black men. Mobs beat and even lynched them.

The published death toll was 119 people, but historians believe the number was as high as 1,200. It took militia forces four days to restore order. The New York draft riots remain the deadliest riots in U.S. history.

draft: the method by which young men and women are conscripted (enrolled) in military service that is required by the government.

lynch: to kill someone without a trial for a real or imagined crime, usually by hanging.

The 1860 census counted 12,414 Black New Yorkers. In 1865, that number was 9,945. Based on what you've learned, what do you think the reasons might have been for the decline in population?

_____

_____

_____

_____

_____

THE GETTYSBURG ADDRESS

Lincoln delivers his now-famous Gettysburg Address.

Historians and others still talk about this speech. You may even have memorized its opening line, "Four score and seven years ago." But why is it important?

On November 19, 1863, Lincoln gave a speech at the Gettysburg battle site in Pennsylvania. That was where General Robert E. Lee had led the Confederacy in its second attack on Northern territory the previous July. Lee's attempt failed, but over the course of two days, as many as 51,000 people lost their lives.

Lincoln arrived at the site to dedicate a national military cemetery to the Union soldiers who had died there. The president was not the featured speaker, and he spoke only ten sentences. But if you ever doubt the potential power of your words, this is a moment to return to. In those ten sentences, Lincoln explained the importance of seeing the war to its end—and of a victory for the Union.

PRIMARY SOURCE: LINCOLN'S ADDRESS

"The world will little note, nor long remember, what we say here, but it can never forget what they did here," he said. *"It is for us the living, rather, to be dedicated here to the unfinished work which they who fought here have so far nobly advanced. It is rather for us to be here dedicated to the great task remaining before*

us—that from these honored dead we take increased devotion to that cause for which they gave the last full measure of devotion—that we here highly resolve [decide] that these dead shall not have died in vain [for no reason]—that this nation, under God, shall have a new birth of freedom—and that government of the people, by the people, for the people, shall not perish [die or disappear] from the earth."

Lincoln was a president in the middle of a civil war. Was his speech about more than honoring the dead? What words in his speech make you think so?

_____

_____

_____

_____

THE OFFICIAL END OF THE WAR, AND A PRESIDENCY

On April 3, 1865, the Union army captured Richmond, Virginia. Five days later, that army attacked and trapped the Confederates as they waited for supplies in Appomattox, Virginia.

The next morning, Confederate General Robert E. Lee and Union General Ulysses S. Grant met in the town's courthouse, and Lee issued a formal surrender. Other Confederate troops soon did the same.

LINCOLN'S LAST SPEECH

On April 11, Lincoln gave a speech at the White House. He said the work ahead would be full of "great difficulty." He also expressed support for limited Black suffrage. Lincoln thought that only "very intelligent" Black men and Black veterans should be able to vote. No one suggested placing these limitations on white men. And no one suggested that any women should be able to vote.

John Wilkes Booth

One person in the crowd listening to the president was a young actor and Confederate sympathizer named John Wilkes Booth. Booth reportedly told his friend Lewis Powell, "That is the last speech he will ever make."

BOOTH ASSASSINATES LINCOLN

On April 14, 1865, Lincoln watched a play from box seats at Ford's Theater in Washington, D.C. with his wife, Mary Todd Lincoln. Booth fired a gun at Lincoln's head and then leaped onto the stage, breaking his own leg in the process. He then yelled Virginia's state motto, "Sic semper tyrannis!" That means "Thus ever to tyrants!" Booth escaped on horseback.

A doctor in the audience heard Mary Todd Lincoln's screams. He rushed to the box to find the president struggling to breathe.

Lincoln died early the next morning, at the age of 56. Twelve days later, Union soldiers found Booth on a Virginia farm. The soldiers shot Booth during the encounter, though historians disagree if the soldiers killed Booth or if he died by suicide.

It turned out that Booth was the leader of a group that had also tried to assassinate Vice President Andrew Johnson and Secretary of State William H. Seward on the same evening. Johnson's would-be assassin lost his nerve and stayed in a hotel bar, drinking. Another man in the group, Lewis Powell, nearly killed Seward. Powell was tried, convicted, and hanged.

RECONSTRUCTION

With Lincoln's assassination, Vice President Andrew Johnson became the seventeenth U.S. president. He was also the first leader of the Reconstruction Era. This was the twelve years after the Civil War during which the government tried to reunite the country.

> **tyrant:** a leader who uses power for selfish and/or cruel purposes.
>
> **assassination:** a murder, usually for political reasons.
>
> **Reconstruction Era:** the twelve-year period immediately following the Civil War. Two of the biggest issues: reuniting the war-torn country, and integrating newly freed Black Americans into the labor market and into society.

BLACK CODES AND RACISM DURING RECONSTRUCTION

Reconstruction was far from successful. Immediately, Southern states clamped down on the four million people now free from enslavement. They passed restrictive "Black codes," meant to suppress Black people's ability to fully participate in white society.

These laws said that Black people could not hold certain jobs. They couldn't carry guns. They couldn't give evidence in court against white people. And marriage between people of different races was illegal.

In addition to the Black codes, the newly formed Ku Klux Klan, a white supremacist organization, terrorized and killed Black people.

SHARECROPPING

White landowners continued to exploit Black laborers. The landowners created sharecropping, a system in which families too poor to own their own land could rent small plots in return for part of the crop they produced. The renters had to pay more money to borrow the landowners' equipment. As a result, sharecroppers often ended up in a ruthless cycle of debt.

THE SHARECROPPING CYCLE OF DEBT

1 Landowners rent small plots of land to Black laborers (sharecroppers). In exchange, the sharecropper agrees to give the landowner a portion of the crop.

2 The sharecroppers buy tools, clothing, seed, and food on credit from the landowner.

3 At harvest, the sharecropper gives the crops to the landowner to sell. The landowner keeps the profit from whatever portion was originally agreed to, and takes additional money for the cost of the tools and clothing.

4 Often, this means the sharecropper now owes more money than their crop made.

5 In order to pay off that debt, the sharecropper promises an even larger portion of crops for the following year.

sharecropping: a system in which families who didn't have enough money to own their own land could rent small plots in return for part of the crop they produced.

MILITARY ORDER IN THE SOUTH

Congress wanted to keep the peace between Blacks and whites in the South. So Congress passed a law that required the military to occupy (oversee and keep order in) certain southern districts. This law reduced violence in the South. It also meant Black men could vote safely.

THE RADICAL REPUBLICANS

Crimes against Black people led to a new faction within the Republican party, called the Radical Republicans. Members of this faction believed Black men should have the same rights as white men. They helped guide Black politicians into positions of power.

The efforts of both the military and the Radical Republicans made voting safer for Black men. In the 1870s, more than 500,000 Black men registered to vote in the South. Thousands of Black men won election to local and state legislatures. Seventeen Black men became members of Congress, including two to the U.S. Senate.

There wouldn't be another Black senator for nearly 100 years. And not until 1993 did a Black woman win election to the Senate.

Black Americans cast their votes for the first time.

Why do you think so many Black men won seats in government in the 1870s? Why do you think it took almost 100 years until another Black man became a U.S. senator?

_____

_____

THE FREEDMEN'S BUREAU

The federal government created the Freedmen's Bureau to help the formerly enslaved. It created schools, set up hospitals, provided jobs and legal aid, and handed out food and clothing. It also created Black colleges and universities.

President Johnson, who was a Southern Democrat from Tennessee, opposed the Freedmen's Bureau. He gave land back to the Confederates that had been promised to Black Americans.

THE FIRST PRESIDENT TO BE IMPEACHED

Lincoln had chosen Andrew Johnson to be his vice president. But Johnson did his best to undo Lincoln's accomplishments.

Johnson consistently vetoed laws that the Republican Congress had passed to protect the formerly enslaved. The Freedman's Bureau act was one such law. He tried to hobble the Republican Party by removing them from government. When he tried to remove Secretary of War Edwin M. Stanton, Republicans in Congress responded by impeaching him—they formally accused him of misconduct with the purpose of removing him from office. The attempt at impeachment was unsuccessful.

YET ANOTHER BROKEN TREATY

After the Civil War, the United States failed to keep its promises to Native Americans. In 1868, the country entered into the Fort Laramie Treaty with a group of Native American nations now known as the Dakota, Lakota, and Nakota.

The treaty established a twenty-five-million-acre reservation west of the Missouri River. It promised that the Black Hills, which these Native American nations consider their spiritual center, were for Native American use only.

FORT LARAMIE TREATY OF 1868

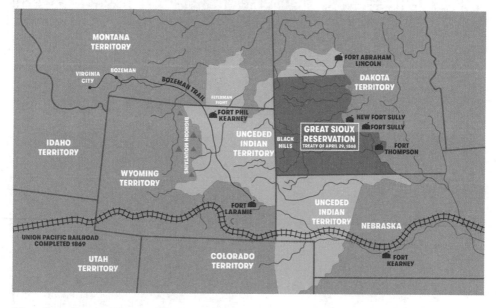

Six years later, General George Custer discovered gold in the Black Hills. The United States refused to honor the treaty. It made the Sioux reservation smaller and forced the Dakota, Lakota, and Nakota, who had been hunters, into a life of farming.

THE DEBATE CONTINUES

The decision has been legally debated ever since. In 1980, the Supreme Court of the United States ruled that what the United States had done was illegal. The court awarded the Sioux more than $100 million in compensation because of the harm and damage to their people. But the Sioux refused the money because the land had never been for sale. Over time, that money has grown to more than $1 billion. The Sioux want their land back instead.

THE BATTLE OF THE LITTLE BIGHORN

According to the terms of the Fort Laramie Treaty, Custer wasn't supposed to be in the Black Hills in the first place. And the 800 fortune-seekers who shortly followed him certainly weren't supposed to be there. Lakota and Cheyenne warriors attacked the prospectors. The United States responded by confining all Lakota, Cheyenne, and Arapaho to the reservation.

The Dakota, Lakota, and Nakota fought back. In 1876, at the Battle of the Little Bighorn, also known as Custer's Last Stand, they had their last military victory. It would result in the United States taking away more of their land.

A COUNTRY NOW CONNECTED, LITERALLY

The United States got its first steam locomotive in 1830. By 1850, companies had laid more than 9,000 miles of track east of the Missouri River. After the first discovery of gold in California in 1849, many people headed west. But they faced a dangerous journey.

Leland Stanford puts in the final spike, completing the transcontinental railroad.

That danger lessened with the completion of the first transcontinental railroad. It connected the existing eastern network in Iowa with San Francisco.

On May 10, 1869, Leland Stanford, founder of the Central Pacific Railroad, drove a ceremonial final gold spike into the tracks.

GOVERNMENT LAND GRANTS

The government was supportive of the railroads. If it became easier to travel West, the growth of the country would be good for the economy. The government gave the railroads something called land grants. That meant that they took millions of acres of public land and gave them to the railroad companies to use. The companies could lay tracks on the land. They could also sell the land to help them raise money.

With the completion of the railroads, people could now get from New York to California in about a week for $65. However, the cost for those who built the railway was high.

ADDICTED TO CHEAP LABOR

Americans continued their tradition of exploiting free or inexpensive labor. Who built the railroads? Irish immigrants, newly freed enslaved people, and as many as 15,000 Chinese laborers.

The work was backbreaking and sometimes deadly. Railroad owners paid Chinese laborers 30 to 50 percent less than white workers. And unlike the white railroad workers, the Chinese workers had to pay for their food and shelter.

THE TELEGRAPH

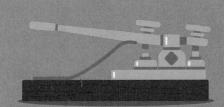

The railroads weren't the only innovation connecting the country. Samuel Morse and others had invented the telegraph in the 1830s, which allowed electric signals to communicate messages. In 1861, the Western Union company had built the first transcontinental telegraph line. During the Civil War, 15,000 miles of telegraph cable had been laid to help the soldiers communicate with each other.

After the war, the telegraph changed the way companies operated. It allowed businesses to run many locations out of a central location.

THE END OF RECONSTRUCTION

In the months leading up to the 1876 elections, race riots took place in the South. These were tied to the Democrats' bid to regain power. To do so, white Southerners planned to prevent Black people from voting. Specifically, the Democrats wanted to terrify Black people with a paramilitary group known as Red Shirts.

In July, Red Shirts surrounded a Black militia stationed to help keep the peace in Hamburg, South Carolina. The Red Shirts killed seven militia members.

Three months later, at a political meeting in Cainhoy, South Carolina, armed Blacks and whites opened fire on each other. Seven more people died. By November, there had been six other disturbances tied to race and politics.

> paramilitary: an armed group that is organized like an army but isn't an official army.
>
> land grant: land given by the government to a specific organization or group of people.

THE ELECTION OF 1876

The fight between presidential hopefuls Republican Rutherford B. Hayes and Democrat Samuel Tilden hardly set a standard for good behavior. On Election Day, Tilden had 184 of the 185 electoral votes he needed to win. He was leading in the popular vote as well. But the Republicans refused to accept defeat. They said Democrats had pressured and frightened Black voters in three southern states, leading to fewer Black men casting votes.

Each side accused each other of fraud—of cheating to steal votes.

Congress stepped in to solve the problem. The lawmakers came up with an informal agreement called the Compromise of 1877. The Democrats agreed to accept Hayes as the victor and said they would respect the civil and political rights of Black men. In return, the Republicans would withdraw the federal troops in the South that had been protecting Black people. The Reconstruction era was over.

CHAPTER 5 VOCABULARY

assassination: a murder, usually for political reasons.

Confederate States of America: also known as the Confederacy or the CSA, this is the collection of states that broke from the Union, prompting the Civil War.

deserted: left the military without permission.

draft: the method by which young men and women are conscripted (enrolled) in military service that is required by the government.

infantry: soldiers who fight on foot, not on horseback.

land grant: land given by the government to a specific organization or group of people.

lynch: to kill someone without a trial for a real or imagined crime, usually by hanging.

paramilitary: an armed group that is organized like an army but isn't an official army.

Reconstruction Era: the twelve-year period immediately following the Civil War. Two of the biggest issues: reuniting the war-torn country, and integrating newly freed Black Americans into the labor market and into society.

scorched-earth policy: a military strategy that involves burning land and crops in order to stop the invading enemy from using those resources.

sharecropping: a system in which families who didn't have enough money to own their own land could rent small plots in return for part of the crop they produced.

subordination: the condition of being less powerful or in a lower class or rank than someone or something else.

tyrant: a leader who uses power for selfish and/or cruel purposes.

white supremacy: the belief that white people are superior to all other people, often connected with actions and violence to enforce that belief.

writ of habeas corpus: the constitutionally protected right of a person who is charged with a crime to appear before a judge.

NOTES

6 THE GILDED AGE AND THE PROGRESSIVE ERA

As railroads continued to open the country, industry boomed, and immigrants flocked to fill new jobs. What were the effects on the United States? Let's investigate.

CHAPTER CONTENTS

BIG CHANGE RIDES THE RAILS

WHAT WAS THE GILDED AGE?

THE SECOND INDUSTRIAL REVOLUTION AND IMMIGRATION

FACTORY WORK

THE RISE OF BIG BUSINESS

THE JIM CROW SOUTH

THE PROGRESSIVE ERA AND THE SOCIAL GOSPEL

BIG CHANGE RIDES THE RAILS

Some of the ways transcontinental trains affected the United States are obvious, but some are less so. For instance: the next time you order something online to be sent to you, thank transcontinental trains for making door-to-door delivery a *thing*.

KEEPING TRACK: THE FIRST TRANSCONTINENTAL RAILROAD, 1869

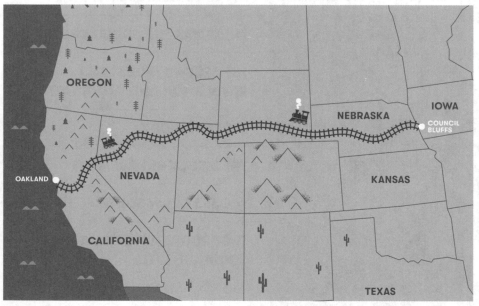

When the transcontinental railroad was completed in 1869, none of the territory west of Iowa were states yet except for Texas, Oregon, Nevada, and California.

DANGEROUS WORK

Working for the railroad could be treacherous. With no government regulations or worker protections in place, 22,000 workers died or suffered injuries in 1889 alone.

THE RAILROAD EFFECT

Let's look at some of the effects train travel had on America.

THE CHANGE	THE EFFECT
It connected the western United States to the rest of the country.	The population in the West soared, helped by the 1862 Homestead Act, which granted nearly 270 million acres of land to applicants. A once-isolated California began transforming into an economic and political power.
It could move giant amounts of products.	By 1880, the railroad was transporting $50 million worth of goods a year. That's equal to more than $1.25 billion now. One year later, the first refrigerated rail-cars allowed meat to be transported without spoiling.
It changed the ways we view space and time.	Suddenly, a country that people could cross in a week didn't seem as overwhelmingly large as it once had. And the need for train schedules brought about the adoption of standard time zones in 1883.
It changed the way we shop.	Now that goods moved quickly and in great bulk, people became less dependent on physical stores. In 1872, the first mail-order catalog business began.
It affected the environment.	People wiped out western forests to provide the wood needed to build the railroad. Wild areas transformed into new towns and cities. Hunters also traveled west and killed tens of millions of buffalo. This hurt the animal population and the Native American groups who depended on them for survival.

 What other ways do you think train travel changed life in America?

_____

_____

_____

_____

HOW INVENTIVE!

Nineteenth-century America also saw the invention of these life-changing items.

- In 1872, Thomas Edison built the first electric typewriter.

- George Eastman introduced paper film and the Kodak camera in 1888.

- In 1876, Alexander Graham Bell spoke the first sentence through his invention: the telephone.

- Thomas Adams opened the first chewing gum factory in 1871.

THE HOMESTEAD ACT

The Homestead Act of 1862 granted 160 acres of public land to any American who applied, and to immigrants who promised to become citizens. In return, they promised to live on it, improve it, and pay a small registration fee. Once the railroads linked the country, the numbers of homesteaders skyrocketed.

Women, including single women, could file claims for land under the Act. However, historians estimate that of the 4 million claims filed under the Homestead Act, Black Americans filed only about 3,500.

THE EXODUSTERS

But even that small number of land claims by Black homesteaders left an impact on the Plains states. Black homesteaders became known as the exodusters, a name that was inspired by the biblical story of Exodus, a journey out of slavery by Jews in Egypt during the time of the pharaohs. This was the first mass migration of Blacks, and the communities established by exodusters remain today.

> exodusters: Black homesteaders became known as the exodusters, a name that was inspired by the biblical story of Exodus, a journey out of Egypt.

HOW EXPANSION WEST HURT MEXICAN AMERICANS

The Treaty of Guadalupe Hidalgo, which ended the Mexican-American War in 1848, added a large amount of land to the United States and 80,000 people to its population. The population grew in the West—California's alone surged from 110,000 to 1.2 million between 1848 and 1890. When the treaty was signed, thousands of Mexican citizens were suddenly living in U.S. territory. The majority chose to become American citizens (a term of the treaty), but many still had neither jobs nor representation within the government.

SUNDAY LAWS

White Californians created "Sunday laws," which forbade "noisy amusements," including festivals and customary Mexican gatherings. California also passed laws that stated police would arrest Hispanic people and Native Americans for being unemployed. This was the same thing that happened to Black people in the Jim Crow South, which you'll read about later in this chapter.

White lawmakers made life extremely difficult, if not impossible, for these new citizens. While they weren't allowed to be unemployed, the law also barred them from various forms of employment. Hispanic men and women could generally find only low-paying, dangerous jobs, particularly in the mining and cattle industries.

SPEAKING OUT AGAINST DISCRIMINATION

Pablo de la Guerra

Pablo de la Guerra, a California state senator, addressed this mistreatment in an 1854 speech. He said, "Remember also that while we accepted the American rule with all candor [honesty] and single heartedness, we are treated as a conquered and inferior race. Our civility [behavior and way of acting] was questioned because we spoke Spanish."

 Who do you think de la Guerra holds accountable for the mistreatment of people of Mexican descent? What evidence do you see that Mexican-Americans were treated as an "inferior" race?

_____

_____

_____

_____

_____

_____

WHAT WAS THE GILDED AGE?

 The author Mark Twain invented the term "Gilded Age" in 1873. It refers to the last years of the nineteenth century and the rise of the first U.S. railroads and of shipping tycoons.

People called some of these men, including Cornelius Vanderbilt and Jay Gould, robber barons because of their greed. Others like Andrew Carnegie, John D. Rockefeller, and Henry Clay Frick used their personal fortunes to benefit the country in some way. (For instance, Carnegie paid for more than 1,600 library buildings in the United States. Your community may still have a Carnegie library!) People were more likely to refer to these multimillionaires with the kinder term captains of industry.

Regardless of what people called them, they built their great fortunes on the backs of immigrants and struggling farmers. These people had begun flocking to cities, such as New York, Boston, St. Louis, and Chicago. They were seeking the new jobs the Second Industrial Revolution was creating.

> **tycoon:** a powerful businessperson.
>
> **robber barons/captains of industry:** both are terms to describe the business tycoons at this time. People who saw these tycoons as greedy might use the phrase "robber baron," and those who thought the tycoons used their wealth for good might use the more positive term "captains of industry."

GARFIELD • ARTHUR • CLEVELAND • HARRISON

GILDED AGE PRESIDENTS

JAMES A. GARFIELD (1881)

The former congressman from Ohio, Garfield (1831–1881) attacked government corruption. He also favored political rights for Blacks and free public education for all Americans. He was assassinated fewer than 200 days after taking office in 1881.

CHESTER A. ARTHUR (1881–1885)

The son of an Irish immigrant, Arthur (1829–1886) oversaw the enactment of the first federal immigration act that excluded "paupers," or poor people, "criminals," and "lunatics" from entering the country.

GROVER CLEVELAND (1885–1889, 1893–1897)

Cleveland (1837–1908) signed the first federal law regulating railroads. He ordered that 500,000 acres of land that President Arthur's administration had taken from Native Americans be returned. However, he also supported the Dawes Act, which allowed the U.S. government to sell Native American land. He is so far the only president to serve two nonconsecutive terms.

BENJAMIN HARRISON (1889–1893)

Harrison (1833–1901) tried to take over Hawaii and make it part of the United States. That would happen in 1898, during the administration of William McKinley. In 1890, Harrison signed the Sherman Antitrust Act in an effort to protect consumers from monopolies. He was the grandson of the ninth president, William Henry Harrison.

> monopoly: a business that doesn't allow for competition. It usually leads to high prices and poor quality and service.

SOCIAL DARWINISM

Social Darwinism was a theory that wealthy white people made popular to justify their privilege at the expense of others. They applied Charles Darwin's theory of evolution to society. Darwin explained that living things that were suited to their environments were most likely to survive. Similarly, social Darwinists insisted that only the strongest and most intelligent people survive.

Just as many white people used Manifest Destiny as an excuse to take land that wasn't theirs, social Darwinism allowed business owners to ignore any social responsibility for their often ruthless actions. According to this theory, if people were poor, that was their destiny. Social Darwinists believed it had nothing to do with the systematic oppression of Black Americans, or with anti-immigration practices or exploitative working conditions.

> social Darwinism: a theory that applied Charles Darwin's theory of evolution to society. Social Darwinists often used this theory to justify racist beliefs.

Why do you think social Darwinism might have been so readily accepted at the time?

_____

_____

_____

_____

_____

_____

_____

_____

THE SECOND INDUSTRIAL REVOLUTION AND IMMIGRATION

Thomas Edison developed the first useful, practical light bulb in 1879.

Advances in manufacturing products, from steel to chemicals—and the increasing demand for those products—helped fuel a huge number of new factories. Many of these got their power from Thomas Edison's Electric Illuminating Company in New York, founded in 1882.

Between 1880 and 1920, the number of factory workers in the country grew from 2.5 million to ten million. Many of these workers were immigrants. In those same years, more than twenty million immigrants arrived in the United States. In this wave of immigration, the new arrivals were mostly from southern, eastern, and central Europe.

ANTI-IMMIGRANT SENTIMENT

These immigrants faced hardships they could not have imagined when they set sail from their homelands. These difficulties included horrible working and living conditions. They also included prejudice from nativists, who believed that these immigrants had diseases and that their poverty was a sign of their inferiority. Nativists seemed to forget that they and their families were relatively recent immigrants as well.

The prejudice toward immigrants was clear from the moment they landed on U.S. soil at intake locations (places where new immigrants officially entered the country). These included Ellis Island in New York and Angel Island in San Francisco. There, the newcomers had to take tests to judge them worthy (or not) of entering the country. These tests included measurements of physical health. But they also included prejudiced tests, guided by a false "science" called eugenics.

EUGENICS

Eugenics was another result of white supremacy. This pseudoscience, which was widely embraced, held that people of certain nationalities and ethnic backgrounds were more intelligent than others. People even believed that they could tell someone's personality through the shape of that person's skull. The skull readings were part of another pseudoscience called phrenology.

Today we know these claims aren't real. Still, they caused long-lasting damage by contributing to deep-seated racist beliefs that still exist among some people today.

pseudoscience: the prefix "pseudo-" means fake or false, so a pseudoscience is a fake science. Often pseudoscience is used to justify racist political or social ideologies.

eugenics: a pseudoscience concerned with "improving" the human race by attempting to prevent people with "inferior" traits—usually unpopular minorities—from reproducing.

nativists: people who believe that new immigrants bring disease and that their poverty is a sign of their inferiority.

What are some ways that people might be able to tell the difference between a pseudoscience like eugenics and real sciences? Why do you think some people in the Gilded Age believed in eugenics?

_____

_____

_____

_____

_____

_____

_____

A nativist and minister, Francis Bellamy, wrote the Pledge of Allegiance in 1892.

CHINESE IMMIGRATION AND PREJUDICE

The wave of Chinese immigrants to the West Coast took place largely from 1838 to 1882. By 1882, Chinese Americans made up one-tenth of the population of California.

Prejudice against Chinese Americans led to the first U.S. law to restrict Immigration. The Chinese Exclusion Act of 1882 forbade Chinese immigration and denied citizenship to Chinese Americans. It stayed law until 1943, when the United States struck down immigration policies based on race or nationality. The definition of which races could live in the United States—and thus be American—still haunts this country.

THE STATUE OF LIBERTY

In 1875, construction began on the Statue of Liberty, a gift from the French to celebrate the freeing of American enslaved people. Chinese American student Saum Song Bo wrote the following letter to a New York newspaper:

> *"That statue represents Liberty holding a torch, which lights the passage of those of all nations who come into this country. But are the Chinese allowed to come? As for the Chinese who are here, are they allowed to enjoy liberty as men of all other nationalities enjoy it? Are they allowed to go about everywhere free from the insults, abuse, assaults, wrongs, and injuries from which men of other nationalities are free?"*

Why do you think Saum Song Bo chose the Statue of Liberty as his subject? How well do you think the Chinese Exclusion Act of 1882 matches up with the ideas the statue stands for?

_____

_____

_____

_____

_____

_____

HOUSING CONDITIONS

Nothing showed the divide between the wealthy and the poor more than how, and where, they lived. Cornelius Vanderbilt made his money in the railroad industry. He owned The Breakers, a 70-room mansion in Newport, Rhode Island—and that was just his summer home.

Urban immigrants, meanwhile, mostly lived in slums and tenements. A tenement is a building that has many apartments but little plumbing. Most tenements were dirty and unsafe. Many family members often lived in a tiny, cramped space. With poor plumbing and air circulation, unsanitary conditions, and people packed together, tenements helped spread disease and cause death. Laws and rules related to construction did little to help. One was that there must be at least one toilet for every 20 people.

These two living situations give a clear look at just how wide the gap was between the wealthy business owners of the time and the working class.

The Second Industrial Revolution transformed the United States from an agricultural economy to an industrial one. By 1900, 40 percent of Americans lived in cities. There were more than 80,000 tenements in New York City alone in 1900, housing more than 2.3 million people.

JACOB RIIS

Photographer and writer Jacob Riis (1849–1914) exposed the awful conditions of tenement and slum living in his 1890 book, **How the Other Half Lives.** As he wrote, "The story is dark enough. . . to send a chill to any heart. . . What are you going to do about it? is the question of today."

What do you think people should have done to help people in these conditions? Who should have helped?

_____

_____

_____

_____

_____

_____

_____

FACTORY WORK

Factory owners and managers rarely enforced safety rules or laws in factories. As a result, workers risked their lives on a regular basis. Between 1880 and 1900, industrial accidents in the United States killed 35,000 and injured another 500,000.

THE RISE OF SWEATSHOPS

In the 1880s, some immigrants sewed garments in their crowded apartments. "Contractors" took advantage of workers by setting up small shops and crowding the workers in. These were the first sweatshops.

Women working in sweatshops faced terrible conditions. They were packed into a tight space and had to work long hours with few breaks.

Bosses required the workers, who were almost all women, to put in up to sixteen hours a day, six days a week, for 20 cents a day. From the 1890s until the 1930s, about half of all manufactured clothing came from contract workers and home workers.

> **sweatshops**: factories with poor working conditions. Workers are crowded in, and they work extremely long hours for very little pay.

 Why do you think people had to work under these conditions?

_____

_____

_____

_____

_____

_____

_____

THE TRIANGLE SHIRTWAIST FACTORY FIRE

In 1911, 146 workers died in only 18 minutes in the Triangle Shirtwaist Factory in New York City. How did so many workers die so quickly? A fire broke out, and workers couldn't escape. They were trapped behind doors that had been locked to keep them from taking breaks they weren't supposed to. Most of the workers were young, female immigrants.

This tragedy received a tremendous amount of newspaper coverage. The scandal helped unions to push for safer working conditions.

CHILD LABORERS

Owners and managers also treated children unfairly. Because children were smaller, they could perform some tasks in factories that adults could not. Factory owners paid them even less than adults made. The children were unable to speak up for themselves, for fear of being fired and losing even the meager wages they were earning.

POLITICAL MACHINES

Political organizations called "machines" tried to convince immigrants to vote for specific candidates. The machines' job was to round up votes for political parties. They would offer financial help to immigrants in exchange for their support.

Immigrants could benefit from this help. Some got jobs building bridges and railroads. But many machines were corrupt. They used violence and took part in voter fraud. One machine filled out voter registration forms for a four-year-old and a dog. The most famous political machine was Tammany Hall in New York City. Its heyday came under William "Boss" Tweed between 1858 and 1871, when Tammany controlled New York City politics through bribery, intimidation, and trading jobs for votes.

WHAT DO UNIONS DO?

A labor union forms when groups of workers come together to protect their interests. By uniting, they can stand up to big businesses and leaders. They can demand safer working conditions or more money. Today, there are more than 14 million U.S. union members. Many teachers, nurses, factory workers, police officers, and firefighters have unions.

STRIKE THAT!

Workers began to go on **strike** to demand better working conditions. Unions' power grew. Between 1881 and 1885, workers carried out more than 500 strikes a year. Here's a timeline of some of the major ones.

> **strike:** stopping work until an employer agrees to changes, usually safety measures, better pay, or better working conditions.
>
> **boycott:** to refuse to buy from or interact with a particular company or group to protest their actions.

MAJOR U.S. STRIKES OF THE GILDED AGE

GREAT RAILROAD STRIKE OF 1877

DATES	WHAT HAPPENED?
July 14–September 4, 1877	Railway workers across the country protested a decrease in wages. Violence and clashes with soldiers left 100 dead.

ATLANTA'S WASHERWOMEN STRIKE

DATES	WHAT HAPPENED?
July–August 1881	Black washerwomen demanded higher wages and better treatment. The strike was successful, in part because white customers didn't want to have to do their own laundry.

HAYMARKET AFFAIR (ALSO KNOWN AS THE HAYMARKET RIOT)

DATES	WHAT HAPPENED?
May 4, 1886	McCormick Harvest Company workers in Chicago protested the company's refusal to create an eight-hour workday. The police responded with violence. A bomb went off, killing several protesters and police officers. Officials put the protest's leaders on trial despite no evidence they were involved in the bombing. The government hanged four of the protest leaders.

SUGAR STRIKE AND THE THIBODEAUX MASSACRE

DATES	WHAT HAPPENED?
November 1–23, 1887	10,000 Black sugar workers in Thibodeaux, Louisiana, struck peacefully. They asked for a daily wage of $1.25. When newspapers falsely reported violence, the government sent in armed soldiers. A local judge put the military in charge of government. When two white plantation guards were shot, white law enforcement members killed over 50 Black people, including women and children uninvolved with the strike.

HOMESTEAD STRIKE

DATES	WHAT HAPPENED?
June 29–July 11, 1892	About 3,500 armed union steel workers in Pennsylvania blocked access to their steel plant, owned by Andrew Carnegie. Carnegie hired a private army called the Pinkerton Detectives. Clashes between detectives and strikers led to the deaths of 12 people before the Pinkertons gave up. Carnegie did not meet the strikers' demands.

PULLMAN STRIKE

DATES	WHAT HAPPENED?
July 1894	George Pullman owned a company that made railroad cars that people could sleep in on overnight trips. He set up a company town in Illinois where his workers lived in housing he owned. He cut their pay but kept their rent the same. His workers went on strike. They had extra help from 50,000 members of the American Railway Union. The workers led a national **boycott**. They stopped all trade heading west of Chicago. President Cleveland argued that the strike was unlawful. He sent soldiers, who killed more than a dozen workers.

Do you think workers should be allowed to go on strike? Are there circumstances under which a strike should not be allowed?

_____

_____

_____

_____

WHAT IS A SCAB ANYWAY?

Scab is a negative word that some people use for union members who refuse to strike and for people who take the jobs of striking workers.

EUGENE V. DEBS

Eugene V. Debs (1855–1926) was head of the American Railway Union. He spent six months in prison for his role in the Pullman strike. While in jail, he embraced the ideas of socialism. He would go on to run as the Socialist Party candidate for president five times.

THE RISE OF BIG BUSINESS

As businesspeople continued to build their wealth, they began to form monopolies. A monopoly has so much power over a certain industry that other businesses can't compete. Monopolies are unfair to other businesses and to consumers, who must buy from just one company. Sometimes businesspeople formed monopolies through trusts.

In 1890, Congress passed the Sherman Antitrust Act. It allowed the government to step in and break up these trusts. Doing this would mean that government would have more control over businesses. But because of its language, the act was difficult to enforce.

FARMERS AND THE FORMATION OF THE POPULIST PARTY

Exploitation of workers wasn't limited to factories. Farmers were angry that they had to depend on the rails to move their crops, so the railway companies controlled farmers' costs. As the railroads expanded, they could transport more crops—so farmers grew more crops. As a result, the price for each individual barrel or bushel of crops got lower.

trust: an agreement between companies to produce and distribute specific commodities or services for their mutual benefit. In the Gilded Age, it meant that companies could team up and dominate the market.

socialism: an economic and political system in which businesses are owned and the government is run by the community as a whole.

THE POPULIST PARTY

Farmers began to meet in groups to discuss their situation. They became more political, but they felt neither the Democrats nor the Republicans supported them. So they formed The People's Party in 1892. Historians also call it the Populist Party.

Mary Elizabeth Lease

Here's what one of the party's future leaders, Mary Elizabeth Lease, said while speaking to a crowd in Topeka, Kansas in 1890: "Wall Street owns the country. It is no longer a government of the people, by the people, and for the people, but a government of Wall Street, by Wall Street, and for Wall Street."

Does this sound like something a politician might say today? Based on what you have learned, what is something else a Populist might say?

_____

_____

_____

_____

POPULIST POSITIONS

Populists backed candidates who supported regulation of the railroads and bimetallism. This plan would make the U.S. dollar payable in silver as well as gold. Populists believed that bimetallism would lead to higher prices because there would be more money in circulation. And getting higher prices for crops would help farmers pay off their debts. Of course, people who weren't farmers didn't want to pay more for the food they bought, fearing inflation.

Populists won positions as governors and even in the U.S. Congress, but the party eventually died out. Some former Populists joined the Democratic Party. This was a blow to Black farmers who had supported the Populists because most Southern Democratic politicians of the time were unapologetically racist.

bimetallism: a policy plan that would make the U.S. dollar payable in both silver and gold.

inflation: an economic term meaning that prices for goods go up, making them more expensive for the consumer.

THE JIM CROW SOUTH

Jim Crow laws were an extension of the Black codes you learned about in Chapter 5. Jim Crow laws were laws passed throughout the United States that required racial segregation. Under segregation, Black people were not allowed to be where white people were.

First enacted in 1877, these laws lasted through the mid-1960s and were especially common in the South. Everything from parks to water fountains, elevators, and cemeteries were segregated. But really, Jim Crow was more than a body of anti-Black laws. It was a way of life. Under Jim Crow, Black people were forced to be second class citizens in every aspect of life, from where they could sit on buses to how they were allowed to speak to white people.

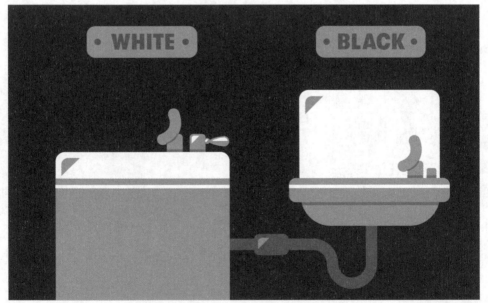

Under Jim Crow laws, everything from water fountains to swimming pools were segregated.

segregation: separating people, usually by race but sometimes by gender or religion.

THE KKK AND LYNCHING

As powerful people allowed white supremacy to thrive in the open, violence against Black people got worse. Groups such as the Ku Klux Klan caused much of this violence. Klan members and other racists would lynch Black men, which means killing them by mob action. They hanged innocent victims from trees in the middle of towns.

Black people were terrified of what would happen if they defied white society. Between 1882 and 1968, more than 3,176 lynchings of Black Americans took place. In Georgia alone, 531 Black Americans were lynched during that time period.

In 1890, Mississippi lawmakers held a meeting to rewrite the state constitution. The man in charge of the meeting, S. S. Calhoon, announced, "We came here to exclude the Negro." That was a clear violation of the Fifteenth Amendment to the Constitution. But nobody spoke up against the changes.

IDA B. WELLS-BARNETT

Ida B. Wells-Barnett (1862–1931) was one of white racism's most fearless enemies. This Black teacher and activist refused to leave a first-class train car in 1884. A conductor threw her out. Then she sued the railroad.

Wells continued expressing her views in print. She became a co-owner of the *Memphis Free Speech and Headlight* newspaper. She strongly opposed school segregation and sexual harassment, and she traveled the South reporting on lynchings.

In one article, Wells-Barnett wrote:

"The city of Memphis has demonstrated that neither [one's] character nor standing [helps] the Negro if he dares to protect himself against the white man or become his rival [competition]. There is nothing we can do about the lynching now, as we are outnumbered and without arms.... There is therefore only one thing left to do; save our money and leave a town which will neither protect our lives and property, nor give us a fair trial in the courts, but takes us out and murders us in cold blood when accused by white persons."

Wells also criticized liberals, including white suffrage leaders, for not taking a stand against racist crimes.

A mob destroyed her newspaper and threatened to kill her in 1892. Wells-Barnett moved north, where she continued her activism.

See page 119 for Wells-Barnett's role in the women's suffrage movement.

EVEN THE SUPREME COURT DEFENDED RACISM

In 1882, a Black man named Homer Plessy refused to sit in a car that was for Black people. This started a legal battle that would end up in the U.S. Supreme Court.

In its 1896 decision in *Plessy v. Ferguson*, the court ruled that segregation was constitutional as long as facilities for Black citizens were "separate but equal" to those for whites. Conditions at the time were clearly separate but unequal. Nonetheless, Plessy lost his case.

THE PROGRESSIVE ERA AND THE SOCIAL GOSPEL

Beginning in the 1890s, activists called Progressives dedicated themselves to fighting for the rights of largely white immigrants and the poor. The Progressives followed a rule called the Social Gospel. This rule held that wealthier Americans were responsible for their fellow citizens. Progressives opposed social Darwinism, which blamed the poor for their fates.

JOURNALISTS FIND THEIR CAUSES

Wells-Barnett wasn't the only journalist working to bring attention to the country's failings. The birth of the Progressive Era gave rise to a new form of journalism called muckraking. Reporters who hoped to improve society wrote about injustices for popular newspapers and magazines.

The term "muckraking" suggests digging through the mud. But muckrakers were vital recorders of the times. They helped bring about important social and governmental reforms. Politicians who didn't like what reporters wrote about them scorned muckrakers. Similarly, some politicians today talk about "fake news."

UPTON SINCLAIR

Upton Sinclair (1878–1968) brought attention to Chicago's meatpacking district with his novel *The Jungle*. The newspaper *Appeal to Reason* originally published it in 1905 as a series of stories.

While *The Jungle* was a fictional account of an immigrant family, the photographs were horrifying. They showed factory floors covered with animal blood. Spoiled packaged meat, Sinclair reported, could contain rats and other disgusting impurities. Sinclair later commented, "I aimed at the public's heart and by accident I hit it in the stomach."

 What do you think Sinclair meant by his comment?

_____

_____

_____

_____

Why It Mattered: *The Jungle* led to the creation of the Food and Drug Administration, a federal agency responsible for testing and approving the food and drug products Americans buy. Sinclair would later focus on working conditions in the coal, oil, and auto industries. He ran for governor of California in 1934 under the EPIC (End Poverty in California) banner.

NELLIE BLY

Nelly Bly (1864–1922) pretended to be mentally ill in 1887. Why? So that doctors would require her to spend ten days at Blackwell Island, a New York asylum (a prison for mentally ill people). She wrote a two-part series called "Ten Days in a Mad House." The *New York World* published it.

Bly showed that the asylum harmed its patients physically and mentally. She also discovered that many of the inmates were not mentally ill. Instead, they were recent immigrants who had gotten caught in the law enforcement system and were unable to communicate.

Why It Mattered: Bly, who was only 23 at the time, persuaded officials to close Blackwell Island. Taxpayers agreed to spend more money on the Department of Public Charities and Corrections to make improvements and prevent the situation from happening again.

IDA TARBELL

Ida Tarbell (1857–1944) exposed Standard Oil's ruthless and corrupt practices in her nineteen-part series, "The History of the Standard Oil Company." *McClure's* magazine published it in 1900.

As a child, Tarbell saw her father's oil production business get swallowed up by Standard Oil, which was a monopoly of the multimillionaire John D. Rockefeller. "They had never played fair, and that ruined their greatness for me," she said.

Tarbell did careful research. She read documents and interviewed employees. She proved the company's success was based on shady business practices.

Why It Mattered: The public's anger when they read her articles helped lead to the company's breakup. The government also renewed its trust-busting efforts.

 If you were a muckraker working today, what would you want to write about?

_____

_____

_____

_____

_____

_____

_____

SETTLEMENT HOUSES

To help white immigrants and the poor, the Progressives founded settlement houses. The idea was that university students and others would set up and live in "open" homes in poor neighborhoods. These activists would welcome neighbors and provide them with education, childcare, and healthcare.

Hull House was one of the earliest settlement houses in the United States. You can still visit the original site in Chicago.

JANE ADDAMS

Jane Addams (1860–1935) opened the first settlement house in the United States in 1889. Addams came from a wealthy family. She was traveling through Europe when she learned about England's settlement houses. Addams returned to Chicago and, along with Ellen Starr, founded Hull House. Addams had attended college. Her houses helped provide employment for working-class graduates, specifically young women.

Addams would go on to set up settlement houses around the country. This included Henry Street Settlement in New York City, which had one of the country's first kindergarten classes. By 1900, there were more than 100 settlements in the United States. Addams won the Nobel Peace Prize in 1931.

FIRSTS FOR WOMEN

In 1840, Catherine Brewer became the first U.S. woman to be granted a bachelor's degree. She graduated from Wesleyan College in Macon, Georgia. Nine years later, Dr. Elizabeth Blackwell would become the first American woman to graduate from medical school.

THE TEMPERANCE MOVEMENT

Jane Addams was one of many Progressives who supported the temperance movement. This movement encouraged Americans to give up drinking alcohol. Their efforts led to the passing of the Constitution's Eighteenth Amendment in 1919. It outlawed the production and sale of alcohol in the United States.

BLACK AMERICANS IN THE PROGRESSIVE ERA

White Progressives were largely focused on helping white people. Black Americans were suffering from segregation, white-inflicted violence, and poverty. Two powerful leaders emerged during the Progressive Era to champion Black rights.

BOOKER T. WASHINGTON

Bio

Washington (1856–1915) was born into slavery in Franklin county, Virginia. Upon emancipation in 1865, nine-year-old Washington found work first in a salt furnace, then a coal mine. Set on getting an education, he enrolled in one of the first Black colleges, supporting himself as a janitor while in school. He then became an educator himself. Washington became the most important spokesman for Black Americans in the late nineteenth and early twentieth centuries.

Beliefs

Washington argued that Black people had to gain economic equality before they could earn political equality. This belief put him at odds with leaders like Du Bois and those who fought segregation.

Accomplishments

Washington wrote numerous books, including *Up from Slavery*, his influential autobiography. He also founded the Tuskegee Normal and Industrial Institute in Alabama, an all-Black college (now Tuskegee University), and served as its first president. Two decades later, he started the National Negro Business League. He advised Presidents Roosevelt and Taft.

A COMPLICATED LEGACY

Today the way people view Booker T. Washington is complicated. Many people today view him as too eager to please white people. Some call him a sellout. But he also wrote letters in code to warn people about lynch mobs, and privately funded legal teams that challenged segregation in court.

W. E. B. DU BOIS

Bio

Born in Great Barrington, Massachusetts, Du Bois (1868–1963) went on to become one of the most important writers, editors, and civil rights activists of the twentieth century. He was a founder of the National Association for the Advancement of Colored People (NAACP) and the editor of its influential magazine, *The Crisis*.

Du Bois ran unsuccessfully as the Progressive Party's candidate for Senate in 1950. He became interested in communism later in his life. He joined the American Communist Party in 1961 before leaving to live in Ghana, an African country.

Beliefs

A teacher, author, and activist, Du Bois (pronounced du-BOYS) disagreed with Washington. He argued that Washington's call to accept prejudice and work hard in order to gain the respect of whites would not stop prejudice. He became a Pan-Africanist: he believed that all people of African descent had common interests and should work together for freedom.

Accomplishments

Du Bois was the first Black man to earn a Ph.D. degree from Harvard. He published a collection of essays titled *The Souls of Black Folk* in 1903. The book introduced the idea of "double consciousness." This means that people facing oppression have a conflict inside themselves.

IN THEIR OWN WORDS

Read these examples of each man explaining what he believed. What do you think?

Booker T. Washington: In an 1895 speech he gave to a largely white audience in Atlanta, Washington said, "The wisest of my race understand that the agitation and questions of social equality is the extremest folly [foolishness] and that progress in the enjoyment of all the privileges that will come to us must be the result of severe and constant struggle rather than artificial forcing. The opportunity to earn a dollar in a factory just now is worth infinitely more than to spend a dollar in an opera house."

W. E. B. Du Bois: As he wrote in *The Souls of Black Folk*, "The equality in political, industrial, and social life which modern men must have in order to live, is not to be confounded [mixed up] with sameness. On the contrary, In our case, it is rather insistence upon the right of diversity; upon the right of a human being to be a man even if he does not wear the same cut of vest, the same curl of hair, or the same color of skin."

How did each of these men approach racial injustice? What do you think of what they achieved?

_____

_____

_____

_____

_____

WOMEN'S VOICES GROW LOUDER

You'll notice that more women were becoming activists during the nineteenth century. They spoke out in large numbers on behalf of many causes. But they were also speaking out for themselves. Specifically, many wanted their right to vote. Read on to learn how their work in the nineteenth century led to their right to vote in the twentieth century.

CHAPTER 6 VOCABULARY

bimetallism: a policy plan that would make the U.S. dollar payable in both silver and gold.

boycott: to refuse to buy from or interact with a particular company or group to protest their actions.

eugenics: a pseudoscience (fake science) concerned with "improving" the human race by attempting to prevent people with "inferior" traits—usually unpopular minorities—from reproducing.

exodusters: Black homesteaders became known as the exodusters, a name that was inspired by the biblical story of Exodus, a journey out of Egypt.

inflation: an economic term meaning that prices for goods go up, making them more expensive for the consumer.

monopoly: a business that doesn't allow for competition. It usually leads to high prices and poor quality and service.

muckraking: a form of reporting in popular newspapers and magazines. Muckrakers exposed injustices.

nativists: people who believe that new immigrants bring disease and that their poverty is a sign of their inferiority.

Progressives: activists and citizens who believed that politicians and the wealthy should be responsible for their fellow citizens.

pseudoscience: the prefix "pseudo-" means fake or false, so a pseudoscience is a fake science. Often pseudoscience is used to justify racist political or social ideologies.

robber barons/captains of industry: both are terms to describe the business tycoons at this time. People who saw these tycoons as greedy might use the phrase "robber baron," and those who thought the tycoons used their wealth for good might use the more positive term "captains of industry."

scab: a negative term for a union member who refuses to strike, and for a person who takes the job of a striking worker.

segregation: separating people, usually by race but sometimes by gender or religion.

social Darwinism: a theory that applied Charles Darwin's theory of evolution to society. Social Darwinists often used this theory to justify racist beliefs.

Social Gospel: the belief that wealthier Americans were responsible for their fellow citizens. (A gospel is a message—often a religious message.)

socialism: an economic and political system in which businesses are owned and the government is run by the community as a whole.

strike: stopping work until an employer agrees to changes, usually safety measures, better pay, or better working conditions.

sweatshops: factories with poor working conditions. Workers are crowded in, and they work extremely long hours for very little pay.

trust: in business, a trust is an agreement between companies to produce and distribute specific commodities or services for their mutual benefit. In the Gilded Age, it meant that companies could team up and dominate the market.

tycoon: a powerful businessperson.

NOTES

7

THE UNITED STATES ENTERS A WORLD WAR

As the United States entered the twentieth century, a war with Spain erupted, women demanded the right to vote, and Theodore Roosevelt rose to power. The country first resisted, and then entered, World War I. Who would succeed, and how? We'll investigate.

CHAPTER CONTENTS

AMERICA'S NEW INTERNATIONAL INFLUENCE

THEODORE ROOSEVELT STEPS INTO THE PRESIDENCY

THE WOMEN'S MOVEMENT GAINS MOMENTUM

THE UNITED STATES ENTERS WORLD WAR I

THE WAR ENDS

AMERICA'S NEW INTERNATIONAL INFLUENCE

Today, the United States is involved in the affairs of many other nations—sometimes, even in their wars. But until the end of the nineteenth century, the country was mostly isolationist. It minded its own business, at least when it came to European affairs. That would change forever with the 1896 election of President William McKinley.

> isolationist: the policy of avoiding alliances and staying out of the affairs of foreign countries.

THE SPANISH-AMERICAN WAR

Spain colonized Cuba in the sixteenth century. In the 1890s, the Caribbean island went to war to claim its independence, much as Americans had done with Britain a century earlier.

The United States sided with Cuba. Americans might have sympathized with another country trying to get out from under a European power. But mostly, the United States was protecting its interest in Cuba's sugar crops.

American companies had bought large areas of land in Cuba for more than $50 million. The companies made twice that amount every year from the products they shipped from Cuba to other places. If the United States supported Cuba, those companies could protect their interests from the Spanish.

THE USS *MAINE*

President McKinley ordered the battleship USS *Maine* to drop anchor in Cuba's Havana Harbor as a show of strength. On February 15, 1898, the ship exploded and killed 268 American shipmen.

The cause of the explosion was never discovered. But Americans, including McKinley, were shocked and angry. On April 25, 1898, Congress officially declared war on Spain.

The USS Maine

THE WAR'S AFTERMATH

The war lasted through the summer and ended with U.S. victory and Cuba's independence. About 3,000 Americans died in that war, but the vast majority of those died of yellow fever and other tropical diseases, not in combat.

The war would affect even more than Cuba's future. Puerto Rico, Guam, and the Philippines became victims when a defeated Spain handed them over to the United States in the Treaty of Paris in 1898. Instead of ruling themselves after a long period of Spanish colonization, these areas fell under the control of the United States.

GAINING CONTROL OF HAWAII

American sugar planters had overthrown Hawaii's Queen Liliuokalani in 1893. But after the Spanish-American War, the United States grew even more aggressive about protecting its sugar interests. In 1898, it officially annexed the Hawaiian islands and claimed them as a U.S. territory.

annex: to take over a country or territory and control its land.

GETTING TERRITORIAL:
THE OUTCOME OF
THE SPANISH-AMERICAN WAR

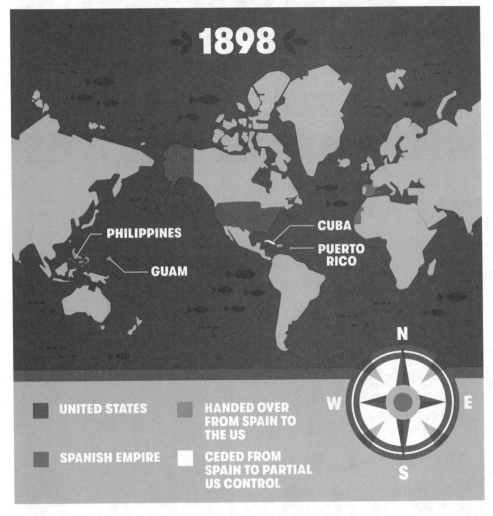

1898

PHILIPPINES

CUBA

PUERTO RICO

GUAM

N
W   E
S

UNITED STATES

HANDED OVER FROM SPAIN TO THE US

SPANISH EMPIRE

CEDED FROM SPAIN TO PARTIAL US CONTROL

It's important to remember that both Spain and the United States were colonizers. Even as power shifted from one to the other, it wasn't by choice of the people living in these colonies.

THEODORE ROOSEVELT STEPS INTO THE PRESIDENCY

On September 14, 1901, President McKinley had just begun his second term when he was assassinated at the Pan-American Exposition in Buffalo, New York. The assassin was 28-year-old Leon Czolgosz, a steelworker and anarchist who rebelled against the government.

At 42, Theodore Roosevelt became the youngest president in U.S. history. He excited the country with his progressive ideas and his forceful foreign policy. When he began his term, the United States was two years into the Philippine War, during which the Philippines fought for its independence.

> anarchist: someone who believes laws, rules, and government are unnecessary and unjust.

Theodore Roosevelt

ROOSEVELT GAINS CONTROL OF THE PHILIPPINES

Roosevelt had been assistant secretary of the Navy during the Spanish-American War. He threw his support behind continuing to fight in the Philippines. He wanted to keep the islands as a refueling station for the U.S. Navy ships in the Pacific. He also held the racist belief that Filipinos were not capable of self-governance.

American soldiers practiced torture and were given the orders to kill anyone older than 10. The Filipino body count was so high that American soldiers used the bodies as defense from enemy bullets. The war ended when Roosevelt ordered a cease-fire on July 4, 1902, and declared victory. The United States would retain control over the Philippines until 1946. Today the Philippines is an independent country.

The war resulted in the deaths of more than 4,200 American soldiers and more than 20,000 Filipino soldiers. An additional 500,000 Filipinos died from war-related causes, including famine and diseases.

 Why do you think the United States fought against independence for the Philippines?

_____

_____

_____

_____

_____

A NEW FORM OF "JOURNALISM" EMERGES

Unlike muckrakers (check the last chapter!), who wanted social reform, a new type of journalist became famous during the Spanish-American War. They used sensationalism to influence popular opinion.

Some news outlets pressed Americans to support the war with a cry to "Remember the *Maine*!" referring to the warship's explosion. Other journalists distorted facts in order to sell papers. For instance, *The New York Journal*, owned by William Randolph Hearst, falsely claimed in 1898 that the destruction of the warship was definitely "the work of an enemy" rather than an accident. (As mentioned previously, it is unclear what led to the explosion.)

YELLOW JOURNALISM

This "fake news" earned the name yellow journalism. The term comes from the comic *Hogan's Alley*, which featured a character known as "the Yellow Kid" because of the color clothing he wore. Joseph Pulitzer's *New York World* newspaper published the comic.

To compete with Pulitzer, Hearst had his art department create its *own* comic featuring a "yellow kid." These two papers' reporting styles thus became known as "yellow journalism."

Pulitzer later became a New York congressman. He left money in his will to Columbia University to establish the Pulitzer Prize. The prize is for excellence in newspaper journalism and the arts.

sensationalism: a type of journalism that greatly exaggerates, or *sensationalizes*, news.

yellow journalism: a style of reporting that distorts facts in order to sell more newspapers or magazines.

AN INDEPENDENT CUBA? NOT SO FAST.

On May 22, 1903, President Roosevelt pressured Cuba into signing the Platt Amendment. This gave the United States the right to have a say in Cuba's government and effectively control it. Cuba may have won its independence from Spain, but the United States had stepped into Spain's place.

"SPEAK SOFTLY AND CARRY A BIG STICK."

Roosevelt summed up his approach to foreign relations with this now-famous phrase. It showed his belief in the importance of negotiation, or **diplomacy**. He believed that when it came time to negotiate, the strength of a country's military force affected its power when making deals with other countries.

For this reason, Roosevelt ordered the construction of sixteen battleships during his eight years in office. The ships earned the nickname "The Great White Fleet" for their color. Roosevelt paraded the ships around the world as a visual reminder of the country's power.

Roosevelt's "Great White Fleet"

ROOSEVELT "SPEAKS SOFTLY"

With the "big stick" taken care of, Roosevelt was now free to show his skill for speaking softly. He gained a reputation for swiftly settling disputes between other countries. When Japan attacked the Russian naval base Port Arthur, Roosevelt's negotiations between the two countries earned him a Nobel Peace Prize in 1906.

Roosevelt also used his powers of persuasion to benefit the United States. He helped keep Europe out of the Western Hemisphere by issuing the Roosevelt Corollary to the Monroe Doctrine. This corollary said that the United States could step in on behalf of Latin American countries that Europe threatened.

THE UNITED STATES EYES LATIN AMERICA

However, the United States sometimes threatened Latin American countries. Colombia rejected the U.S. proposal for building a canal through the isthmus of Panama. The isthmus of Panama has the Pacific Ocean on one side and the Atlantic on the other. Building a canal through Panama meant that ships in the Atlantic would not have to travel around all of South America to reach the Pacific.

Roosevelt responded to Colombia's rejection by supporting Panama's fight for independence from Colombia. As a reward, Panama gave the United States permission to build, own, and control the Panama Canal. The United States had full control of the canal until 1979.

> **diplomacy:** the act of negotiating and keeping good relations between the governments of different countries.
>
> **corollary:** a statement that logically follows another statement that has been proven to be true.
>
> **isthmus:** a narrow piece of land surrounded by water.

THE PANAMA CANAL

The Panama Canal opened in 1914. It was an incredible feat of engineering.

The United States built the canal by digging across the Central American isthmus of Panama at its narrowest point (only 50 miles!). Then workers built a series of watertight chambers, called locks, to lift or lower ships from one section to the next.

One of the most important and ambitious construction projects in American history, the canal let the United States control almost all trade between the Pacific and Atlantic oceans. It also gave the U.S. Navy easy access to the country's new territories in the Pacific.

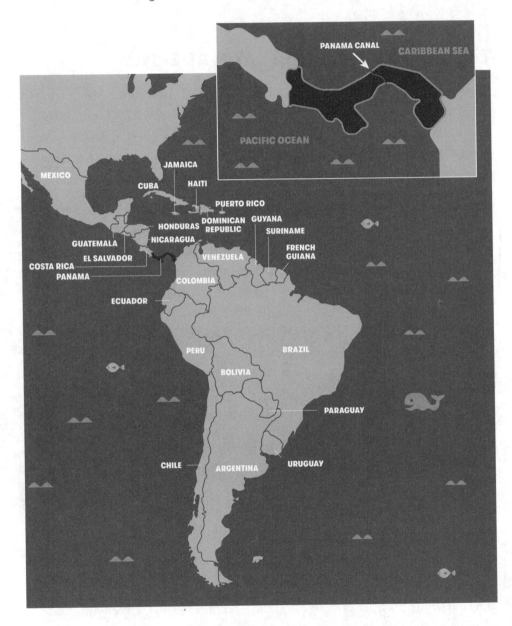

PRESIDENT ROOSEVELT'S ECONOMIC REFORMS: A SQUARE DEAL

Theodore Roosevelt believed that the government's job was to balance the economic forces of businesses and workers.

Roosevelt was a powerful "trust buster." In other words, he broke up large companies that prevented competition and kept prices high. (You learned about trusts in Chapter 6.)

For example, Roosevelt forced the breakup of a railroad combination in the northwest by relying on the Sherman Antitrust Act. During a coal strike in 1902, he pressured wealthy businesspeople on Wall Street to threaten to sell coal companies' stocks. Selling the stocks helped end the strike and helped get the workers higher pay.

WHAT EXACTLY IS A STOCK?

A *stock* is a small piece of a company that people can buy or sell. People who buy stocks make money if the stock price rises or if the company issues a dividend, which is a small payment to stockholders. But stock prices can also fall, which can leave stockholders poorer if they have to sell at a low price.

THE SQUARE DEAL

These actions were part of Roosevelt's policy called the Square Deal. He wanted to champion hardworking Americans, or, as he said, "my favorite formula—a square deal for every man." Women and children also benefited from the Square Deal, especially because the quality and purity of foods and drugs improved.

A SELECTION OF SQUARE DEAL PROGRAMS

WHEN	WHAT IT WAS	WHAT IT DID
1903	Bureau of Corporations	Investigated businesses that sold products across state lines in order to identify possible monopolies. The Bureau didn't have the power to enforce anti-monopoly laws, though.
1906	Hepburn Act	Gave the (already existing) Interstate Commerce Commission control over how much it cost to ship items from state to state by railroad.
1906	Pure Food and Drug and Meat Inspection Acts	Outlawed the sale of misbranded or contaminated food and drugs across state lines. Became the foundation for the nation's first consumer protection agency, the Food and Drug Administration (FDA).

ROOSEVELT AND CONSERVATION

Historians refer to the Square Deal as the "three C's."

- Consumer protection: making sure the products people buy are safe and the labels are accurate.

- Corporate oversight: watching over businesses to make sure they obey the laws and keep prices reasonable.

- Conservation: taking care of land, water, and air so they are not polluted.

Roosevelt established 150 national forests, 51 bird reserves, four national game preserves, and five national parks. These took up more than 230 million acres of public land.

> **conservation:** the protection of natural resources such as air, land, animals, and water so they are not used up or destroyed by pollution or overhunting.

 Some of the land protected by new conservation laws was in North Dakota, South Dakota, and Florida. Do you remember who these lands used to belong to, and how they became "public"? Hint: go back and review Chapter 3.

_____

_____

_____

_____

_____

_____

_____

_____

THE BULL MOOSE PARTY

The Progressive Party's official mascot was the bull moose, which party members wore proudly on campaign buttons like this one.

President William Howard Taft, who had served as vice president under Roosevelt, won election in 1908 with Roosevelt's help. But the former president thought Taft did not do enough to break up trusts, so he campaigned against Taft's renomination in 1912.

Roosevelt wanted to run for president in place of Taft, but the Republican Party said no. So he formed the Progressive Party, or "Bull Moose Party," which sought to introduce a minimum wage for women and a national health service, and to give voters more direct control over the government.

Roosevelt's new party split the Republican vote. He and Taft lost to the Democrat Woodrow Wilson.

WOODROW WILSON: REGULATING BUSINESS

Like Roosevelt, Wilson kept an eye on big businesses. He broke up monopolies and formed the Federal Trade Commission to enforce antitrust laws and protect consumers. The establishment of the Federal Reserve Bank in 1913 gave the government, rather than companies, control over the supply of money and interest rates. This made the economy more secure.

With Wilson's encouragement, Congress also passed the Sixteenth Amendment in 1913. This allowed the federal taxation of Americans' income. The tax was graduated, meaning people who earned higher incomes had to pay higher taxes than those who earned less. Income tax quickly became the biggest source of money for the federal government.

A CONSTITUTIONAL AMENDMENT

The Seventeenth Amendment, passed in 1913, gave the people the right to elect the two U.S. senators from their state. Before that, state legislators had selected senators, who often protected those legislators' own political interests.

THE WOMEN'S MOVEMENT GAINS MOMENTUM

On March 3, 1913, the day before Wilson's inauguration, a 65-year-long fight for women's right to vote resulted in a march in Washington, D.C.

Organized by Alice Paul (1885–1977) and the National American Woman Suffrage Association (NAWSA), the march was led by lawyer and activist Inez Milholland, who rode a white horse up Pennsylvania Avenue. More than 5,000 suffragists followed in her path. They demanded that the Nineteenth Amendment become part of the Constitution so women could have the vote and a voice in the country's government.

> suffragist: someone who fights to give the right to vote to those who don't yet have it.

On March 3, 1913, women took to the streets in Washington, D.C., to fight for their own voting rights.

IDA B. WELLS-BARNETT MARCHES

One of those suffragists was journalist Ida B. Wells-Barnett—you read about her in Chapters 5 and 6. Wells-Barnett had cofounded the Alpha Suffrage Club in 1913 to campaign for the right of Black women to vote in Chicago. When she arrived at the march, the organizers told her to move to the back of the line. She asked the white Illinois marchers to support her, but they refused.

Wells-Barnett protested by saying she wouldn't march. But halfway through, she came out of the crowd and stepped in *front* of the Illinois group, marching between two white suffragists.

FALLOUT FROM THE MARCH

Around 500,000 spectators watched the march. Many of them were in town for the president's inauguration. While many cheered, some attacked the marchers. More than 100 women went to hospitals with injuries.

Refusing to be discouraged, Paul and the NAWSA activists continued to press for the vote. They criticized Wilson in the press, and posted protestors wearing banners and holding signs outside the White House and in nearby Lafayette Square for more than two years, putting "silent sentinel" protesters outside the White House gates. This tactic had never been tried before. It would be another seven years before the U.S. Congress passed the Nineteenth Amendment in 1919, which gave women the right to vote after it was ratified by two-thirds of the states and became part of the Constitution in 1920.

KNOW YOUR WOMEN'S MOVEMENT ACTIVISTS

Helen Keller

HELEN KELLER

Helen Keller (1886–1916) was already famous for championing people with disabilities. She was among the marchers in Washington. Keller became blind and deaf when she was about a year and a half old. As an adult, she graduated from college and wrote several books. A cofounder of the **American Civil Liberties Union**, she supported women's suffrage, access to birth control, and **pacifism**.

> **American Civil Liberties Union (ACLU):** a nonprofit organization formed in 1920 that works to protect "the individual rights and liberties guaranteed to every person in this country by the Constitution and laws of the United States."
>
> **pacifism:** the belief that people should not use war or violence to solve problems.

Inez Milholland

INEZ MILHOLLAND

Milholland (1886–1916) grew up in London and New York in a wealthy family. She became a war correspondent and activist for pacifism. Several top law schools refused to let her attend because she was a woman. However, she graduated from New York University's law school. She used her degree to fight for workers' rights.

Hallie Quinn Brown

HALLIE QUINN BROWN

Also marching was Brown (1849–1949), an African American suffragist, activist, and writer. Brown championed temperance (drinking little or no alcohol) and civil rights. Well-known for her public speaking skills, Brown became president of the National Association of Colored Women.

The only other Black marchers (other than Wells-Barnett, who joined halfway through) were 22 founders of Howard University's Sigma Theta sorority. The march organizers forced them to the back of the parade.

A WHITE AFFAIR

American suffragists largely fought for white women's right to vote, as witnessed by the makeup of the march. The Nineteenth Amendment says nothing about race. However, in practice, only white women got to vote at first. In spite of the passage of the Fifteenth Amendment in 1870, many Black people were prevented from voting until the federal Voting Rights Act passed in 1965.

Most nonwhite people faced voter suppression, which Jim Crow laws supported. In 1926, a group of Black women tried to vote in Birmingham, Alabama. Election officials beat them. Voter suppression continues to this day in the form of strict ID requirements that many people can't provide, deleting large numbers of people from the voter rolls—and even making it illegal to bring food or water to people standing on long voter lines!

People with Asian ancestry were not allowed to vote until 1952. Legal barriers preventing Native Americans from voting weren't removed until 1962.

BLACK VOTING RIGHTS

The Fifteenth Amendment, passed in 1870, stated that no man could be denied the chance to vote because of race. But some states continued to suppress African Americans' votes. They did this by enacting laws that allowed poll taxes and literacy tests.

Also, huge numbers of Black voters stayed away from the polls (voting places) because of threats and violence from some white people.

voter suppression: creating and enforcing policies and practices that make it harder for people to vote. Literacy tests and poll taxes are forms of voter suppression.

poll tax: a fee that someone has to pay if they want to vote. Like the literacy test, a way to prevent minorities and poor people from voting.

literacy tests: an exam that supposedly shows whether the test taker can read, but is really meant to keep minorities and poor people from voting. Test makers designed the literacy tests to be confusing and difficult to pass.

THE UNITED STATES ENTERS WORLD WAR I

Wilson had promised to keep the country out of World War I when he was running for reelection in 1916. His campaign slogan was "He kept us out of war!" But he would soon reverse his position. Why? Because of a telegram and a sinking ship.

GERMANY PROVOKES THE UNITED STATES

On April 4, 1917, the United States entered into war against Germany. Germany had gone back on its promise to restrict submarine attacks in the North Atlantic and the Mediterranean, specifically on passenger and merchant ships.

In February and March, German submarines had sunk several U.S. ships, killing civilians (non-soldiers) as well as soldiers. In addition, Wilson had found out that Germany tried to make an alliance with Mexico that would hurt the United States.

This marked the United States' official declaration of war. But prior to that, the federal government had loaned Great Britain $2 billion to fight Germany. It also kept them supplied with wartime goods.

Providing these supplies led to more jobs and higher wages in the United States. As the war continued, the prosperity of the U.S. economy became increasingly tied to British success.

THE ZIMMERMANN TELEGRAM

Germany reached out to Mexico, offering a deal. In return for Mexico's support, Germany promised that Mexico would get back parts of Texas, New Mexico, and Arizona it had lost during the Mexican-American War.

The British discovered this by intercepting and decoding the Zimmermann Telegram. (It got that name because the German foreign minister, Arthur Zimmermann, sent it to Mexico.) But the British didn't immediately share the details with the Americans.

The British feared the Germans would find out that Britain had cracked their codes. But the fighting got worse, and the British realized they needed more help. They sent the telegram to Wilson. It was part of his decision to ask the U.S. Congress to formally declare war.

THE *LUSITANIA*

Many Americans had been in favor of entering the war since 1915. That was when the Germans attacked and sank the *Lusitania*, a U.S. passenger ship that was also carrying military supplies.

Part of Germany's war strategy was preventing supplies from reaching its enemies. The Germans accomplished this goal using armed submarines called U-boats. The captain of the *Lusitania* was about to set sail from New York Harbor for Liverpool, England, on May 1, 1915. He found out that U-boats had just sunk three British liners—large ships that carry many passengers. The captain nevertheless set out across the Atlantic.

The Lusitania

On May 7, the *Lusitania* approached southern Ireland. A U-boat destroyed it with a single torpedo. A total of 1,198 passengers died, including 124 Americans. When the press reported the event, many Americans felt outraged at Germany's attack and the deaths of civilians.

Few newspapers reported that wartime supplies (including weapons and ammunition) were on the ship. Even fewer reported that the ship's captain had received a warning about the trip's dangers. Do you think this would have changed people's feelings? Why or why not?

_____

_____

_____

_____

_____

_____

THE RUSSIAN REVOLUTION

Another reason Wilson decided to join the war was the Russian Revolution. In 1917 the Bolsheviks, a **communist** revolutionary group, overthrew Tsar Nicolas II. Wilson believed that entering the war would help make the world "safe for democracy" by helping to keep communist revolutions from spreading to other countries.

communist: someone who believes there should be no privately owned property. In a communist country, the people (through the government) own all land and factories.

A WORLD DIVIDED

WORLD WAR I ALLIANCES

More than 30 nations were involved in World War I. Here are the main members of the two alliances.

ALLIED POWERS:		CENTRAL POWERS:	
France	Japan	Austria-Hungary	Ottoman Empire
Great Britain	Russia	Bulgaria	
Italy	United States	Germany	

 U.S. fighting mainly took place on the Western and Eastern fronts between the Allied Powers and the Central Powers. The Western Front spanned from Belgium to Switzerland. The Eastern Front was on the border of Austria-Hungary and Russia. There was also fighting in Southwest Asia and North Africa.

front: an area where armies or other military forces are fighting.

AN INTERNATIONAL WAR QUICKLY BECOMES PERSONAL

Most of the war took place in Europe. However, it had a dramatic and lasting effect on Americans.

More than 4.7 million American men and women served in the war. About 2.8 million of those served overseas. A stunning 53,402 were killed in action. More than 63,000 people serving in the armed forces died from war-related causes, including cholera, dysentery, and other diseases. Also, more than 200,000 were wounded.

Soldiers fought in trenches that quickly spread disease, as had happened in the Civil War. But now the military had deadlier weapons. New seaborne and airborne weapons allowed sides to kill each other from greater distances. Chemical weapons, including mustard gas, were so powerful that even gas masks were often ineffective. Both sides also used military tanks, a new automotive technology.

BLACKS' AND NATIVE AMERICANS' ROLES AS SOLDIERS

U.S. military units continued to be segregated, as they had been during the Civil War. More than 380,000 Black Americans gave their service.

Many of them were eager to show their patriotism and be recognized as full citizens, a right many white Americans had denied by passing laws that discriminated against Black citizens.

One branch of the military, the Marines, barred Black men. The Navy allowed them but often made them serve in low-status, backbreaking jobs. Black people in the armed forces frequently faced racism from whites.

THE HARLEM HELL FIGHTERS

One of the most celebrated Black units was the 369th United States Infantry. People nicknamed it the "Harlem Hell Fighters." This unit served alongside French soldiers. The Hell Fighters were the first unit to reach the Rhine River, a crucial waterway for Germany. More than 170 of its 191 members received French Legion of Honor medals for serving in the trenches.

UNSUNG WAR HEROES: BLACK DOCTORS AND FEMALE DOCTORS

Tending to the sick and wounded in the Black infantries were 104 Black doctors who volunteered for service. Most had graduated from the country's three Black colleges that specialized in training Black men to become doctors.

Female doctors were not allowed to serve as enlisted members of the army unless they signed on as nurses. But they still found ways onto the front lines. In 1918, an Iowan newspaper called the *Evening Times-Republican* reported that 33 percent of the country's registered female doctors had volunteered. Some signed on as "contract" doctors (which meant they weren't officially enlisted). Others served with the French army.

Dr. Caroline Sandford Finley headed an all-female U.S. hospital service in France. She earned the rank of lieutenant in the Medical Corps of the French army. The French and English government rewarded her with medals of honor for her service.

Native American code talkers used native languages to communicate U.S. military messages that Germans couldn't understand.

NATIVE AMERICANS AND THE WAR EFFORT

Native Americans wouldn't be considered U.S. citizens until 1924. Still, more than 12,000 volunteered to serve in the war. They generally served as scouts and snipers, based on the stereotype that they were natural navigators and warriors. Like the Black soldiers who fought, they too hoped that their efforts would lead to citizenship.

Native Americans were indispensable for their work as code talkers. They used at least six native languages to send messages that the Germans could not understand because the languages were unknown to them. Choctaw and Cherokee code talkers played key roles in a military campaign called the Meuse-Argonne Offensive (see page 250).

In 1920, General John Pershing wrote, "The North American Indian took his place beside every other American in offering his life in the great cause, where as a splendid soldier, he fought with the courage and valor of his ancestors."

 Remember that in the nineteenth century, boarding schools had forced Native American students to speak English and to try to forget their Native languages. Does the story of the code talkers make you feel any different about the importance of preserving language and culture?

_____

_____

_____

_____

A COMANCHE SOLDIER IS RECOGNIZED

Army Private Calvin Atchavit, a Comanche soldier from Oklahoma, received a Distinguished Service Cross for "extraordinary heroism in action" in France on September 12, 1918. Despite having a wounded right arm, he shot and killed one enemy soldier and took another prisoner.

PROPAGANDA: A NEW FORM OF COMMUNICATION

While U.S. forces were busy fighting across the Atlantic, the government was trying to control people's feelings and behaviors at home.

Officials believed that increasing support for the war was essential. President Wilson created the Committee of Public Information to help. The CPI published propaganda that called antiwar sentiment unpatriotic.

Many newspapers got their information from the CPI. The agency picked statistics to make it look as though Allied forces were winning regardless of the reality.

THE ESPIONAGE ACT

The government also further restricted the rights of immigrants. This was a form of xenophobia, which means prejudice against people from other countries. Congress said that immigrants "born under other flags" might oppose the war because they supported their homeland.

In 1917, Congress passed the Espionage Act. This law made it illegal to obstruct the draft, weaken the armed forces through spying, or print "unpatriotic" information.

The government censored seventy-four newspapers under this law, endangering the First Amendment right to free speech.

THE SEDITION ACT

Even *speaking* negatively about the United States became illegal with the Sedition Act of 1918. This law criminalized criticism of the government, military, or Constitution. Union leader Eugene Debs went to prison for his antiwar speeches. So did fellow socialist Charles Schenck. He distributed antiwar pamphlets that encouraged Americans to disobey the draft.

Schenck's case reached the Supreme Court, which ruled against him. Justice Oliver Wendell Holmes defended the Sedition Act in 1919, saying that a person cannot yell "Fire!" in a crowded movie theater without cause. While it was not a part of the Court's official ruling, this example boiled down to: When the country is at war, stop making trouble.

100 DAYS IN 1918

In the summer of 1918, America fought alongside the Allied powers—principally, Great Britain, France, Russia, Italy, and Japan—in a series of battles known as the Hundred Days Offensive. Their opponents were the Central powers: Germany, Austria-Hungary, and the Ottoman Empire (modern-day Turkey). These are some of the key events and conflicts of that hundred-day period.

propaganda: information that is designed to support a particular point of view, even if that information is exaggerated, unproven, or false.

Sedition Act: a 1918 law that made it illegal to criticize the government, the military, or the Constitution.

xenophobia: prejudice against people from other countries.

censor: to remove the parts of a message that officials believe could harm society. Can apply to letters, books, magazines, movies, etc.

THE HUNDRED DAYS OFFENSIVE (1918)

AUGUST

AUGUST 8-11

In the brutal **Battle of Amiens**, Allied forces of 75,000 attacked the Germans in France with more than 500 tanks and 2,000 planes. The Allied victory helped turn the tide of the war, but more than 27,000 people died.

AUGUST 21-SEPTEMBER 2

The **Second Battle of the Somme** helped turn the tide of the war, as the Allies were able to disrupt the German supply line near the Somme River. Two years earlier, the Battle of the Somme had slogged on for five months, resulting in more than a million killed or wounded for the British, French, and German armies combined.

SEPTEMBER

SEPTEMBER 26-NOVEMBER 11

The **Meuse-Argonne Offensive** was the largest effort by American forces in the war. It involved more than a million U.S. soldiers. The Americans won by cutting vital German railroad connections in France. More than 26,000 American soldiers were killed.

SEPTEMBER 29

This day brought a deciding victory for the Allies. Their forces broke through the last line of German defenses. It was a heavily armed zone that ran for several miles in northern France near the Belgian border.

NOVEMBER

NOVEMBER 11

Kaiser Wilhelm of Germany stepped down. The two sides came to an **armistice**, or an agreement to stop fighting.

FRENCH FIGHTS

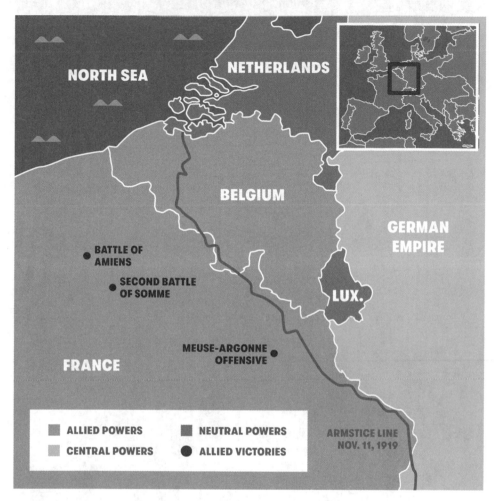

NORTH SEA

NETHERLANDS

BELGIUM

GERMAN EMPIRE

LUX.

BATTLE OF AMIENS

SECOND BATTLE OF SOMME

MEUSE-ARGONNE OFFENSIVE

FRANCE

ALLIED POWERS

CENTRAL POWERS

NEUTRAL POWERS

ALLIED VICTORIES

ARMSTICE LINE NOV. 11, 1919

Take a look at this map to see where the Hundred Days Offensive battles took place.

armistice: an agreement to stop fighting.

President Wilson delivers his Fourteen Points speech.

THE WAR ENDS

PRESIDENT WILSON'S FOURTEEN POINTS

In January 1918, President Wilson gave a speech to Congress and outlined his vision for international peace. Today people know it as the Fourteen Points speech. Many of its ideas came from the country's Progressive moment.

For example, Wilson and the Progressives favored self-determination, meaning that people should rule themselves rather than submitting to colonizers. Wilson also wanted free trade, which means that governments don't put many taxes or tariffs on goods sold across international borders.

In the speech, Wilson suggested forming a League of Nations. Wilson's points became the basis for negotiations between the Allies and Germany.

> League of Nations: a political organization established at the end of World War I designed to prevent more wars. An early version of the United Nations.

A GLOBAL PANDEMIC HITS

World War I ended in 1918. But the world was facing a new threat: a global pandemic known as the Spanish flu. Between 1918 and 1919, this flu killed 50 million people worldwide and 675,000 in the United States.

Health care workers tried desperately to contain the flu. When World War I officially ended on November 11, 1918, doctors advised that large groups shouldn't attend gatherings that were celebrating the Allied victory.

THE TREATY OF VERSAILLES

Five months after his speech, Wilson went to France to meet the leaders of Great Britain, Italy, and France and sign the Treaty of Versailles (pronounced ver-SIGH). The 1919 treaty redrew Germany's borders. It also held the country responsible for war reparations. This meant the Germans had to pay back the money other countries had spent fighting the war. That total cost to Germany was a staggering $33 billion.

In addition, Germany was no longer allowed to have a large military force. Germany also gave up 13 percent of its land and all of its colonies in China, the Pacific, and Africa, to the Allied nations. Germany and its defeated partners (including Austria-Hungary, Turkey, and Bulgaria) did not have representatives at the table.

The humiliation of the Germans and its economic ruin would help fuel the rise of Adolf Hitler and World War II less than twenty years later.

> reparations: payments for damages or harm caused.

By 1920, 48 countries had joined the League of Nations. But because Wilson was unable to get the approval of the Republican-majority Congress, the United States was not one of them.

THE GREAT MIGRATION BEGINS

Black veterans returned home from fighting on behalf of their country only to be met by an increase in race-fueled hatred. During the summer of 1919 alone, there were at least 97 lynchings; 13 of the men killed were World War I veterans. With mounting attacks by whites on Black men, police refused to act. The resulting bloodshed was called the Red Summer.

Black people had few defenses against the hatred encouraged by Jim Crow laws. So they moved out of the South in huge numbers in what we now call the Great Migration. By 1920, the Black population in Chicago alone had grown by 500 percent.

CHAPTER 7 VOCABULARY

armistice: an agreement to stop fighting.

American Civil Liberties Union (ACLU): a nonprofit organization formed in 1920 that works to protect "the individual rights and liberties guaranteed to every person in this country by the Constitution and laws of the United States."

anarchist: someone who believes laws, rules, and government are unnecessary and unjust.

annex: to take over a country or territory and control its land.

censor: to remove the parts of a message that officials believe could harm society. Can apply to letters, books, magazines, movies, etc.

communist: someone who believes there should be no privately owned property. In a communist country, the people (through the government) own all land and factories.

conservation: the protection of natural resources such as air, land, animals, and water so they are not used up or destroyed by pollution or overhunting.

corollary: a statement that logically follows another statement that has been proven to be true.

diplomacy: the act of negotiating and keeping good relations between the governments of different countries.

front: an area where armies or other military forces are fighting.

isolationist: someone who believes that his or her own country should not be involved with other countries.

isthmus: a narrow piece of land surrounded by water.

League of Nations: a political organization established at the end of World War I designed to prevent more wars. An early version of the United Nations.

literacy test: an exam that supposedly shows whether the test taker can read, but is really meant to keep minorities and poor people from voting. Test makers designed the literacy tests to be confusing and difficult to pass.

pacifism: the belief that people should not use war or violence to solve problems.

poll tax: a fee that someone has to pay if they want to vote. Like the literacy test, a way to prevent minorities and poor people from voting.

propaganda: information that is designed to support a particular point of view, even if that information is exaggerated, unproven, or false.

reparations: payments for damages or harm caused.

Sedition Act: a 1918 law that made it illegal to criticize the government, the military, or the Constitution.

suffragist: someone who fights to give the right to vote to those who don't yet have it.

sensationalism: a type of journalism that greatly exaggerates, or *sensationalizes*, news.

voter suppression: creating and enforcing policies and practices that make it harder for people to vote. (See literacy test and poll tax, above.)

xenophobia: prejudice against people from other countries.

yellow journalism: a style of reporting that distorts facts in order to sell more newspapers or magazines.

NOTES

8

FROM ROARING TO WARRING: THE '20S, '30S, AND '40S

These three decades gave birth to jazz, Hollywood glamour, and the Harlem Renaissance. They also brought a devastating economic depression and World War II. How? Let's do some digging.

CHAPTER CONTENTS

THE ROARING TWENTIES

THE STOCK MARKET CRASHES

FDR: A NEW PRESIDENT AND A NEW DEAL

THE SEEDS OF WORLD WAR II

TWO VICTORIES FOR THE ALLIES

THE ROARING TWENTIES

The decade earned its name thanks to the great times that many Americans were having with World War I behind them. The economy was booming. The nation's wealth more than doubled between 1920 and 1929. And lots of people spent their money having fun.

Women were finally allowed to join the party, politically and socially. They gained the right to vote with the passing of the Nineteenth Amendment in 1920. Poorer women had always worked, but millions of middle-class women took up office jobs, earning paychecks. Previously, most of the jobs widely available to women had been doing manual labor in textile mills and other factories. Many worked in the homes of wealthy people as servants.

Birth control became more widely available, so many women began to experience the benefits of both family planning and sexual freedom in their personal lives. Some women, nicknamed flappers, cut their hair and wore short dresses. For the first time in U.S. history, some women felt free to drink and smoke in public.

NEW TECHNOLOGIES BRING NEW OPPORTUNITIES

Both men and women benefited from the rise of new industries that created a flood of job opportunities. Automobiles were being mass-produced, and air travel took off. There was also a boom in highway and housing construction—made easier by inventions like the bulldozer and concrete mixers—as more people moved from farms to cities.

The 1920s brought life-changing inventions. Many were possible because of easier access to electricity.

NEW INVENTIONS

VACUUM CLEANERS

James Murray Spangler, a store janitor in Ohio, invented the first portable electric vacuum cleaner in 1907. He sold the design to William Henry Hoover. The two of them worked together until Spangler died in 1915. "Hoovering" became another word for vacuum cleaning.

WASHING MACHINES

As these became more widely available, women gained hours in their days when they no longer had to wash their family members' clothes by hand. Scholars link the invention of washing machines to middle-class women being able to spend more time fighting for their rights.

ELECTRIC REFRIGERATORS

The first refrigerators cost about $1,000, which was twice as much as the cost of a new car! They replaced the icebox, which used—you guessed it—a big block of ice to keep food cool.

FROZEN FOODS

Clarence Birdseye studied wildlife for the U.S. government in Canada from 1912 until 1915. He worked alongside Indigenous Inuits. They showed him how they froze fish, fruits, and vegetables that would still taste good months later. In 1928, Birdseye invented the first machine to freeze food.

STICK-ON BANDAGES

Earle Dickson invented these when he noticed that his wife, Josephine, kept getting cuts and burns when she cooked. In 1921, he brought his design to his bosses at Johnson & Johnson, where he worked as a cotton buyer.

SUNGLASSES

Sam Foster began selling mass-produced sunglasses on a boardwalk in Atlantic City, New Jersey, in the 1920s. Sunglasses got even more popular in the 1930s, when Bausch & Lomb started making sleek "aviators" for military pilots.

TELEVISIONS

In 1925, Scottish inventor John Logie Baird transmitted the first image of a human face on a television. Two years later, 21-year-old American Philo T. Farnsworth created the first electronic television.

LOUDSPEAKERS

With the invention of the first electronic loudspeakers, audiences could hear actors talking. What was the first line in a "talkie"? It was "Wait a minute! You ain't heard nothing yet!" spoken by Al Jolson in *The Jazz Singer* (1927).

A LIFE SAVER

In 1928, Dr. Alexander Fleming invented the antibiotic penicillin, the first drug to kill bacterial infections. Before this, getting strep throat didn't mean staying home and eating ice cream; it meant having to worry about whether you were going to die.

FACTORIES BECOME MORE EFFICIENT

Thanks to Henry Ford's installation of the first assembly line in 1913, cars became more affordable. Building a Model T now took one and a half hours instead of twelve. By 1924, America was producing 88 percent of the world's cars, and 20 percent of American families owned one. Other manufactured products also became more affordable to the average person, as assembly lines and other innovations made mass production more common.

Economic prosperity contributed to the decline of unions, which were already suffering from the pro-business policies of the government. Powerful, big businesses wanted less government, and the government listened. The result was increased union suppression. It became more difficult for workers to form and join unions, as well as for unions to win strikes.

THE RADIO BRINGS IT HOME

The introduction of the home radio changed people's lives. It was the first time that a national audience could hear news and entertainment almost immediately. Radio dramas including *The Lone Ranger* and *The Shadow* thrived.

For many families, the radio became the center of home life. Baseball's World Series was first broadcast on the radio on October 1, 1921. The New York Giants defeated Babe Ruth's Yankees.

PROHIBITION AND THE RISE OF THE SPEAKEASY

 Think back to the Progressive Era (Chapter 7). Many reformers championed the idea of temperance (not drinking alcohol). Women were powerful in the movement. Some acted because of religious beliefs. Others wanted to protect themselves and others from abuse at the hands of drunk male family members. In the early twentieth century, this led to Prohibition, the Eighteenth Amendment that outlawed the making and selling of alcohol beginning in 1920.

Many Americans supported Prohibition and obeyed the rules. But by the early 1920s, lawbreakers had created illegal speakeasies. Often hidden in basements, these "secret" clubs provided alcohol and entertainment in the form of jazz music. White and Black audiences gathered together, many mingling socially for the first time.

Secret clubs called speakeasies made it possible for people to gather in defiance of Prohibition.

assembly line: a factory process that breaks up production into specialized tasks.

speakeasy: an illegal and secret club that provided alcohol and entertainment during the Prohibition era.

Behind the scenes, speakeasies were also responsible for the rise of organized crime families. They made money bootlegging alcohol. One of the most famous bootleggers was Al Capone. He headed the Chicago mafia and earned as much as $60 million a year—nearly $900 million in modern currency.

mafia: an organized group of people doing criminal activities.

bootlegging: illegally making, importing, or selling alcohol.

THE HARLEM RENAISSANCE

In the 1920s, New York City became home to a group of Black artists whose work celebrated Black experiences and criticized the country's racism. They were responsible for what was called the Harlem Renaissance. During this time, the Manhattan neighborhood became a thriving Black cultural community. (The Harlem Renaissance, or "rebirth," was named after the Italian Renaissance, a period between 1400 and 1600 when culture thrived.)

Harlem benefited from the Great Migration. It also had cultural stars, including the writers Zora Neale Hurston, Langston Hughes, Alain Locke, and Countee Cullen (who was married to W. E. B. Du Bois's daughter). Actors Paul Robeson and Ethel Waters also called the neighborhood home, as did the painters Aaron Douglas, Jacob Lawrence, and Romare Bearden.

THE TEAPOT DOME SCANDAL

In a shift from previous presidencies, Warren G. Harding (1865–1923) promised "less government in business and more business in government" when he ran for election in 1920. During his term (1921–1923), Congress slashed taxes, established a federal budget, and passed the Fordney-McCumber Tariff. This tariff stimulated the U.S. economy by encouraging Americans to buy goods made in the United States rather than abroad.

While Harding may have had good business sense, he had terrible taste in colleagues. He chose his friend Albert Fall to be Secretary of the Interior, which means Fall was in charge of managing federal land. In the Teapot Dome Scandal, Fall was caught offering government-owned oil fields in Teapot Dome, Wyoming, to the company that would pay *him personally* the most money. Harding tried, but failed, to cover up the scandal.

Harding died of a heart attack in 1923. Vice President Calvin Coolidge took over the presidency and led the congressional investigation into the Teapot Dome scandal.

GROWING ANTI-IMMIGRATION SENTIMENT

Harding placed limits on the number of immigrants who could enter the United States. It wasn't a hard sell. Immigrants often received harsh treatment. Also, the nativist sentiment you read about in Chapter 6 continued to increase.

SACCO AND VANZETTI

Unfair treatment of immigrants was clear in the case of Nicola Sacco and Bartolomeo Vanzetti. A jury found them guilty of the deaths of two men during a 1920 robbery. There was little evidence—witnesses described the robbers as "two Italian men," at a time and place where there were many Italian immigrants. Sacco and Vanzetti had no criminal records. However, they were anarchists who carried guns and had made false statements after their arrests.

Many people throughout the world believed that the jury found Sacco and Vanzetti guilty for their anarchist beliefs, not because there was strong evidence linking them to the crime. Protests over the injustice of their trial eventually reached the Massachusetts Supreme Court. But that court refused to overturn the decision—even after someone else confessed. On August 23, 1927, authorities electrocuted Sacco and Vanzetti.

Protesters took to the streets to demand the charges against Sacco and Vanzetti be dropped, but ultimately, they were unsuccessful.

THE KKK RIDES HIGH

A white supremacist terrorist group called the Ku Klux Klan continued to gain power. Its violent hate crimes multiplied. It continued to persecute Black Americans in the South. But it also made immigrants, Jews, and Catholics targets of its campaign of terror and murder.

Estimates put KKK membership during the 1920s between 3 million and 8 million. This made it the largest private organization in the country, with representatives in local, state, and national politics. In 1925, 30,000 Klansmen marched in a rally in Washington, D.C.

THE OSAGE MURDERS

In the early 1920s, no less than twenty-four members of the Osage nation in Oklahoma were killed. (The Osage are a Native American people.) Some of the murders were clearly violent. Others weren't obviously murders. Listed causes of death included "indigestion." It turned out that the indigestion likely came from poison.

Alarmed Osage members asked for government intervention. The U.S. Bureau of Investigation sent agents. These agents discovered that a wealthy rancher named William K. Hale was the ringleader of a group trying to steal the Osage's newfound wealth.

Osage land had valuable oil beneath the surface, and the Osage's income had totaled more than $30 million in 1923. That would be nearly $500 million today.

Hale was sentenced to life in prison in 1929, but authorities allowed him to leave prison in 1947. He lived another 15 years.

 Why do you think William Hale might have thought he could steal from the Osage? Do you think his punishment was fair?

_____

_____

_____

_____

_____

THE TULSA MASSACRE

On May 30, 1921, a Black teenager named Dick Rowland entered an office building in Tulsa, Oklahoma. He fled the building after a white elevator operator, Sarah Page, screamed. Although the exact details of what happened in the elevator are disputed, historians later determined that Rowland likely tripped and stepped on Page's foot. Police arrested him the next day, and a newspaper falsely reported he had tried to sexually assault her.

What followed over the next two days is now called the Tulsa Massacre. Around 1,500 white men went to the courthouse, demanding the police turn Rowland over so they could lynch him. About 75 armed Black men also went to the courthouse. Fighting broke out, and city officials gave some white men weapons and permission to act.

White men shot an unarmed Black man in a movie theater before storming a neighborhood called Greenwood, home to some 10,000 Black people. The men damaged or destroyed as many as 1,256 houses as well as a hospital, churches, and a school. People had called Greenwood the

"Black Wall Street" because the Black people who lived there had been prosperous. When the National Guard arrived, they arrested many Black men. They put some 6,000 people under armed guard.

AFTER THE MASSACRE

Authorities eventually dropped the charges against Rowland. The Oklahoma Bureau of Vital Statistics noted that 36 people had died, 26 of whom were Black. But historians now believe that the death toll was closer to 300 and that 8,000 people were made homeless.

Why was the official number so low? Officials destroyed paperwork in an effort to cover up the events. The local newspaper removed its false story from its archives.

In 2012, lawmakers introduced a bill in the state senate, demanding that Oklahoma schools teach students about the massacre. The bill didn't pass.

LINDBERGH AND EARHART: AVIATION PIONEERS

Amelia Earhart

In 1926, Amelia Earhart became the first female pilot to fly across the Atlantic. On May 21, 1927, Charles Lindbergh became the first person to complete a solo transatlantic flight. He landed his plane, the Spirit of St. Louis, in Paris 33 hours after leaving New York.

Both aviators became international heroes. People marveled at their skill and bravery. They also admired the technological advances that made travel faster and made the world feel a little smaller.

THE STOCK MARKET CRASHES

At the beginning of the 1920s, the United States enjoyed a thriving stock market. Banks and individuals invested large amounts of money in stocks. Some believed that the value of stocks would never decline and that stockholders would get richer and richer.

A stock is something you buy that represents ownership in a company (review Chapter 7 if you need to!). Companies issue stock as a way of raising money. They promise shareholders a return on their investment in the form of an increase in the stock price or sometimes a small share of a company's profits, called a dividend. Units of stocks are known as shares.

Depending on how much you pay for your shares, if a company makes big profits (and its share price goes up), you make money. If the company fails (and the stock price falls), you lose money.

stock: a financial instrument or tool that represents a share of ownership in a company.

share: the term used to describe a single unit of stock.

THE MARKET SLOWS

In the second half of the decade, the economy began to slow. Farmers struggled with low crop prices and high equipment costs. The construction, steel, and automobile industries all shrank.

Banks wanted to get the economy going again. They began to issue credit with high interest rates. Credit is money that a business or bank allows someone to borrow for a while. In exchange, the borrower pays interest.

This means the borrower promises to return all the money after a certain period, plus a little extra money.

> **credit:** money that a business or bank allows someone to borrow for a set period of time.
>
> **interest:** money that is earned or paid back on a loan in addition to the amount of the original loan.

MORE PEOPLE BUY IN

Business was slowing down. But the stock market was still soaring. So individuals joined the banks in investing money in the market. Sometimes people bought stocks with borrowed money. They were sure the stocks would rise in value and they would be able to pay back what they had borrowed, plus interest.

In September 1929, many businesspeople realized that Americans were struggling. These businesspeople figured out that companies' shares were not worth what others had paid for them. They started selling *their* stocks.

A month later, the public noticed. They began a stampede of getting rid of their stocks.

A DOWNWARD SLIDE

The market began to slide. In other words, people started selling because they no longer believed that what they had bought was valuable. Bankers started buying stocks to keep the market steady, but that worked for only a few days.

There was a massive stock market crash on Tuesday, October 29, 1929. People panicked and traded more than 16 million shares, often selling for pennies on the dollar. The loss totaled $14 billion (more than $207 billion in today's money). Some people lost every dollar they had—and every dollar they had borrowed.

This financial panic was the first major event in a long period of economic suffering called the Great Depression. It lasted from 1929 until about 1939.

BANK RUNS

More than 9,000 banks closed during the Great Depression, including 4,000 banks in 1933 alone.

Banks make investments, just as people do—only they do it with money that belongs to their customers. They keep only enough on hand to allow people to withdraw their money when they need it.

When the stock market crashed, many thousands of people wanted their money *all at once*. The banks often didn't have enough money on hand to give it to them. Experts call this a **bank run**.

During the Great Depression, more than 9,000 banks failed because of bank runs just between 1930 and 1933. If you showed up after the doors closed, you were out of luck.

In response, the federal government created the Federal Deposit Insurance Corporation in 1933. It still guarantees that people can get their money from the federal government if their bank fails.

During the Depression, production in American factories declined 47 percent. Unemployment grew from 1.6 million in 1929 to a peak of 15 million by 1933. Black Americans were disproportionately affected, with 50 percent unemployed at some points during the crisis.

PRESIDENT HERBERT HOOVER

Herbert Hoover

Hoover (1874–1964) was president from 1929 until 1933. He had run the Food Administration during World War I under President Wilson. Back then, Hoover made sure that U.S. troops around the world had enough food—a massive and complex project.

But Hoover believed that poor people could overcome hard times without help from the government. This idea is called laissez-faire. Hoover came to the idea naturally. Orphaned at the age of nine, he went on to become a multimillionaire as a mining engineer.

Hoover believed in goodwill. He asked business leaders to keep up production and not fire workers. But after a while, these pleas failed. Hoover eventually asked Congress to help farmers avoid mortgage foreclosures.

laissez-faire: a policy of non-interference usually applied to business or economics. The term means "let it be" or "leave it alone" in French.

bank run: occurs when a large number of bank customers want to withdraw their money all at once and banks don't have enough money on hand to give to the people trying to withdraw it.

mortgage foreclosure: a mortgage is a loan that a bank gives someone to buy a house. If that person can no longer pay back the loan, the bank can take possession of their house or land, in what's called a mortgage foreclosure.

CONGRESSIONAL AID

Hoover also asked Congress to pass laws to keep some prices steady. He wanted states to provide relief (food or money) for people who didn't have enough to eat. He reluctantly signed the Hawley-Smoot Tariff. This law made European goods more expensive so that people would be more likely to buy American goods.

But European governments struck back. They put high tariffs on imported American goods. The result was a disastrous decline in overseas demand for American goods and a standoff in international trade.

Between 1931 and 1933, the number of unemployed increased from seven million to 11 million. In the 1932 election, Hoover lost to Franklin D. Roosevelt.

As people lost their homes, they set up shacks and temporary homes in Hoovervilles like this one.

LOST HOMES AND SHANTYTOWNS

People could not pay their home mortgages. Banks forced some 250,000 people out of their homes in 1932 for nonpayment. The following year, home foreclosures reached the rate of 1,000 a *day*.

Thousands of shantytowns, or crude, temporary homes in streets and parks, sprang up in St. Louis, Washington, D.C., Chicago, New York, and other cities. People called them Hoovervilles because of what they saw as the president's failings.

shantytown: a temporary home in the streets or in a park. Shantytowns popped up across the United States during the Great Depression.

THE DUST BOWL

Further west, the lumber and mining industries suffered due to lack of demand. New farming practices helped cause massive dust storms in the Great Plains. Overplowing and overgrazing destroyed the deep-rooted prairie grass that had held the rich topsoil in place. When a drought hit, the winds blew up "black blizzards"—dust clouds so thick that some people and animals actually choked to death. During this period, the region became known as the Dust Bowl.

The Dust Bowl affected 125 million acres of land throughout the 1930s. In 1933 alone, more than 200,000 farms went into foreclosure.

Eventually the federal government sent in teams that planted long lines of trees. These trees reduced wind speeds and helped the land recover.

HELP FOR THOSE IN NEED

To help people who were going hungry, private citizens and churches provided soup kitchens, which offered free food to people in need.

MOVIES BRING COMFORT—AND BECOME A BIG BUSINESS

Movies had come a long way since the silent films of the 1920s. The 1930s brought economic ruin to many Americans. But movie theaters were still a place to escape, with films like *Scarface* (1932), *King Kong* (1933), and *The Wizard of Oz* (1939).

Movies allowed Americans to dream of glamorous lives in tuxedos and top hats. Hollywood, the center of the American film industry, became the world's dream factory. American movies became among the country's most successful and influential exports.

soup kitchen: a place that provides free meals to those who can't otherwise afford them. Soup kitchens became a symbol of the Depression.

FDR: A NEW PRESIDENT AND A NEW DEAL

In 1933, Franklin Delano Roosevelt—a distant cousin of former President Theodore Roosevelt—began what would be a twelve-year presidency. The first Democratic president since Wilson, Roosevelt (known as FDR) focused on connecting with ordinary Americans rather than business leaders. He supported reforms that he hoped would help people get back on their feet again.

FIRESIDE CHATS

In his inauguration speech, FDR said "The only thing we have to fear is fear itself." One week after that, FDR gave his first fireside chat. These were radio programs in which he spoke to Americans directly about the issues of the day. At the time, radio was the main source of news and entertainment for most families.

During the first fireside chat, he urged people to put their savings back into banks in an attempt to make the economy steadier. Within a month, almost three-quarters of banks had reopened. These fireside chats would prove crucial when it came to explaining his philosophy: the New Deal, which he described as "relief, recovery, and reform."

Roosevelt developed polio, an illness that causes paralysis, in 1921. He was 39. FDR used a wheelchair in private, but he masked his condition in public by leaning on other people or using a cane. He asked the press not to photograph him in motion.

Why do you think Roosevelt didn't want the American people to see him in a wheelchair?

_____

_____

_____

_____

_____

ELEANOR ROOSEVELT

President Franklin D. Roosevelt and First Lady Eleanor Roosevelt

Eleanor Roosevelt was far more than First Lady. She was an activist and diplomat. As a young woman, she was involved in social reform, teaching in a settlement house. (You learned about settlement houses back in Chapter 6.) She was also a member of the National Consumers League. This progressive organization fought to end unsafe working conditions and protect consumers from harmful products.

CIVIL RIGHTS WARRIOR

Eleanor Roosevelt fought fiercely for civil rights. In 1939, a famous Black opera singer named Marian Anderson wanted to perform in Washington, D.C.'s largest concert hall. A group called the Daughters of the American Revolution refused to rent the hall to a Black artist. In response, Roosevelt quit the group and moved the concert to the Lincoln Memorial. About 75,000 people attended the concert.

Eleanor Roosevelt resisted racism in other ways. When Alabama local officials ruled that a series of public meetings would be segregated, Roosevelt carried a folding chair and set it up in the middle of the aisle.

THE NEW DEAL

FDR wanted the New Deal to bring back a booming economy. He did this by encouraging Congress to pass specific laws and create social services. Today, we take many of these for granted, including a minimum wage and payments for retired or disabled people. The New Deal also led to the widespread belief that the government is responsible for people's economic welfare.

THE FIRST HUNDRED DAYS

This term refers to FDR's efforts in his first months as president. During this time, he accomplished many goals, including:

 Asking Congress to end Prohibition (Taxes on alcohol brought money to the government.)

 Setting up the Tennessee Valley Authority (TVA) to build hydroelectric dams along many rivers in the southeast; this created jobs and inexpensive power.

 Giving workers the right to form unions and bargain as a unit for better working conditions and wages.

Over the next eight years, FDR created dozens of federal programs to help Americans. Here are some of the most important.

EIGHT YEARS OF NEW DEALS

Agricultural Adjustment Act	Wheat, tobacco, corn, and dairy farmers were paid not to produce for a year in order to improve prices.
Federal Deposit Insurance Corporation (FDIC)	The government guaranteed personal bank accounts, up to $250,000 per depositor.

Civilian Conservation Corps	The government hired young, single men to work on public projects, such as parks and public buildings. Some CCC workers planted the trees that helped end the Dust Bowl.
Securities and Exchange Commission	The government gained more authority and control over the stock market—but not complete control.
Social Security Act	Workers and employees paid a payroll tax. The money provided income for retired and disabled people.
Works Progress Administration	The WPA created millions of jobs building highways and bridges, and in the arts. Your community may still have WPA buildings, murals, or other artwork.
Fair Labor Standards Act	The FLSA ended child labor other than on farms. It also set a minimum wage and limited the workweek to forty hours.
The Federal Housing Administration	The FHA helped millions of Americans to become homeowners.

BLACK AMERICANS AND THE NEW DEAL

FDR had won the allegiance of many Black Americans by campaigning on a platform of economic renewal. He opposed the poll tax, spoke out against lynching, and met with Black leaders.

New Deal programs helped poor Black people. But because of segregation and economic divides, people of color often lacked access to most of them. In fact, because of racist practices, Black Americans were the last to receive aid, in whatever form, and the first to lose it. For instance, the Agricultural Investment Act applied only to landowners. That meant that Black sharecroppers and tenant farmers didn't benefit from it.

To this day, white Americans remain the largest beneficiaries of America's welfare system. This is partly because about 60 percent of the U.S. population is white.

By overseeing the New Deal, FDR was taking power away from Congress. Congress reacted by asking whether the Constitution allowed the New Deal programs. The Supreme Court struck down some but not all of FDR's programs.

A WOMAN IN THE CABINET

Frances Perkins

First Lady Eleanor Roosevelt encouraged her husband's administration to hire women. FDR made Frances Perkins his Secretary of Labor—the first female cabinet member.

In 1911, Perkins had witnessed the Triangle Shirtwaist Factory fire, in which 146 workers died. (You learned about this fire in Chapter 6.) She spent her political life crusading for workers' rights.

Many people considered Perkins assertive and dynamic. But she said later of her first cabinet meeting, "I wanted to give the impression of being a quiet, orderly woman who didn't buzz-buzz all the time. . . I knew that a lady interposing an idea into men's conversation is very unwelcome. . . I just proceeded on the theory that this was a gentleman's conversation on the porch of a golf club, perhaps. You don't butt in with bright ideas."

Despite the sexism that she faced as a woman, Perkins had no end of bright ideas. We have her to thank for the minimum wage, a 40-hour workweek, and Social Security. One idea she wasn't able to see through was national health care.

Why might women be expected to hang back professionally? Do you think they still are? What do you think of the way Perkins handled her first meeting?

_____

_____

_____

_____

_____

_____

_____

_____

fascism: a political system in which a dictator uses peoples' fears and weaknesses to gain total power. Fascist leaders often make scapegoats of immigrants, minorities, and those who dissent.

dictator: a leader who has total power and is not accountable for his or her actions.

scapegoat: someone who is blamed for something he or she didn't do. Historically, immigrants and people of color are often used as scapegoats for a country's problems.

THE SEEDS OF WORLD WAR II

FASCISM RISES IN EUROPE

World War I had ravaged Europe economically, and Europe was experiencing its own depression. People grew angry about their governments' inability to protect them from war and poverty. As a result, Europe saw a rise of fascism. This is a political system in which a leader plays on peoples' fears and weaknesses, convincing them that only he or she can protect them from their enemies. Conveniently, everyone who is not favored by the leader is an enemy, especially immigrants and minorities. Fascist governments usually have these qualities:

- The leader is a dictator, which means he or she has total power. The dictator's main interest is in becoming more powerful rather than helping citizens.

- Citizens have no voice—unless they support the leader. The dictator forbids protests and cracks down on opponents.

- Newspapers, magazines, and other news organizations must say what the dictator wants them to say. The dictator calls journalists or newspapers who are critical of him traitors or liars—and in some cases, jails or kills them.

- The dictator often scapegoats immigrants and minorities. In other words, the dictator blames and punishes them for every problem, regardless of the real cause.

During the 1920s, Benito Mussolini became the dictator of Italy. Adolf Hitler rose to power as the leader of the Nazi party and was named the Chancellor of Germany. Joseph Stalin became the communist dictator of the Soviet Union.

These countries were characterized by extreme nationalism. In other words, they each believed their country was better than other countries. Their aggression toward other nations grew, and in the process they violently targeted Jewish people and other minorities.

nationalism: the belief that one's nation is superior to others, often based on ethnicity, language, or religion.

FASCIST REGIMES

AMERICA AND THE COMING EUROPEAN WAR

Germany was beginning to claw back military power it had given up at the end of World War I. On September 1, 1939, it invaded Poland, breaking the Treaty of Versailles (page 254). Two days later, France and Britain declared war on Germany. By late 1940, the war was being fought on both British and French soil.

The United States hung back. It relied on a series of Neutrality Acts that Congress had begun passing in 1935. These laws made it illegal to sell or transport war materials to enemy countries.

However, the United States did support Britain with the passing of the Lend-Lease Act in 1941. This law stated that the United States could ship war supplies to a country that was "vital to the defense of the United States." So even though the United States was not officially part of the war, it could ship much-needed guns, bullets, tanks, trucks, food, and other materials to Britain with the promise that Britain would pay for those supplies later. The Lend-Lease Act was also open to China and the Soviet Union, but Britain gained the most from it.

A STRIKE ON PEARL HARBOR

On December 7, 1941, Japan targeted the military base at Pearl Harbor in Hawaii. Japanese fighters damaged or destroyed close to 20 ships and more than 300 airplanes. The attack was deadly: 2,403 sailors, soldiers, and civilians were killed, and 1,000 more were wounded.

On December 8, Roosevelt received Congress's approval to declare war on Japan. FDR called December 7 "a date which will live in infamy." Japan's allies, Germany and Italy, then declared war on the United States.

THE FOUR FREEDOMS

In 1941, FDR appeared before Congress and made a speech about raising taxes in order to fund the Allied Powers. In the "Four Freedoms Speech," he outlined his beliefs about human rights. The Four Freedoms were:

- Freedom of speech and expression
- Freedom of worship
- Freedom from want
- Freedom from fear

But these beliefs didn't always carry into action. The United States refused to shelter many Jewish refugees who were fleeing Nazi violence and persecution. And after Japanese troops attacked Pearl Harbor, FDR created internment camps. In these isolated, poorly built camps, 112,000 people of Japanese descent lived as prisoners. Authorities sent them there based on the nationalist belief that they might aid Japan. Nearly 70,000 of the people interned were American citizens.

> **internment camps:** isolated camps where the U.S. government imprisoned people of Japanese descent during World War II.

From 1942 to 1945, U.S. policy dictated that all people of Japanese descent (including U.S. citizens) would be imprisoned in internment camps.

WORLD WAR II ALLIANCES

AXIS POWERS	ALLIED POWERS
Germany	France
Japan	Great Britain
Italy	the United States
	the Soviet Union

A MIGHTY MILITARY EFFORT

Some American men and women volunteered for military service. The government also drafted some men, which means it required men to serve in the military. In total, 16 million Americans fought in World War II. Of those, 75 percent served abroad in Europe, North Africa, the Pacific, and Southwest Asia.

As in World War I, units remained segregated:

- Some 22,000 Chinese Americans signed up to serve.

- Japanese Americans were facing more racism than ever after Pearl Harbor, but they formed the 442nd Regimental Combat Team. It is one of the most decorated in U.S. history.

- The Tuskegee Airmen were the first Black military fighter pilots. During World War II, they flew more than 15,000 missions and earned more than 150 Distinguished Flying Crosses.

- About 350,000 women served in the war. Black women weren't allowed to join the effort until 1944, and Black nurses could tend only to Black soldiers.

Rosie the Riveter

Representing the five million women who joined the American job force between 1940 and 1945, Rosie the Riveter became an icon during the war with her "can-do" image. Her rolled-up sleeve showed her flexed bicep, and her hair was tied back so it wouldn't get caught in machinery.

KEY BATTLES OF WORLD WAR II

BATTLE OF MIDWAY

DATES	WHAT HAPPENED?
June 3–6, 1942	The United States and Japan fought in the air and at sea in the Pacific. The United States defended its base on Midway Island (which is about halfway between Japan and the United States) and established its dominance.

BATTLE OF STALINGRAD

DATES	WHAT HAPPENED?
August 23, 1942–February 2, 1943	More than two million soldiers and civilians died in this epic battle between the Soviet Union (or USSR) and Axis powers trying to take over the city. Soviet troops successfully fought back, making it Germany's first public defeat. While the United States wasn't directly involved in this battle, it was a turning point in the war.

INVASION OF NORMANDY, OR "D-DAY"

DATES	WHAT HAPPENED?
June 6, 1944	Around 156,000 American, British, and Canadian forces landed on the beaches of Normandy in northern France. As a result, troops liberated France from Germany two months later.

BATTLE OF THE BULGE

DATES	WHAT HAPPENED?
December 16, 1944–January 25, 1945	Americans fought back as Germany tried to divide the Allied troops in Belgium. The masses of troops looked like a big bulge. Americans suffered their greatest loss, with more than 70,000 casualties, but they were able to drive the Germans back. This was Hitler's last large-scale attack.

BATTLE OF IWO JIMA

DATES	WHAT HAPPENED?
April 16, 1945– May 2, 1945	Americans and Japanese forces fought over this Japanese island, which had important airstrips for landing planes. The Allies won control, with only about 250 of the 18,000 Japanese soldiers surviving. About 7,000 Americans died.

THE BATTLE OF BERLIN

DATES	WHAT HAPPENED?
April 16, 1945– May 2, 1945	After the United States and Britain pushed German forces back to Germany, the Soviet army surrounded Berlin. Hitler and Eva Braun, whom he had married 40 hours earlier, died by suicide on April 30th. The Nazis surrendered the city. The Allies had won the war in Europe.

The Invasion of Normandy

Roosevelt died on April 12, 1945, and Vice President Harry S. Truman became president.

TWO VICTORIES FOR THE ALLIES

THE ALLIES LIBERATE EUROPE

The Allies declared victory over Germany on May 8, 1945. Allied forces liberated the concentration camps. The Nazis had rounded up, imprisoned, and killed six million Jews, whom they blamed for many of Germany's problems. This hatred of Jews is known as antisemitism. They also killed Romani people (Gypsies), people with physical or mental disabilities, gay people, as well as millions of civilians from surrounding countries such as the Soviet Union, Poland, and Serbia. Today we call this period of fascist terror the Holocaust.

A TERRIBLE DISCOVERY

Harold Porter was a medic in the 116th Evacuation Hospital. After arriving at the Dachau concentration camp, he wrote to his parents. He told them, "when we reached the furnace house we came upon a huge stack of corpses piled up like kindling, all nude so that their clothes wouldn't be wasted by the burning. . . there were both women and children in the stack in addition to the men." He added, "There is a rumor circulating which says that the war is over. It probably is—as much as it ever will be. . . it's difficult to celebrate anything with the morbid state we're in."

concentration camps: prison camps where Nazis enslaved and murdered their victims: Jewish people, Romani people, individuals with physical or mental disabilities, and gay people among them.

antisemitism: the hatred of Jews, and/or the desire to harm them. Often includes prejudiced or stereotyped views about Jews and Judaism.

Holocaust: the reign of violence, antisemitism, and fascism that took place under the Nazi party in Europe during World War II.

THE BOMBING OF HIROSHIMA

The Axis powers in Europe had surrendered. But the Japanese army had yet to do the same. The U.S. Navy continued to attack Japanese-held islands in the Pacific and was closing in on Japan itself.

In July, the leaders of Britain, the Soviet Union, and the United States met. They came up with the terms of Japan's surrender, known as the Potsdam Declaration. The Japanese agreed to all the conditions but one: they wanted Emperor Hirohito to remain in power. The Allies' response: nothing less than "prompt and utter destruction" if they didn't comply completely.

On August 6, 1945, the United States dropped an atomic bomb on the city of Hiroshima. It killed about 150,000 Japanese. Three days later, the United States dropped another on the city of Nagasaki, killing 75,000. Shigeko Matsumoto, who was in Nagasaki, shared his story:

> "[T]he sky turned bright white. My siblings and I were knocked off our feet and violently slammed back into the bomb shelter. We had no idea what had happened. As we sat there shell-shocked and confused, heavily injured burn victims came stumbling into the bomb shelter en masse [in large numbers]. Their skin had peeled off their bodies and faces and hung limply down on the ground, in ribbons. Their hair was burnt down to a few measly centimeters from the scalp."

JAPAN SURRENDERS

The bombs' radiation would go on to kill tens of thousands more. On August 14, Hirohito surrendered on behalf of Japan. Hirohito was allowed to stay in power. The secretary of war of the United States called the atomic bombs "the most terrible weapon ever known in human history."

The explosion over Nagasaki

Many people around the world criticized the United States for using atomic bombs against an enemy. It remains the only nation on Earth to have done so. President Truman believed it was necessary to use the bombs to end the war as quickly as possible and save the lives of Allied soldiers and civilians. However, many historians now believe Japan was planning to surrender before the United States dropped the bombs.

CHAPTER 8 VOCABULARY

antisemitism: the hatred of Jews, and/or the desire to harm them. Often includes prejudiced or stereotyped views about Jews and Judaism.

assembly line: a factory process that breaks up production into specialized tasks.

bank run: occurs when a large number of bank customers want to withdraw their money all at once and banks don't have enough money on hand to give to the people trying to withdraw it.

bootlegging: illegally making, importing, or selling alcohol.

concentration camps: prison camps where Nazis enslaved and murdered their victims: Jewish people, Romani people, individuals with physical or mental disabilities, and gay people among them.

credit: money that a business or bank allows someone to borrow for a set period of time.

dictator: a leader who has total power and is not accountable for his or her actions.

fascism: a political system in which a dictator uses peoples' fears and weaknesses to gain total power. Fascist leaders often make scapegoats of immigrants, minorities, and those who dissent.

Holocaust: the reign of violence, antisemitism, and fascism that took place under the Nazi party in Europe during World War II.

interest: money that is earned or paid back on a loan in addition to the amount of the original loan.

internment camps: isolated camps where the U.S. government imprisoned people of Japanese descent during World War II.

laissez-faire: a policy of non-interference usually applied to business or economics. The term means "let it be" or "leave it alone" in French.

mafia: an organized group of people doing criminal activities.

mortgage foreclosure: A mortgage is a loan that a bank gives someone to buy a house. If that person can no longer pay back the loan, the bank can take possession of their house or land, in what's called a mortgage foreclosure.

nationalism: the belief that one's nation is superior to others, often based on ethnicity, language, or religion. In its extreme form, the belief that other nations must be dominated using military power.

scapegoat: someone who is blamed for something he or she didn't do. Historically, immigrants and people of color are often used as scapegoats for a country's problems.

shantytown: a temporary home in the streets or in a park. Shantytowns popped up across the United States during the Great Depression.

share: the term used to describe a single unit of stock.

soup kitchens: places that provide free meals to those who can't afford them otherwise. Soup kitchens became a symbol of the Depression.

speakeasy: an illegal and secret club that provided alcohol and entertainment during the Prohibition era, the period between 1920 and 1933 when the production and sale of alcoholic drinks were banned in the United States.

stock: a financial instrument or tool that represents a share of ownership in a company. Corporations issue stock to raise money to conduct business; investors buy stock if they believe the company will increase in value.

NOTES

FROM THE COLD WAR TO CIVIL RIGHTS

Soldiers returned from the war to two very different realities. For many, it was a time of great prosperity. Most Black people, though, didn't share that experience. Against the backdrop of the Cold War with the USSR, the civil rights movement began. How do these things relate? Let's figure it out!

CHAPTER CONTENTS

AMERICA AFTER WORLD WAR II

A COLD WAR SETS IN

THE COLD WAR IN THE UNITED STATES

THE CIVIL RIGHTS MOVEMENT

AMERICA AFTER WORLD WAR II

 Immediately following World War II, the United States underwent huge changes. The victory in the war fueled a sense of optimism. The United States was now a world leader. The poverty of the Great Depression was gone. The sacrifices of wartime were no longer necessary. The result was a period of tremendous economic growth.

THE G.I. BILL

Millions of Americans benefited from the G.I. Bill (formally known as the Servicemen's Readjustment Act of 1944). It paid for college and training programs, and it provided low-interest loans and mortgages. It was extremely popular. But in most cases, the white administrators in power favored white people and denied the benefits of the G.I. Bill to Black Americans. Black people didn't have the same access to colleges and universities as white Americans.

REDLINING

In addition, banks and mortgage companies legally denied home loans to Black people with what were known as **redlining** practices. Officials at banks refused to give loans to Black home buyers, literally drawing red lines on maps around poor neighborhoods.

In the suburbs of New York and northern New Jersey, the G.I. Bill backed 67,000 mortgages. Fewer than 100 of those went to people of color. By 1950, suburban growth was ten times more than that of cities. Only 2 percent of those homes built with G.I. Bill loans belonged to people of color. The result was a growing racial divide where white people benefited and Black people did not.

THE SUBURBS EXPAND RAPIDLY

With their newfound prosperity, white people left America's cities in droves for the **suburbs**. Many returning soldiers and their families were eager to leave behind city life for their own private homes with yards in spacious new developments. Racial fears also fueled the departure of whites for newly built, affordable houses in suburban communities that were intentionally racially segregated.

Making the move all the easier was the Interstate Highway Act (1956). This law resulted in thousands of miles of new highways. White people could commute quickly to their new homes, but the construction of the highways demolished many Black neighborhoods.

redlining: the practice by banks and mortgage companies of refusing to invest in minority communities or loan money to Black or Brown people looking to buy homes in white neighborhoods.

suburbs: areas outside of urban centers that usually have more spacious developments.

THE BIRTH OF FAST FOOD

Soon, conveniences like fast-food restaurants began to pop up in suburban towns across the country. A businessman named Ray Kroc bought a small hamburger chain in Southern California run by the McDonald brothers and duplicated it in suburban towns all over America. In doing so, Kroc created the first and largest fast-food empire in the world.

TOO GOOD TO BE TRUE?

Millions of people built lives they hoped would be as perfect as the white picket fences that surrounded their new homes. Media images and ads painted pictures of wholesome happiness, with smiling middle-class white mothers tending to their hard-working husbands and carefree children. But this was far from the truth for many—especially for people of color and those who needed two incomes in order to afford that house with the picket fence.

Women who had enjoyed newfound freedoms during the war discovered that they suddenly had fewer options for work. Men returning from the war took back the jobs some women had filled. Most women were limited to lower-paying jobs, such as typists, teachers, and secretaries. Women of color had even fewer choices.

The only thing unifying the country was a growing terror of another country.

A COLD WAR SETS IN

First of all, what is a cold war? It happens when countries go to war with each other with every means possible except for actually fighting in a direct battle against each other. Here's how the Soviet Union and the United States ended up locked in one.

The Americans and Soviets had been allies in World War II. Then, their bond came from fighting a common enemy. But even during the war there were tensions. The two countries were more like "frenemies," political style.

TENSIONS RISE

Stalin, the Soviet leader, resented the fact that the United States and Britain had waited so long to open a battlefront in France with the Germans. Had they done this earlier, it would have divided the German army and forced it to fight on two fronts, relieving pressure on the Soviet army.

The Soviet Union suffered by far the most military and civilian deaths of any nation during the war—an estimated 24 million people died. Stalin never missed a chance to remind his allies of this sacrifice.

As the war drew to a close, the Soviets and the United States (supported by Britain and France) each scrambled to liberate German territory before the other could. Both sides wanted to control as much territory as possible. The Soviets seized the Eastern European nations of Estonia, Latvia, and Lithuania. They wanted to create a buffer zone against possible attacks from Western Europe and the United States.

A MEETING IN YALTA

When victory in World War II seemed very likely, the leaders of the United States, Britain, and the USSR met at the Crimean resort of Yalta, in what is now known as the Yalta Conference. There, they formed a plan to divide German territory into four occupation zones. Each of the Allied nations would control one zone.

As for the German capital city of Berlin, located in the USSR Zone, the victors would divide it into four sectors. The United States, Soviet Union, Britain, and France would each occupy one.

With the Germans defeated, the differences between the ideologies of the United States and the USSR created a giant separation. Each country feared the other's search for control and authority. Both began stockpiling weapons and trying to politically outmaneuver each other. The United States and USSR never met in a head-on conflict of their own. However, they were constantly fighting for power.

 The United States and USSR may not have engaged in any open wars against each other directly, but the Cold War did lead the United States to enter into multiple armed confrontations with other countries.

WARRING IDEOLOGIES: COMMUNISM AND CAPITALISM

The USSR was a communist country. It had an all-powerful ruler in its dictator, Stalin. He controlled its citizens' rights and punished anyone who disagreed with how the country was run.

The Soviet government ran the country's economy and all businesses. It wanted trading partners and military allies who had the same kind of system. Likewise, the United States wanted to trade with countries that shared its system of capitalism. Both wanted trading partners they could control.

BUILDING SPHERES OF INFLUENCE

The two nations did whatever they could to build up their own sphere of influence. This might include the threat of military force, but more often it involved promises of foreign aid, favorable business deals, and diplomacy. Countries as far-flung as Korea in East Asia, Cuba and Grenada in the Caribbean, Afghanistan in Central Asia, and the African nation of Angola became part of the two countries' battle for power.

What do you think made the building of "spheres of influence" in the Cold War different from building alliances in earlier periods in U.S. history?

_____

_____

_____

_____

ideologies: systems of ideas or beliefs, usually political and/or economic in nature. Two ideologies that are often at odds with each other are capitalism and communism.

communism: an economic and political system under which there is no private property. In theory, communism is meant to result in public ownership and control, but in practice communist revolutions have resulted in dictatorships.

capitalism: an economic and political system in which private individuals and groups own land, factories, and goods—the government owns few or none of these things.

sphere of influence: a Cold War term referring to the countries and regions that the USSR and United States wanted to affect, sway, and control politically.

OFF AND RUNNING: THE ARMS RACE

In 1949, the Soviets began testing their own atomic bomb. In 1950, a U.S. government report suggested a 400 percent increase in spending on weapons and other systems to defend the country. President Truman said the United States would build an even more destructive weapon called the hydrogen bomb. The Soviets also started work on a similar bomb.

COLD WAR ALLIANCES IN EUROPE 1949

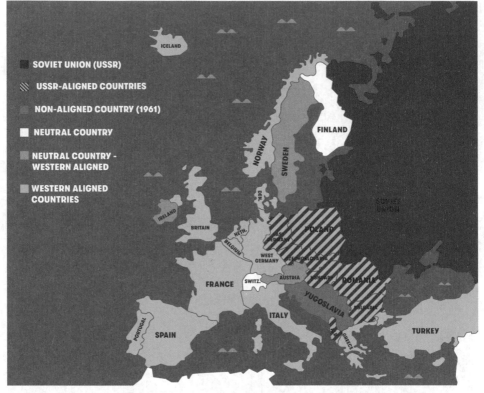

- **SOVIET UNION (USSR)**
- **USSR-ALIGNED COUNTRIES**
- **NON-ALIGNED COUNTRY (1961)**
- **NEUTRAL COUNTRY**
- **NEUTRAL COUNTRY - WESTERN ALIGNED**
- **WESTERN ALIGNED COUNTRIES**

ICELAND, FINLAND, NORWAY, SWEDEN, SOVIET UNION, DEN., IRELAND, BRITAIN, NETH., BELGIUM, EAST GERMANY, POLAND, WEST GERMANY, CZECHOSLOVAKIA, AUSTRIA, HUNGARY, ROMANIA, FRANCE, SWITZ., YUGOSLAVIA, BULGARIA, ITALY, ALB., GREECE, PORTUGAL, SPAIN, TURKEY

In 1947, the Soviets had succeeded in annexing Eastern European countries and making them into satellite states. This map shows which European countries were aligned with the United States and which were aligned with the USSR.

satellite state: a country that is officially independent, but is actually controlled by another country.

Immediately after World War II, the American government put its money where its mouth was. With the 1948 Marshall Plan, the United States provided more than $15 billion to Western European countries rebuilding after the war. (That would be the same as $161 billion today.)

This wasn't just an act of generosity. It was a way of ensuring that these countries could fight communist influences. Also, it was a financial and political connection to the United States. A year earlier, Congress had provided $400 million to Greece and Turkey, which sat close to the Soviet border.

BERLIN: A DIVIDED CITY

After World War II, the Soviets controlled East Berlin. Great Britain, France, and the United States controlled West Berlin. Over the next few years, the United States provided financial support to rebuild European countries. As a result, the Soviets became increasingly worried about losing influence.

In 1948, the Soviets struck back. They blocked access to West Berlin (see map). This meant shutting off food and medical supplies to its 2.5 million residents. The Allies spent much of the next year delivering food and supplies by airdrops in what became known as the Berlin Airlift. This was the first major standoff of the Cold War. Some American pilots dropped packages of donated candy and chocolate from their planes for children isolated in West Berlin. These pilots got the nickname the Candy Bombers.

Seeing West Berliners thriving, East Germans "voted with their feet." An estimated 3.5 million East Germans fled to West Germany in search of a better, freer life. By 1961, as many as 1,000 East German residents were leaving every day.

THE BERLIN WALL

The East German government and their Soviet backers were embarrassed by this. They wanted to keep East German citizens from leaving. Suddenly, with no warning, they built a wall on the border between East and West Berlin on the night of August 12 to 13. They built almost the entire thing in one night!

The Berlin Wall separated the U.S.-controlled West Germany from the Soviet-controlled East Germany.

The Berlin Wall became a guarded stretch of 96 miles that separated not only the city but also families. One year after its completion, U.S. President John F. Kennedy stood before the wall on the West Berlin side and gave a famous speech in which he said, "Ich bin ein Berliner," or "I am a Berliner." He meant that West Berlin was a symbol of democracy, like America, as opposed to the communism on the other side of the wall.

PRESIDENT DWIGHT D. EISENHOWER

A decorated World War II hero, Eisenhower won huge electoral victories in 1952 and 1956. A Republican, he defeated Democratic nominee Adlai Stevenson both times. Eisenhower wanted to lead the country "down the middle of the road,"—not too conservative, not too liberal—calling his politics Modern Republicanism.

Eisenhower stimulated the economy with the Federal-Aid Highway Act. The largest public funding in U.S. history, the act gave $25 billion to build more than 40,000 miles of four-lane interstate highways. Like the earlier Interstate Highway Act, many of these highways destroyed Black neighborhoods. Yet Eisenhower would also sign civil rights legislation.

BUILDING UP THE MILITARY

Eisenhower's military strategy emphasized developing nuclear weapons and air power over building up the army or navy. It included the idea of brinkmanship. This is essentially a staring contest that could end with a blink, or all-out war.

> brinkmanship: a Cold War military strategy meaning that each side would go to the brink (edge) of war in order to force the other to back down.

THE COLD WAR IN THE UNITED STATES

Some Americans feared communists at home as well as in the Soviet Union. In 1945, the House Un-American Activities Committee (HUAC) began investigating stories of communist activity in the United States. Americans feared that communists lived among them. They also feared that someone might call them a communist unjustly.

JOSEPH MCCARTHY AND THE RED SCARE

Senator Joseph McCarthy led HUAC. In a speech in 1950, McCarthy announced that communists had secretly become a part of every area of the United States, from college professors to members of the entertainment industry. McCarthy said there were even communists working in the U.S. State Department. The senator warned of a Red Menace. The "red" referred to the color of the Soviet flag.

COMMUNIST PARTY ORGANIZATION USA—FEB 9, 1950

Senator Joseph McCarthy

The accused person would receive a subpoena. Just being subpoenaed resulted in thousands of people losing their jobs. Employers were scared they would lose business if they had people working for them who were even suspected communists. Government officials also encouraged people to report on each other.

Fears of communism were so great that McCarthy and HUAC were able to destroy innocent peoples' lives without any evidence whatsoever.

THE RED SCARE AND HOLLYWOOD

Hollywood was hit particularly hard. Walt Disney and Ronald Reagan, who was then a movie actor, both appeared before the committee to discuss their colleagues' activities. Silent-movie star Charlie Chaplin was among those forced to defend themselves against charges of being communists.

The Hollywood Ten was a group of screenwriters, producers, and directors who refused to cooperate with the committee. They then went to prison for contempt of Congress (in other words, disobeying Congress). The Hollywood studios blacklisted the ten, even though the studios never said so officially.

Red Menace: a term used in the United States to describe the threat of communism.

subpoena: an official notice directing a person to appear before a court or legal committee.

blacklist: a list of people that companies (such as Hollywood studios) would refuse to hire, usually because of their political beliefs.

Alger Hiss was a State Department official accused of being a member of the Communist Party and spying for the Soviet Union. A court found him guilty and sentenced him to prison. After that, some Americans were convinced that Senator McCarthy was right when he said communists had become part of the government itself.

In his 1950 speech, McCarthy claimed there were 57 members of the State Department who were communists. He said these employees were worse than foreign spies. McCarthy added, "We are dealing with a far more sinister type of activity because it permits the enemy to guide and shape our policy."

 What do you think McCarthy's hunt for communists says about the importance of evidence? Why do you think people might have gone along with him even in the absence of evidence?

_____

_____

_____

_____

_____

_____

_____

_____

THE END OF THE MCCARTHY ERA

Senator McCarthy didn't act alone. Some members of the government backed him. And while President Eisenhower criticized him privately, he never spoke up against him in public.

The tide turned against McCarthy in 1954. That was when he accused an Army lawyer, Joseph Welch, of hiring a man who was a communist. In attacking an attorney for the armed services, the senator had gone too far. As McCarthy accused the supposed communist on the Senate floor, Welch demanded, "Have you no sense of decency, sir? At long last, have you left no sense of decency?"

Soon after, the journalist Edward R. Murrow exposed the senator's brutal and unfair methods on his popular television news show. That was the beginning of the end of McCarthy's power. Congress officially punished McCarthy later that year.

McCarthy's methods became known as McCarthyism. The disgraced senator died from complications of alcoholism in 1957.

> **McCarthyism:** refers to the campaign in the 1940s and 1950s led by Senator Joseph McCarthy to expose people with communist sympathies and remove them from government and other positions of importance. It has come to mean any campaign that uses unproven facts, rumors, and bullying methods to eliminate supposed enemies.

> One of HUAC's members was California representative Richard Nixon, who would go on to become president of the United States.

THE COLD WAR COMES TO SCHOOLS AND BACKYARDS

The United States and the USSR were each determined to have more nuclear weapons than the other side had. Both countries started testing their bombs in unpopulated places.

Americans became worried about nuclear warfare. Schools practiced drills where children hid under their desks. People who could afford it built bomb shelters in their backyards.

THE COLD WAR LAUNCHES INTO SPACE

The United States and the Soviet Union took their feud into space, each determined to be the first nation to set foot on the moon.

When the Soviets successfully launched the world's first artificial satellite, Sputnik, in 1957, worry turned into panic. Americans had thought that they were more advanced than the Soviets. Now Americans worried about spies in the skies.

One year after Sputnik, the United States launched its own satellite, Explorer I. The "space race" was on. President Dwight Eisenhower created the National Aeronautics and Space Administration (NASA) in 1958.

But the Soviets won the next round. They launched the first person into space in April 1961. The United States got its man into space one month later. And Americans won a major victory when Neil Armstrong became the first person to set foot on the moon on July 20, 1969.

ONE FOR YOU, AND ONE FOR ME: THE BUILDUP TO THE KOREAN WAR

As the Allied powers and the Soviet Union divided up much of the world after World War II, it was an even split, and it seemed that no territory was too small.

Berlin is an example of where the division was hyperlocal. Former neighborhoods were literally divided between the communists, who controlled the eastern part, and the U.S. and its Cold War allies, who controlled the western part.

Mostly, it happened on a much larger scale. Korea had been part of the Japanese empire. After Japan lost the war, North Korea became a communist state (supported by the Soviet Union). The south became a republic supported by the United States.

A "HOT" WAR

In 1950, North Korea attacked South Korea. Americans became scared that the Soviets (and thus communism) were becoming too powerful. So the United States sent nearly 1.8 million soldiers to the region to fight for South Korea.

This became what was known as the first "hot" war of the Cold War. There was actual fighting supported by both the Soviets and the United States, even though the USSR and the USA did not fight each other directly.

Another name for this situation is proxy war. A proxy is a stand-in.

> **satellite:** a human-made object sent into space to orbit the planet.
>
> **proxy war:** active fighting influenced by two superpowers (the United States and the USSR), but without their direct military involvement.

THE KOREAN WAR

The war lasted three years. During that time, more than five million people were killed. The United States lost almost 40,000 soldiers, and another 103,000 were wounded. But the death tolls among soldiers and civilians in both Koreas were even higher.

Altogether, at least 2.5 million people died in the war. Neither side really won victory. Korea remains divided to this day.

STILL DIVIDED: NORTH AND SOUTH KOREA

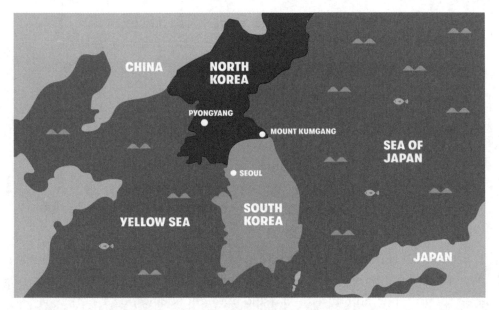

The United States believed in a strategy called containment when it came to communism. There was a worry that if one country "fell" to communism, it would have a domino effect and lead other surrounding countries to communism as well.

containment: a Cold War strategy intended to stop communism from spreading from one country or region to another.

THE CIVIL RIGHTS MOVEMENT

While historians date the civil rights movement as beginning in the 1950s, the movement didn't come out of nowhere.

Emancipation after the Civil War meant that Black people achieved freedom from slavery. But the Jim Crow laws that whites enacted denied Black people equality. They faced racism at every turn throughout the country—not just in the South. And Black soldiers, one million of whom served in World War II, returned from the war to a country that did anything but welcome them as heroes.

A **grassroots** movement began to grow in the South. It was called the civil rights movement.

> **grassroots: the actions or ideas of ordinary people as opposed to those being promoted by rich or powerful individuals or organizations.**

BROWN V. BOARD OF EDUCATION AND PAULI MURRAY

Brown v. Board of Education was a 1954 Supreme Court decision that legally ended segregation in schools. It was based on the work of Dr. Pauli Murray, an attorney. While she was in law school, Murray (1910–1985) had the idea to challenge Jim Crow laws using the equal protection clause of the Fourteenth Amendment to the Constitution.

NAACP attorney Thurgood Marshall argued the case in front of the Supreme Court and won. He called Murray's 1950 book on the subject, *States' Laws on Race and Color*, the "bible" of *Brown v. Board of Education*. Marshall later became the first Black Supreme Court justice.

Brown v. Board of Education was a big win that helped to spark the civil rights movement. But it's important to note that the Supreme Court's decision was vague. It held that integration must happen "with all deliberate speed," giving school districts the out they needed to stall the process.

Pauli Murray

Murray later cofounded the National Organization for Women. She also became the first Black female Episcopal priest in the United States. Despite her many accomplishments, Murray later wrote in a 1970 essay, "If anyone should ask a Negro woman in America what has been her greatest achievement, her honest answer should be, 'I survived!'"

THE MURDER OF EMMETT TILL

On August 28, 1955, 14-year-old Emmett Till was visiting relatives in Money, Mississippi, when two white men kidnapped and brutally murdered him. They accused him of whistling at one of their wives. She later said she had made up a false story about him. But her admission came too late.

Till's body was found in a river three days later. Officials tried to dispose of his body. But his mother, Mamie Till Mobley, got a court order to have his remains sent back to Chicago. The casket arrived padlocked, but Mobley insisted it stay open for his funeral, saying, "Let the people see what they did to my boy."

The world saw. A photograph of Till in his casket ran in *Jet* magazine, which covered news and culture related to Black Americans, motivating more people to join the civil rights movement.

An all-white jury found Till's murderers not guilty. The men went on to profit from the murder when they sold their story to an author who wrote a book about it.

A MOTHER'S DETERMINATION

Mamie Till Mobley remained an activist for the rest of her life. "We cannot afford the luxury of self-pity," she said decades after her son's murder. "Our top priority now is to get on with the building process. . . We must teach our children to weather the hurricanes of life, pick up the pieces and rebuild. We must impress upon our children that even when troubles rise to 7.1 on life's Richter scale [used to measure earthquakes], they must be anchored so deeply that, though they sway, they will not topple."

SIT AND BE COUNTED

In the following table are three of the most important protests in the civil rights movement.

DECEMBER 1, 1955	
ROSA PARKS AND THE MONTGOMERY BUS BOYCOTT	Inspired by the story of Emmett Till, Rosa Parks became a civil rights activist in the segregated city of Montgomery, Alabama. Parks was a 42-year-old Black woman sitting in the designated Black section at the back of a crowded bus in Montgomery. The bus driver ordered her to give up her seat when a white man boarded. When she refused, police arrested her. Black community leaders responded by forming the Montgomery Improvement Association (MIA), led by Baptist minister Dr. Martin Luther King, Jr. The group held a 381-day-long boycott of the bus system.
FEBRUARY 1, 1960	
SIT-IN AT A GREENSBORO LUNCH COUNTER	Four Black college students in Greensboro, North Carolina, refused to leave a restaurant when the manager wouldn't serve them because of their skin color. This led to hundreds of people protesting segregation in what is known as the Greensboro sit-ins. By April, more than 50,000 students had joined similar sit-ins across the country.

THE FREEDOM RIDERS

Even though the Supreme Court had ruled it unconstitutional in 1960, bus terminals throughout the South were still segregated in 1961. In response, seven Black and six white activists set out on a bus from Washington, D.C., to various Southern cities. White protestors and police subjected the "Freedom Riders" to violence, beating them and bombing their bus.

The Freedom Riders made a global television audience aware of the secrets of the Jim Crow South. There would be dozens more Freedom Rides throughout the year.

sit-in: a type of protest in which people would literally sit in a business and refuse to leave until their demands were met.

CLAUDETTE COLVIN

Nine months before Rosa Parks refused to move from her seat, 15-year-old Claudette Colvin was arrested for doing the same on a bus, also in Montgomery, Alabama. She later explained, "My head was just too full of Black history. . . . It felt like Sojourner Truth was on one side pushing me down, and Harriet Tubman was on the other side of me pushing me down. I couldn't get up." (Remember: Truth and Tubman were antislavery activists from the 1800s.)

Why did Parks become famous when Colvin did not? The NAACP focused on Parks's story instead of Colvin's. They believed that the white media would view Parks more sympathetically. Colvin and three other Black students, who had also refused to give up their seats, became the plaintiffs (the people bringing the lawsuit) in the court case that would overturn bus segregation in Alabama.

DR. MARTIN LUTHER KING, JR.

Dr. King was a young pastor when he helped organize the Montgomery bus boycott. He dedicated himself to the cause of civil rights. He also championed the rights of the working class and oppressed people around the world.

Dr. Martin Luther King, Jr.

His determination and leadership would change the course of the country's history, but the cost to him and his family would be great. People bombed and burned his house, and he and his family received many death threats. He was also targeted by J. Edgar Hoover and the FBI.

DR. KING'S LEADERSHIP

King, who helped found the Southern Christian Leadership Conference (SCLC), believed in nonviolent protests. When he was organizing the bus boycotts after Parks's arrest, he asked, "Are you able to accept blows without retaliating. . . to endure the ordeals of jail?"

He led by example. King was always speaking out—he traveled 780,000 miles around the country in 1957 alone, giving 208 speeches. White authorities frequently threw him in jail.

King would play an important part in the Civil Rights Act of 1964. This act outlawed discrimination based on race, sex, nationality, and religion. He won a Nobel Peace Prize that same year.

DYING FOR THE VOTE

Civil rights activists weren't just beaten. The names of some of the 41 people murdered during the movement are inscribed on the Civil Rights Memorial in Montgomery, Alabama. Among them are Black men who organized other Black people to vote.

Reverend George Lee was one of the first Black people registered to vote in Humphreys County, Mississippi. He publicly encouraged others to do the same. White officials offered to protect him if he would end his voter registration efforts, but he refused.

Lee was murdered in May 1955. No one was ever prosecuted for his murder.

Three months later, Lamar Smith, who also organized Black voters, was killed by a white man on a courthouse lawn in broad daylight. Although dozens of people witnessed the shooting, none of them would admit to seeing a white man kill a Black man. The killer was never charged.

MALCOLM X

Malcolm X's father was a minister and civil rights activist whose activism prompted death threats by white supremacists. His childhood house was burned down. Two years after that, when his father was found dead, his mother had an emotional breakdown and was placed in a mental institution. Malcolm X and his siblings were split up and sent to foster homes and orphanages.

Malcolm X

In 1946, Malcolm X began serving ten years in prison for a burglary charge. During this time, he became a devoted follower of the Nation of Islam. Founded in 1930, the Nation of Islam is a political and religious organization that is dedicated to improving the lives of Black Americans. When he was released, Malcolm X's articles and speeches about the group gained him national attention. Membership in the Nation of Islam grew from 500 in 1952 to 30,000 in 1963.

BY ANY MEANS NECESSARY

As a leader of the civil rights movement, Malcolm X disagreed with Dr. Martin Luther King, Jr.'s position regarding pacifism. (Remember what pacifism is? Check back in Chapter 7.) Instead, Malcolm X encouraged Black Americans to protect themselves against white aggression "by any means that are necessary."

In 1964, Malcolm X founded the Organization of Afro-American Unity. It stated that the enemy of justice was not the white race but the institution of racism.

Malcolm X faced years of death threats. Three men shot him 15 times on February 21, 1965, while he was giving a speech in New York. He was 39 when he died.

What do you think Malcolm X meant when he blamed racism, rather than white people, for social injustice?

_____

_____

_____

_____

_____

_____

_____

_____

Malcolm X used an initial for his last name in order to stop the tradition of Black people having the last name of their enslavers. He chose the initial "X" to symbolize his lost African name.

LEGAL ACTIONS: MAJOR EVENTS DURING THE CIVIL RIGHTS MOVEMENT

 **BROWN V. BOARD OF EDUCATION** legally ended segregation in schools.

 President Eisenhower signed **THE CIVIL RIGHTS ACT OF 1957.** It said that anyone who tried to prevent someone else from voting could be prosecuted. It also established the Civil Rights division of the Department of Justice, which created a formal commission to look into voter fraud and suppression.

 **THE CIVIL RIGHTS ACT OF 1964** dismantled Jim Crow policies and laws by ending segregation in public spaces. It also banned discrimination in the workplace based on race, color, religion, sex, or national origin.

THE TWENTY-FOURTH AMENDMENT abolished poll taxes. As you learned in Chapter 7, a poll tax was a fee that people had to pay in order to vote. Typically, authorities charged only Black people with these taxes. They were meant to discourage Black people from voting.

 **THE VOTING RIGHTS ACT OF 1965** suspended literacy tests for voters. Again, authorities typically gave these only to people of color. The act also allowed the government the right to intervene on behalf of any voter facing discrimination.

THE FAIR HOUSING ACT made it illegal for landlords to discriminate against someone based on race or color, religion, sex, national origin, family status, or disability.

THE LITTLE ROCK NINE

Just because authorities pass laws doesn't mean that people obey them. Three years after segregation of schools was legally overturned, nine Black students showed up at the formerly all-white Central High School in Little Rock, Arkansas. Known as the Little Rock Nine, they were met by the state's National Guard and a screaming mob.

White parents in Little Rock, outraged about the integration of schools, yell at members of the Little Rock Nine.

They didn't make it inside the building for two weeks, and then were removed for their own safety. President Eisenhower eventually ordered federal troops to escort them to and from classes. But even armed troops couldn't protect the students from harassment.

JOHN F. KENNEDY BECOMES PRESIDENT

Kennedy was only 43 when he took office in 1961. Though he served less than three years, he became one of the most quoted U.S. presidents because of the way he expressed his vision for American society. "Ask not what your country can do for you," he challenged Americans in his first speech as president. "Ask what you can do for your country."

He called for new civil rights legislation and launched programs to expand the economy. He also continued the Cold War with the Soviets by supporting a coup (a military takeover of the government) in Cuba to overthrow its communist leader, Fidel Castro. The coup, known as the Bay of Pigs, failed.

THE CUBAN MISSILE CRISIS

A year later, relations between the United States and the Soviet Union grew even more tense. The United States found out that the Soviets were installing nuclear weapons on the Caribbean island of Cuba, in close firing range of the United States. The confrontation, known as the Cuban missile crisis, pushed the United States and the Soviet Union to the brink of nuclear war. However, the two powers reached a settlement. The United States agreed to remove its missiles from Turkey if the Soviets did the same in Cuba.

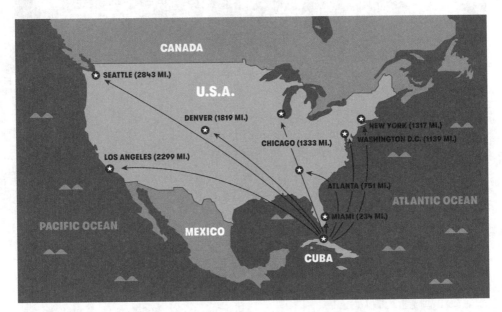

Even though no nuclear missiles were ever fired at the United States, this map shows why Americans were so nervous. Cuba was much too close to the U.S. mainland for comfort!

THE MARCH ON WASHINGTON

On August 28, 1963, some 250,000 people marched in Washington, D.C. to support civil rights. They wanted Congress to pass the Civil Rights Act, which had stalled.

Before the march, President Kennedy met with its organizers and expressed his concern about violence. He said, "We want success in the Congress, not just a big show at the Capitol." The leaders agreed to end the march at the Lincoln Memorial rather than the Capitol, so that Congress wouldn't feel threatened.

Speakers included NAACP president Roy Wilkins, actor Ossie Davis, and activist Daisy Lee Bates. Dr. King spoke last, delivering what became known as his "I Have a Dream" speech.

ANOTHER PRESIDENTIAL ASSASSINATION

Kennedy was assassinated in Dallas, Texas, on November 22, 1963. He was riding in a presidential motorcade when Lee Harvey Oswald shot him.

THE SELMA TO MONTGOMERY MARCH

On February 18, 1965, state troopers armed with clubs attacked a peaceful protest against voter suppression in Marion, Alabama. When a young Black demonstrator named Jimmie Lee Jackson tried to protect his mother from being beaten, a state trooper shot and killed him.

In response, Dr. King and the SCLC organized a 54-mile march from Selma, Alabama, where they were organizing Black voters, to the state's capital, Montgomery. On March 7, more than 600 people marched, led by activists Hosea Williams and future congressman John Lewis. They got no farther than Selma's Edmund Pettis Bridge before state troopers arrived bearing whips, tear gas, and nightsticks. The troopers injured scores of people, with seventeen requiring hospitalization.

Captured on television and seen by millions all over the world, the event became known as "Bloody Sunday."

Selma was in Dallas County, Alabama. In 1964, 50 percent of the population was Black, but only 2 percent of registered voters were Black.

A NEW PRESIDENT LENDS HIS SUPPORT

Lyndon B. Johnson, who had become president after Kennedy's assassination, appeared on television several days later. He gave his support to the protesters and asked Congress to support the Voting Rights Act of 1965. "There is no Negro problem," he said. "There is no Southern problem. There is no Northern problem. There is only an American problem. . . . Their cause must be our cause too. Because it is not just Negroes, but really it is all of us, who must overcome the crippling legacy of bigotry and hatred."

On March 21, 1965, 2,000 people, led by Dr. King, set out again. This time they had protection from the army and National Guard troops, thanks to President Johnson. Nearly 50,000 supporters met the marchers when they arrived in Montgomery four days later.

Dr. King stood on the steps of the state capitol. He said, "No wave of racism can stop us. . . Like an idea whose time has come, not even the marching of mighty armies can halt us. We are moving to the land of freedom. . . I know you are asking today, 'How long will it take?'" He continued, "How long? Not long, because the arc of the moral universe is long, but it bends toward justice."

On April 4, 1968, a sniper shot King dead in Memphis, Tennessee. Like Malcolm X, King was 39 when he was killed.

Dr. King gave this speech more than 50 years ago. Do you think he imagined we would be further along than we are now? What do you think has changed?

_____

_____

_____

_____

_____

_____

CHAPTER 9 VOCABULARY

baby boomers: the generation born between 1945 and 1964. The name comes from the huge boom (increase) in births during this time.

blacklist: a list of people that companies (such as Hollywood studios) would refuse to hire, usually because of their political beliefs.

brinkmanship: a cold war military strategy meaning that each side would go to the brink (edge) of war in order to force the other to back down.

capitalism: an economic and political system in which private individuals and groups own land, factories, and goods—the government owns few or none of these things.

communism: an economic and political system under which there is no private property. In theory, communism is meant to result in public ownership and control, but in practice communist revolutions have resulted in dictatorships.

containment: a Cold War strategy intended to stop communism from spreading from one country or region to another.

grassroots: the actions or ideas of ordinary people as opposed to those being promoted by rich or powerful individuals or organizations.

ideologies: systems of ideas or beliefs, usually political and/or economic in nature. In this chapter, you read about two ideologies that were at odds with each other: capitalism and communism.

McCarthyism: refers to the campaign in the 1940s and 1950s led by Senator Joseph McCarthy to expose people with communist sympathies and remove them from government and other positions of importance. It has come to mean any campaign that uses unproven facts, rumors, and bullying methods to eliminate supposed enemies.

proxy war: active fighting influenced by the two superpowers (the United States and the USSR), but without their direct military involvement.

redlining: the practice by banks and mortgage companies of refusing to invest in minority communities or loan money to Black or Brown people looking to buy homes in white neighborhoods.

Red Menace: a term used in the United States to describe the threat of communism.

satellite: a human-made object sent into space to orbit the planet.

satellite state: a country that is officially independent, but is actually controlled by another country.

sit-in: a type of protest where people would literally sit in a business and refuse to leave until their demands were met.

sphere of influence: a Cold War term referring to the countries and regions that the USSR and United States wanted to affect, sway, and control politically. This far-reaching global power was called a sphere of influence.

subpoena: an official notice directing a person to appear before a court or legal committee.

suburbs: areas outside of urban centers that usually have more spacious developments. In the decades following World War II, many white people left big cities to live in suburbs, bringing their wealth with them.

10 WAR AND DISILLUSION-MENT

When the United States started fighting in a war in Vietnam, a small country thousands of miles away, many Americans rose up in protest—especially young people. Their reactions would affect the fight for rights for decades to come. How did this happen? Let's investigate.

CHAPTER CONTENTS

THE VIETNAM WAR

THE WAR AT HOME

GROWING DISTRUST AND ACTIVISM

THE EQUAL RIGHTS AMENDMENT

BIG-TIME MONEY TROUBLES

THE PRESIDENCY OF JIMMY CARTER

THE REAGAN ERA

THE AIDS CRISIS BEGINS

PRESIDENT GEORGE H. W. BUSH

THE VIETNAM WAR

Put simply, the United States became involved in the Vietnam War because of another war: the Cold War.

Vietnam was once a French colony. It fought a war for independence from France after World War II. Ho Chi Minh, a communist, led the independence forces. The United States wanted to make sure that Vietnam did not become a communist country and fall under the control of the Soviet Union.

Because Vietnam was a small and poor country, the U.S. government hoped to convince the American public that a war to crush the rebels would be a quick and easy fight. Instead, it dragged on for more than a decade and killed three million people. The United States finally withdrew the last of its combat troops in 1973. More than half of the dead were Vietnamese civilians, and 58,000 Americans died.

NORTH AND SOUTH VIETNAM

China

NORTH VIETNAM

Laos

★ HANOI

Gulf of Tonkin

DEMILITARIZED ZONE

LINE OF DEMARCATION

Thailand

Cambodia

SOUTH VIETNAM

★ SAIGON (HO CHI MINH CITY)

THE DOMINO THEORY

After World War II, Vietnam split into two countries. The South, led by Ngo Dinh Diem, had the backing of the French (and, quietly, the United States). The North, led by Ho Chi Minh, was communist. Therefore, it got support from the Chinese and Soviets.

The North declared independence in 1946. It defeated the French in a decisive battle in 1954, driving them out of the country.

With the French gone, President Kennedy was concerned that if one country fell to communism, others would follow. This was known as the domino theory.

In 1961, Kennedy increased U.S. aid to South Vietnam. By 1962, Kennedy had sent 9,000 troops there, just in case.

THE GULF OF TONKIN RESOLUTION

On August 7, 1964, less than a year after Kennedy's assassination, President Johnson received congressional approval for full-scale U.S. involvement in Vietnam. This was called the Gulf of Tonkin Resolution. Only days earlier, two U.S. naval destroyers had been attacked in the Gulf of Tonkin, off the Vietnam coast—or so Secretary of Defense Robert McNamara told Congress. Years later, historians gained access to documents that showed McNamara had purposely misled Congress about the incident to justify the United States entering the war.

> domino theory: the idea that if one country fell to communism, its neighbors and allies would follow.

FIGHTING CONDITIONS

Vietnam was filled with dense jungles. Soldiers often couldn't see their targets—or who was targeting them. The temperature could be more than 100 degrees, and soldiers were carrying backpacks that weighed more than 70 pounds.

The United States relied on its own air force. It dropped more than two million tons of bombs in Southeast Asia. The United States also used toxic chemicals including napalm, which had the nickname "liquid fire," and Agent Orange.

napalm: a chemical weapon also known as "liquid fire" used by the United States in the Vietnam War.

Agent Orange: a plant-killing chemical used by the United States in the Vietnam War to remove jungle vegetation where the enemy could hide and to destroy crops they could eat.

Thousands of Vietnamese civilians died because of these chemicals. Their long-term effects—cancers, severe psychological and neurological problems, birth defects, and more—still affect Vietnamese people and U.S. veterans of the Vietnam War today.

American troops faced brutal fighting conditions, including dense jungles, toxic chemicals, and an enemy that knew the land.

 What do you think the effects of wars might be on the people living in war-torn countries years after the war has ended?

_____

_____

_____

_____

_____

EVADING THE DRAFT

Vietnam disproportionately affected Black people and poor people. Between 1964 and 1973, the government drafted 2.2 million soldiers. People who were in college didn't have to worry about the draft. Also, with the right connections and money, it was possible to get out of military service with a doctor's note that claimed you had ulcers, anemia, or a foot ailment. More than half a million men got out of service, including future presidents Bill Clinton, George W. Bush, and Donald Trump.

Also, 40,000 draft evaders ran away to Canada between 1965 and 1975. They were safe there because Canada considered them immigrants, not criminals.

In 1966, Secretary of Defense Robert McNamara launched a program called Project 100,000. It targeted poor men for recruitment into the military. Its purpose was to solve two problems at once: reduce unemployment in the United States and increase the number of soldiers available to fight in Vietnam. Project 100,000 put thousands of poor men into the war—40 percent of them Black Americans.

draft evaders: people who (often illegally) found ways to get out of being drafted to the U.S. army. Also called draft dodgers.

THE FIRST INTEGRATED TROOPS

The Vietnam War was the first time in U.S. history that Black soldiers and Native American soldiers fought alongside white American soldiers in fully integrated units. The soldiers of color endured racism and harassment. Military officials often sent Black soldiers to the front lines first and promoted white soldiers to higher ranks more quickly.

JOURNALISTS AND TELEVISION BRING THE WAR "HOME"

For the first time, television journalists embedded with troops. That means they lived with the soldiers. These journalists were able to take photographs and film footage that Americans could watch on the nightly news. Incidents involving U.S. soldiers murdering women and children and burning villages—or being wounded or terrorized themselves—were beamed into people's living rooms.

After watching the images, many Americans began joining marches and protests against the war. Who organized these events? Groups such as Students for a Democratic Society (SDS), the Black Panthers, the Asian-American Political Alliance, and the Chicano Movement.

OPPOSITION TO THE WAR

In 1967, Dr. Martin Luther King, Jr. publicly opposed the war in Vietnam. He pointed out the large numbers of Black soldiers being killed. In addition, the war was costing the U.S. billions of dollars a year. The government could have spent that money on health care, housing, and food at home.

During a protest in Chicago that drew more than 5,000 people, King called the war "a blasphemy against all that America stands for." (*Blasphemy* means a terrible insult to God.)

By 1968, a poll showed that only 35 percent of Americans approved of President Johnson's handling of the war. That same year,

Americans had learned about the My Lai massacre. In that event, U.S. soldiers had slaughtered more than 504 villagers.

Many hippies protested the American military presence in Vietnam.

HIPPIES

In 1967, *Time* magazine published a cover story on hippies. They were a movement made up of mostly young, white, middle-class people. Hippies disagreed with the war and the government. They encouraged people to "question authority." They preached "free love" and promoted peace. Many experimented with drugs as a way of expanding their minds and rebelling against authority.

Loving v. Virginia, a 1967 Supreme Court ruling, reversed state laws that made interracial marriage illegal.

THE WAR AT HOME

THE 1968 DEMOCRATIC NATIONAL CONVENTION

Americans felt growing fury against the government in general, and about the war in particular. This played out on the political stage of the Democratic Convention that summer. The convention, where Democrats chose their candidate for president, was held in Chicago.

Added to the outrage was grief over Dr. Martin Luther King, Jr.'s assassination that April, as well as the June assassination of John F. Kennedy's brother, former United States attorney general Robert F. Kennedy. At the time of his assassination, Robert Kennedy had been seeking the Democratic presidential nomination.

THE WHOLE WORLD IS WATCHING

Thousands of protesters flocked to Chicago, even though its mayor denied them a permit to gather. Tension between police and protestors grew. Police beat the protesters with clubs and used tear gas on them, in full view of television crews from around the world. This led the crowd to chant, "the whole world is watching," which became a rallying cry for the antiwar movement.

THE OUTCOME OF THE CONVENTION

The delegates were divided between an antiwar group and supporters of Vice President Hubert Humphrey, who was running in Johnson's place. (Johnson withdrew from the race because of his deep unpopularity.)

Humphrey won the nomination. But the violence led antiwar delegates to leave the building and join the protesters outside in a candlelight vigil. The Democratic Party was in tatters. That left the field open for Republican Richard M. Nixon to become the country's next president.

THE CHICAGO EIGHT

Police arrested more than 650 protesters, including a group known as the Chicago Eight (later the Chicago Seven). This was the first time a court put people on trial under the country's new anti-riot law.

One of the Eight, Black Panther co-founder Bobby Seale, hadn't helped plan the protest and was there for only two days of the convention. He kept objecting that his lawyer was in the hospital. Unlike the other defendants, Seale had no one to represent him. So Seale, the only Black defendant in this trial, spoke to represent himself.

In response, the judge ordered him to appear before the jury bound, gagged, and tied to a chair. Then he sentenced Seale to four years in prison for contempt and removed him from the trial.

People around the world felt horror at seeing a man tied up and gagged in a courtroom.

The charges against Seale were later dropped.

Bobby Seale in the trial against the Chicago Eight

The jury found the remaining members innocent of conspiracy, but five were found guilty of causing violence. Two years later, a higher court overturned their convictions.

THE BLACK PANTHERS

The Black Panthers, or Black Panther Party, was founded in 1966 by Seale and Huey P. Newton. The purpose of the group was to confront police brutality against Black people after police in San Francisco killed Matthew Johnson, an unarmed black teenager.

Members dressed in black berets and leather jackets. They made armed patrols of cities. They worked not only to end police brutality but to increase housing and job opportunities for Black people. Also, they opened health clinics in Black communities and started free breakfast programs for schoolchildren.

FBI SURVEILLANCE

There were conflicts within the Panther organization. This often led to violence, both with the police and with one another. The FBI began investigating the Panthers. J. Edgar Hoover, the FBI director, called them "one of the greatest threats to the nation's internal security."

The FBI tried to discredit the Panthers, including through negative media coverage. They also took away the Panthers' free breakfast programs in schools. The FBI spied on members and weakened the group by turning members against each other.

THE MURDER OF FRED HAMPTON

The government even resorted to murder. In 1969, in a nighttime raid, Chicago police killed two Black Panthers while they slept. One of those killed was Fred Hampton, the 21-year-old deputy chairman of the Illinois chapter of the Black Panther Party. Hampton was an effective speaker and leader. The FBI had determined that he could help unify the Black movement—a development that Hoover wanted to prevent.

In 1982, as the result of internal conflicts and external pressure, the Black Panthers officially dissolved.

Why do you think the FBI wanted to discredit the Black Panthers?

_____

_____

_____

_____

THE AMERICAN INDIAN MOVEMENT

In 1968, a group of Native American activists gathered in Minneapolis, Minnesota, and founded the American Indian Movement (AIM). AIM spoke out against the racism directed at Native Americans. AIM members fought for job opportunities, better housing for Native Americans living in cities, and the right to reclaim tribal lands.

In 1972, AIM organized the Trail of Broken Treaties march in Washington, D.C. The group took over the Bureau of Indian Affairs building to protest its policies. Much as they had done to the Black civil rights movement, the FBI and CIA tried to suppress the group.

When the Trail of Broken Treaties marchers arrived at the Bureau of Indian Affairs, they put up a tepee on the lawn and promoted their 20-point plan.

OCCUPYING WOUNDED KNEE

In February 1973, AIM leader Russell Means organized the group to occupy the Native American community in Wounded Knee, South Dakota, to protest its allegedly corrupt government. AIM took eleven people hostage, demanding a Senate investigation of the Bureau of Indian Affairs and some reservations.

The FBI sent agents, and a 71-day siege followed. Two Native Americans were killed and 1,200 were arrested. The event drew international attention to mistreatment of Native Americans. AIM leaders went to trial but were found not guilty.

THE LGBTQ+ COMMUNITY RISES UP

As more Americans grew unhappy with how the government was affecting their lives, they took a lesson from the civil rights marchers in the 1950s and 1960s as well as Vietnam protesters. For the LGBTQ+ community, this meant speaking up publicly for their civil rights.

Gay people suffered discrimination socially and legally. Being gay was illegal in many states. And gay people had no legal remedy when people committed hate crimes against them.

In 1953, President Eisenhower had issued an executive order that named homosexuality as grounds for firing people from federal positions. By the 1960s, more than 5,000 people had lost their jobs because of that rule. That same decade, states began passing laws making it illegal for bars to serve gay people.

> LGBTQ+: an acronym (formed from the first letter of each word) that includes people who identify as lesbian, gay, bisexual, transgender, or queer (or questioning). The plus sign indicates inclusion of people who hold other marginalized gender identities.

THE STONEWALL RIOTS

Just as speakeasies had found a way around Prohibition, bar owners—again, many of them connected to organized crime—did the same with gay bars. One was the Stonewall Inn, a New York City gay bar owned by the mafia.

On June 28, 1969, police officers raided the bar and arrested 13 people. Within minutes, people were rioting on the street, with some members of the police, patrons, and a writer for the *Village Voice* newspaper stuck inside. The protests were started mainly by trans women of color, including Marsha P. Johnson. Five days of protests followed, and the *Village Voice* published a story about what had happened.

Several gay rights groups grew out of this event. On its one-year anniversary, thousands of people joined the first gay pride parade. They marched from the Stonewall Inn to Central Park, chanting, "Say it loud, gay is proud!"

In 1972, Kathy Kozachenko became the first openly gay American to be elected to local government. She won a seat on the city council in Ann Arbor, Michigan.

In 1977, activist Harvey Milk was elected to the San Francisco board of supervisors. Milk was a champion of gay rights. In 1978, a former city supervisor assassinated him and Mayor George Moscone at City Hall.

Harvey Milk

THE SECRET BOMBING OF CAMBODIA

From 1969 until 1970, American B-52 planes loaded down with bombs took thousands of side trips from Vietnam. They dropped 110,000 tons of bombs on its next-door neighbors, Cambodia and Laos. The North Vietnamese had established camps in these countries.

President Nixon approved the mission, but he didn't tell Congress or the public. He knew the reaction to bombing a neutral country would be negative.

THE KENT STATE MASSACRE

When news outlets reported the story, people were outraged. Tens of thousands of people marched unharmed in Washington, D.C., and Boston. But on May 4, 1970, National Guardsmen shot and killed four students during an antiwar protest at Kent State University in Ohio. One of the students did not even attend the protest. She was walking to class when a stray bullet struck her.

In response, more than four million students at 450 universities went on strike. Also, another march of 100,000 people mobilized in Washington. On May 14, police shot 14 students during a protest at Mississippi's Jackson State University, a historically Black institution. Two of the students were killed. The deaths at Jackson State got far less attention than the deaths at Kent State.

 Do you think a government should have to tell citizens if it's fighting a war in another country? Why or why not? Should the president have to tell Congress? Remember, it's in the Constitution that Congress must decide how the government spends taxpayer money.

_____

_____

_____

_____

THE END OF THE VIETNAM WAR

In 1972, after a final failed attempt to take South Vietnam, the North was ready to compromise. When the South rejected a proposed peace treaty, the United States responded with an attack on targets in the North. These became known as the Christmas Bombings.

In January 1973, the United States and North Vietnam signed a treaty, and the United States was officially out of the war. The North and South would continue to fight for another two and a half years. The North won and reunified the country.

American soldiers returned home traumatized from the war. Some of their fellow Americans criticized them for having killed innocent people.

GROWING DISTRUST AND ACTIVISM

THE PENTAGON PAPERS

Distrust of the government continued to swell with the publication of the Pentagon Papers in 1971. An economist and former military analyst named Daniel Ellsberg leaked secret documents. The documents showed that the United States had been secretly increasing its military efforts in Vietnam since the early 1950s.

Three men acting on behalf of the Richard Nixon White House broke into Ellsberg's psychiatrist's office. They wanted to steal Ellsberg's file in hopes of finding something to make him look untrustworthy.

The *New York Times* began printing parts of the Pentagon Papers. The Nixon administration tried to stop these reports. The case went all the way to the Supreme Court. The court ruled in defense of a free press. It said that the newspaper could continue publishing the papers.

> **leak:** to reveal a secret document to one or more media sources.

THE WATERGATE SCANDAL

On June 17, 1972, police arrested five men for breaking into the Democratic National Headquarters in Washington, D.C. In October, journalists Bob Woodward and Carl Bernstein published a newspaper story about the burglary.

According to the article, an anonymous source known as "Deep Throat" had told the reporters that the FBI believed the burglary was the work of President Nixon's aides. The aides were trying to get information to help Nixon win the 1972 election.

CONGRESS INVESTIGATES

The men included two former CIA employees and a former FBI agent. They pleaded guilty to conspiracy, burglary, and hiding a recording device in the DNC headquarters.

Four of Nixon's top aides resigned, and Congress began an investigation. Congress found out that Nixon recorded all his White House conversations. Nixon had denied his role in Watergate convincingly enough to win reelection easily. But Congress insisted that he turn over the tapes. He refused. Again, the case went all the way to the Supreme Court, which ruled that Nixon had to turn over the tapes.

 Remember the balance of powers in the Constitution? Check Chapter 2 for a refresher.

Before the Senate could begin impeachment proceedings against the president, Nixon announced his resignation.

A "SMOKING GUN"

On the tapes, Nixon could be heard saying that he knew about the break-in and he ordered a cover-up to hide evidence from investigators. So on August 9, 1974, Congress began the process of impeachment. This led Nixon to resign (quit) his position as president.

Vice President Gerald Ford was now in charge. Ford angered many Americans when he issued Nixon a **presidential pardon**, which meant Nixon wouldn't go on trial for any crimes related to Watergate. Ford said that Watergate had been a "long national nightmare" and that putting Nixon on trial would have further divided the country.

In 1977, Nixon gave the following defense of his actions: "When the president does it. . . that means that it is not illegal."

> **presidential pardon:** the use of executive power to protect someone from punishment for a crime. Basically, a "Get Out of Jail Free" card.

 Do you think U.S. presidents should have to follow the same rules or laws as ordinary citizens? Why or why not?

_____

_____

_____

_____

_____

_____

THE EQUAL RIGHTS AMENDMENT

In 1923, the National Woman's Party had called for legal equality as well as laws to make it illegal to discriminate based on gender. It would take close to another half a century to even approach this goal. But in the 1960s and 1970s, feminism became a widespread political movement.

Feminist activists included Gloria Steinem, Betty Friedan, and U.S. representatives Bella Abzug and Shirley Chisholm. Congress approved the Equal Rights Amendment in 1972. This would have been an amendment to the Constitution that forbade discrimination based on gender. Congress then sent it to the states for ratification.

Three-quarters of the fifty state legislatures must vote in favor of a constitutional amendment for it to be ratified. That's thirty-eight states. Thirty-one states backed the amendment—seven short of the minimum needed to make it part of the Constitution.

Since then, the federal government and all states have passed legislation to protect women's legal rights. But the Equal Rights Amendment is still not part of the Constitution.

> feminism: a movement that fights for gender equality. Focuses on issues such as women's suffrage, women in the workplace, violence against women, and more.

FEMINISTS DIVIDE

Just as they had during the suffrage movement, white activists didn't always represent the interests of all women, but rather those of middle-class white women. In response, Black activists and women of color developed their own definitions of feminism and fought for themselves. Writers like bell hooks, Alice Walker, and Patricia Bell-Scott looked at

how racism and differences in class affected the movement. Author and educator Shirley Chisholm focused her congressional campaign on women voters. She became the first Black congresswoman.

When she was elected, Chisholm hired only women for her office. She ran for president in 1972 but lost. Afterward, she said "I ran. . .

Shirley Chisholm

despite hopeless odds, to demonstrate the sheer will and refusal to accept the status quo."

ROE V. WADE

When "Jane Roe" (real name Norma McCorvey) became pregnant with her third child, she wanted to have an abortion. This was illegal in the state of Texas, where she lived. So she sued the Dallas County district attorney, Henry Wade. She argued that the Texas law banning abortion was unconstitutional.

In 1973, the Supreme Court agreed. The court's decision made a woman's access to safe and legal abortion a constitutional right. The ruling is still hotly debated.

abortion: a medical procedure to end a pregnancy.

status quo: Latin phrase meaning "the way things currently are."

Why do you think people have such strong opinions about *Roe v. Wade?*

_____

_____

_____

BIG-TIME MONEY TROUBLES

Remember how the United States experienced economic booms after World War I and World War II? After Vietnam, the opposite happened.

RUNAWAY INFLATION

During the 1970s, the United States experienced some of the highest inflation rates in history. The government printed more money to try to stimulate the economy. But because there were more dollars, each dollar was worth less.

This meant the cost of goods skyrocketed. Someone who might have been able to afford to buy a house before couldn't even afford to take out a mortgage. Interest rates had risen nearly 20 percent.

> **inflation:** an economic term that describes a widespread increase in prices. The purchasing power of the dollar goes down and the prices of goods and services go up.

 You learned about mortgages and interest back in Chapter 8. Flip back if you need a refresher.

AN OIL CRISIS

In 1973, the United States was getting nearly 48 percent of its oil supply from Saudi Arabia and other countries allied with it. These Middle Eastern countries had been in conflict with Israel since that nation's founding, with the support of the United States, in 1948.

The United States supported Israel in a brief but intense war (called the Yom Kippur War because it began during the Jewish holiday). After that, Saudi Arabia and its allies in the Organization of Petroleum Exporting Countries (OPEC) refused to ship the supply of oil that the United States needed.

GAS PRICES SKYROCKET

The result was an energy crisis. The price of gas soared. And even if people could afford to buy gas, they had a hard time finding any. Americans waited hours in long lines at gas stations.

It wasn't just gasoline. The oil crisis drove up the prices of nearly all manufactured goods. (Factories run on oil, and nearly all plastics are made primarily from oil.) Even the prices of non-manufactured goods, such as farm products, rose. How would milk get to stores when trucks didn't have gas to make the trip?

WHITE FLIGHT

Meanwhile, New York City almost went bankrupt. Police officers, firefighters, teachers, and other city workers lost their jobs because the city couldn't pay their salaries. This left poor and vulnerable communities with even fewer resources. By the late 1970s, more than 820,000 people had left the city for the suburbs in a movement known as white flight.

white flight: the mass movement of white people as they left cities to live in suburbs in the decades following World War II.

CITIES FEEL THE RESULTS

As more white people began paying taxes in the suburbs, cities had less money. City neighborhoods became more segregated. Poor neighborhoods suffered increases in poverty and crime, and many more urban schools lost the funding they desperately needed. This problem persists to this day.

By 1975, the country's rate of unemployment for Black Americans was nearly 15 percent, but it was 8 percent for whites. President Ford suggested a tax cut and then a tax hike. None of it helped. In 1976, he lost the presidential election to Georgia's Democratic governor, Jimmy Carter.

Public funding for a school is largely determined by the property taxes of the area where a school is. That means that schools in areas with higher property values usually receive more money per student than schools in less expensive areas.

THE PRESIDENCY OF JIMMY CARTER

Carter, a former peanut farmer, wanted to make the government "competent and compassionate."

- During his term, there was an increase of nearly eight million jobs.

- He decreased the federal budget, and he established a national energy policy to confront the energy shortage.

- Carter also improved the environment, expanding the national park system by 103 million acres.

- He created the Department of Education, and he appointed record numbers of Blacks, Latinx, and women to government jobs.

CARTER AND FOREIGN AFFAIRS

President Jimmy Carter

A champion of human rights, Carter urged South Africa to end apartheid. With the 1978 Camp David Accords, he helped Egypt and Israel reach a peace agreement.

However, like previous presidents, Carter backed dictatorships. He continued U.S. support for oppressive governments in Iran, Nicaragua, the Philippines, and Indonesia in an effort to protect American interests there.

apartheid: the legal segregation and unjust, brutal treatment of Blacks in South Africa.

In 2002, Carter won the Nobel Peace Prize. The prize committee recognized his decades-long efforts to solve international conflicts.

THE IRAN HOSTAGE CRISIS

One conflict Carter struggled to solve was the Iran hostage crisis. In 1979, oil-rich Iran was in the middle of a revolution. The Islamic fundamentalists who led the revolution to overthrow the shah (king), wanted the government to reflect the beliefs of Islam.

> fundamentalist: someone who strictly follows religious traditions exactly as they are written.
>
> hostage: a person held prisoner by an individual or group who demands that certain conditions are met before the captured person is released.

WHERE IS IRAN?

The shah's family had been in power in Iran for decades. They wanted a Western-style government with less focus on religion. The United States supported the shah because he allowed access to Iran's economy and its oil.

After the revolution, the shah fled the country. The anti-American Ayatollah Ruhollah Khomeini took power. An ayatollah is a Muslim religious leader.

THE SHAH COMES TO THE UNITED STATES

That November, Carter allowed the shah to come to the United States for cancer treatment. This enraged many Iranians, who were already furious about years of American interference. Crowds attacked the U.S. embassy in Iran's capital city, Tehran, on November 4.

Iranians took more than sixty Americans hostage. They released fourteen hostages after a few weeks. But Carter's efforts to free the remaining hostages failed for more than a year. A U.S. military effort also failed.

SETTLING THE CRISIS

Finally, in January 1981, the two countries came to an agreement. The United States agreed to stay out of Iran's business and unfreeze eight billion dollars in Iranian money that was in U.S. banks. In return, Iran released the hostages. They did so the next day, when Ronald Reagan became the next president of the United States.

In 1979, the Soviet Union invaded Afghanistan (a country in Southwest Asia) to support that country's communist government, which was fighting non-communist Muslims. The United States backed the Muslim groups and boycotted the 1980 Moscow Olympics.

THE REAGAN ERA

Reagan had been a Democrat before switching parties in 1962. His campaign pledge in 1980 was to restore "the great, confident roar of American progress and growth and optimism." Also, he wanted Americans to rely less on the government.

REAGANOMICS

Guided by an economic plan dubbed "Reaganomics," he cut taxes for corporations and the rich. Reagan believed that the wealthier people at the top become, the more they help society by spreading some of that wealth around. This is called the trickle-down theory. Instead, the gap between the wealthy and the poor grew. By 1983, 22 percent of Black Americans were unemployed, compared to 9 percent of white Americans.

Reagan believed it was not the government's job to help poor people. He took money from social and welfare programs to fund the military. He cut spending on Medicaid, food stamps, and school lunches. Medicaid is a government-sponsored program that pays for medical care for people who are very poor. Reagan also rolled back affirmative action programs. These programs promote the hiring of people in marginalized groups and women in job fields that have been dominated by white men.

Reagan's cuts to social and welfare programs were not enough to make up for the huge increase in military spending. By the time Reagan left office, the federal debt had almost tripled, from $998 billion in 1981 to $2.857 trillion in 1989.

A big federal deficit can be good because the money can be used to stimulate the economy. But if it gets too big, the leaders of other countries and other people owed money might begin to doubt that the country can repay its debts.

REAGAN REELECTED

Reagan easily won a second term. He showed his strength as a negotiator when he hammered out a treaty with Soviet leader Mikhail Gorbachev to eliminate certain nuclear missiles. He also continued American support of anticommunist uprisings in Central America, Africa, and Asia. In addition, he supported dictators who were not communists.

THE FALL OF THE BERLIN WALL

In 1987, Reagan stood in front of the wall separating East and West Berlin and said, "General Secretary Gorbachev, if you seek peace, if you seek prosperity for the Soviet Union and Eastern Europe. . . tear down this wall." The wall would come down two years later, but it had little to do with the speech. That's when the Soviet Union's declining power led to its dismantling. Masses of East and West Berliners wrecked the wall in 1989, and two years later, the Soviet Union dissolved, breaking up into the individual countries they had been before the Russian revolution in 1917.

President Reagan gives a speech at the Berlin Wall.

The fall of the Berlin Wall was a huge celebration, as residents on both sides of the wall brought sledgehammers, chisels, and anything they could get their hands on to break the barrier down to rubble. If they had done the same thing only days earlier, East German police would have shot them. Now, people collected pieces of the rubble as souvenirs. Suddenly, families and friends who had been prevented from seeing each other for decades were allowed to reunite. Germany itself was formally reunited the following year.

THE IRAN-CONTRA AFFAIR

In 1980, Iranian-backed terrorists took Americans hostage in Lebanon. U.S. officials made a secret deal to sell Iran $48 million in weapons in exchange for the hostages' release. Then the U.S. government used $18 million of that money to secretly support a war in Nicaragua, a country in Central America. In that country, a rebel group called the Contras were fighting the Sandinistas—a socialist party that had overthrown the dictator Anastasio Somoza DeBayle. The United States supported Somoza (as he was known), and officials wanted to protect American financial interests in Nicaragua.

All this took place in secret. Why? Since the Iranian Revolution, the United States had a trade embargo in place against Iran. An embargo happens when one country makes it illegal for its people to trade goods with another country. So it was illegal to sell those weapons. As for the Nicaraguan War, Congress had previously told Reagan they wouldn't support it. When word got out, the Iran-Contra affair became a black mark on Reagan's presidency.

THE WAR ON DRUGS

Reagan and his wife, Nancy Reagan, launched a campaign that encouraged Americans to "just say no to drugs." The Reagans took up where Nixon had left off in his presidency's war on drugs. But because of laws and policies that favored white people, whites who were caught using drugs could often get a free pass, while Black people often suffered punishment.

That didn't change when Reagan left office.

- A 1995 study showed that 66 percent of users of the illegal drug crack cocaine were white and only 8 percent were Black. Still, police focused their drug raids on Black neighborhoods.

- Between 1988 and 1993, drug arrests of Blacks were five times higher than whites.

- The average prison sentence for Black Americans was almost 50 percent longer than whites.

- A 2015 study showed that nearly 80 percent of the people serving time for drug offenses in federal prison as a result of the war on drugs were Black or Latinx.

What do you think are some ways to make sure that laws are applied equally to people of all races?

_____

_____

_____

_____

_____

_____

_____

_____

_____

_____

THE AIDS CRISIS BEGINS

In 1981, the first case of Acquired Immunodeficiency Syndrome (AIDS) was diagnosed in the United States. Caused by the HIV virus, AIDS would cause havoc in the gay community. AIDS had killed more than 20,000 Americans by 1987, without a single public mention by President Reagan.

At first, no one understood how AIDS spread, and there were no treatments. AIDS killed members of Black and Latinx communities at higher rates than members of white communities, just as COVID-19 would do decades later.

GAY MEN BECOME ACTIVISTS

The Gay Men's Health Crisis, cofounded by activist and playwright Larry Kramer, mobilized in New York in 1982. Its goal was to help those affected by the disease. The group called on the government and the Food and Drug Administration to find a cure.

Another group called ACT UP—which stood for AIDS Coalition to Unleash Power—staged protests and "die-ins" to bring attention to government inaction. A die-in was an event where protesters gathered and lay down on the ground as if dead, to represent those who had died from AIDS.

AIDS TAKES ITS TOLL

Mark S. King, a gay man, said of the time, "It was like a *Twilight Zone* episode where everyone in town just starts disappearing. It was the bank teller at your bank who wasn't there one day. It was your favorite bartender. It was the guy who did your hair. They just stopped being there."

President Reagan and many state and local leaders were slow to react to what some of them referred to as "the gay plague." Reagan issued an executive order in 1987 to put together an advisory committee and fund research into how best to combat the disease.

ACT UP members march to protest the U.S. response to the AIDS crisis.

Acquired Immunodeficiency Syndrome (AIDS): a disease caused by the HIV virus that attacks the human immune system, which is responsible for fighting off diseases.

THE SCIENTIFIC COMMUNITY STEPS IN

In 1987, scientists were able to determine that HIV is transmitted through bodily fluids. AIDS does not spread by shaking hands or casual contact.

Scientists developed medicines that could delay the onset of AIDS and lessen its symptoms. Getting HIV is no longer a death sentence, but it is still a complex medical condition that can be difficult (and expensive) to treat. About 700,000 Americans have died from AIDS, as have 35 million people across the world.

PRESIDENT GEORGE H. W. BUSH

Reagan's former vice president, George H. W. Bush, cruised into the next presidency. Bush benefited from Reagan's high approval rating. In Bush's first speech as president, the conservative Republican promised to use American strength "as a force for good." Let's take a look at the two military interventions under Bush.

A TALE OF TWO INVASIONS

INVASION OF PANAMA, 1990

WHY	EFFECT
The United States supported the overthrow of Panama's military dictator, Manuel Noriega. At one time, Noriega had worked with the CIA to fight communism in Central America. When tensions between Noriega and the United States threatened America's access to the Panama Canal, some 21,000 U.S. military troops overthrew the government.	The United States protected its interests by ensuring that the next president, Guillermo Endara, was an ally. Noriega was flown to the United States, where a court found him guilty of illegally selling drugs and several related charges. It was the first time that a U.S. jury convicted a foreign leader.

OPERATION DESERT STORM, JANUARY 17–FEBRUARY 28, 1990

WHY	EFFECT
Iraqi president Saddam Hussein ordered the invasion of Kuwait in 1990. Neighboring Arab countries including Saudi Arabia and Egypt feared they might be next, and asked for Western help. The United States, dependent on Kuwaiti oil, sent in 540,000 troops. They pummeled Iraqi forces. This became known as the first Persian Gulf War. With Iraq defeated, Bush ordered a cease-fire.	Iraq returned to its previous borders and agreed to get rid of its nuclear, biological, and chemical weapons. Scuffles with Iraq continued for years. By 2003, U.S. forces fought the second Persian Gulf War, after the U.S. government had lied that Iraq had weapons of mass destruction.

Do you think these are examples of using American strength for good? Why or why not?

_____

_____

_____

_____

In Operation Desert Storm, U.S. forces struck Iran in a campaign to pressure Iraq to leave Kuwait.

ALL THIS AND AN OIL SPILL, TOO

On March 24, 1989, a ship called the *Exxon Valdez* ran aground in Alaska. It spilled 11 million gallons of oil into the waters and caused massive environmental damage.

A TIMELINE OF THE GEORGE H. W. BUSH PRESIDENCY

JUNE 4–5, 1989 Bush spoke out strongly against the massacres in China's Tiananmen Square. During that conflict, the communist Chinese government killed as many as 10,000 pro-democratic protesters. Bush also stopped sales of American weapons to China.

NOVEMBER 17, 1989 Bush signed the Fair Labor Standard Amendments, raising the minimum wage to $4.25 per hour.

NOVEMBER 21, 1989 Bush signed a new anti–drug abuse law. It provided more than $3 billion in funding for anti-drug programs, treatment facilities, education, federal prison expansion, and law enforcement.

JUNE 1, 1990 Bush and Soviet President Mikhail Gorbachev signed an arms reduction agreement. The United States promised to get rid of 25 percent of its chemical weapons, and the Soviet Union agreed to eliminate 40 percent of its stockpile.

JULY 26, 1990 Bush helped protect the rights of more than 43 million Americans by signing the Americans with Disabilities Act. This act forbids discrimination against people who have disabilities. It affects workplaces, transportation, and public accommodations. Many of the wheelchair ramps you see today exist because of the ADA. This law also helps people who are blind or have poor vision, people who are deaf or have hearing impairments, and many other individuals.

OCTOBER 22, 1990 Bush vetoed the Civil Rights Act of 1990, which would have strengthened civil rights laws. He said it would "introduce the destructive force of quotas" into the country's employment system. A year later, Bush signed a Civil Rights Act that makes it easier for employees to sue for discrimination.

NOVEMBER 29, 1990 By signing the Immigration Act of 1990, Bush allowed 700,000 immigrants a year to enter the country—a significant increase.

On October 15, 1991, Clarence Thomas was confirmed as a Supreme Court justice. During Thomas's Senate confirmation hearings, law professor Anita F. Hill accused Thomas of sexual harassment. The Senate judicial committee, led by then-Senator Joseph Biden, ignored Hill's accusations.

Anita Hill

THE PRESIDENTIAL ELECTION OF 1992

During his term, George H. W. Bush agreed to raise taxes after publicly promising not to. Republicans were not happy about this. Also, Americans in general were not happy about finding themselves back in an economic recession.

Bush ran against the Democratic governor Bill Clinton of Arkansas. Clinton's campaign boiled down to a sign that hung in its headquarters: "It's the economy, stupid." Billionaire Ross Perot also hopped into the fray. He ran as an independent, drawing support from Republicans and Democrats.

On January 20, 1993, Bill Clinton was sworn in as the forty-second president.

> **quota:** a specific limit or required amount of something.
>
> **recession:** a slowdown in the economy that can result in lost jobs. Less severe than a depression.

CHAPTER 10 VOCABULARY

abortion: a medical procedure to end a pregnancy.

Acquired Immunodeficiency Syndrome (AIDS): a disease caused by the HIV virus that attacks the human immune system, which is responsible for fighting off diseases. It is transmitted through bodily fluids.

Agent Orange: a plant-killing chemical used by the United States in the Vietnam War to remove jungle vegetation where the enemy could hide and to destroy crops they could eat.

apartheid: the legal segregation and unjust, brutal treatment of Blacks in South Africa.

delegate: a person selected to represent a group of people in a political assembly, such as a convention.

domino theory: the idea that if one country fell to communism, others would follow.

draft evaders: people who (often illegally) found ways to get out of being drafted to the U.S. army. Also called draft dodgers.

embassy: an office or residence where an ambassador representing a foreign country works.

feminism: a movement that fights for gender equality. Focuses on issues such as women's suffrage, women in the workplace, sexual violence, and more.

fundamentalist: someone who strictly follows religious traditions exactly as they are written.

hostage: a person held prisoner by an individual or group who demands that certain conditions are met before the captured person is released.

inflation: an economic term that describes a widespread increase in prices. The purchasing power of the dollar goes down and the prices of goods and services go up.

leak: to reveal a secret document to one or more media sources.

LGBTQ+: an acronym (formed from the first letter of each word) that includes people who identify as lesbian, gay, bisexual, transgender, or queer (or questioning). The plus sign indicates inclusion of people who hold other marginalized sexual or gender identities.

napalm: a chemical weapon also known as "liquid fire" used by the United States in the Vietnam War.

presidential pardon: the use of executive power to protect someone from punishment for a crime. Basically, a "Get Out of Jail Free" card.

quota: a specific limit or required amount of something.

recession: a slowdown in the economy that can result in lost jobs. Less severe than a depression.

status quo: Latin phrase meaning "the way things currently are."

trickle-down theory: the belief popularized by President Ronald Reagan that laws and policies benefiting the wealthy help everyone, as wealth will "trickle down" to those at the bottom in the form of jobs and overall prosperity.

vigil: a serious event where people come together to pray or to remember something or someone.

white flight: the mass movement of white people that took place in the 1950s, 1960s, and 1970s as they left cities to live in suburbs.

PROSPERITY AND CONFLICT

The world became more interconnected and faster thanks to the invention of the internet. Cooperation between governments increased global trade. But it wasn't a time of peace. The United States suffered terrorist attacks on its home soil and continued fighting in the Middle East. Let's take a look at how—and what—the United States was doing.

CHAPTER CONTENTS

THE PRESIDENCY OF BILL CLINTON

A WAR AGAINST CRIME, ON U.S. SOIL

SCANDAL AND IMPEACHMENT

THE GEORGE W. BUSH ERA

THE WAR ON TERROR

THE SECOND TERM OF THE BUSH PRESIDENCY

THE PRESIDENCY OF BILL CLINTON

AN ECONOMIC BOOM

During Bill Clinton's two-term presidency (from 1993 until 2001), the economy grew in leaps and bounds. Unemployment hit new lows, inflation was at its lowest in thirty years, and more people owned homes than ever before. In 2000, the Labor Department announced that the nation's business economy had grown each month for more than nine years, the longest unbroken period of growth in American history until the 2010s.

The internet became widely used for the first time, leading to an explosion of new businesses that used it to make money. Investors poured money into buying stocks in these new tech companies, hoping to get rich. (Ultimately, not all did: When many tech startups failed, people lost their money. This was the "dot-com bubble.")

Bill Clinton

CLINTON'S RECORD

Clinton had a mixed record in terms of what he got done. He tried to overhaul health care and restrict handgun sales, but he didn't have much luck in those areas. He had better success when it came to protecting the environment. He proposed policies that preserved national parks, cleaned up toxic waste dumps, and protected drinking water. He also focused on education reforms, helping low-performing schools with additional money.

WORKING WITH REPUBLICANS

In 1996, Clinton lessened the federal government's power and handed it over to the states when he signed the "Welfare to Work" bill. The bill made it more difficult for millions of people to receive benefits. But signing it made him popular with the Republicans. And he needed at least some Republicans on his side if he was going to get anything done in Congress.

He did this because in 1994, the Republicans had swept the midterm elections after signing something called the Contract with America. They promised to lower taxes and reduce the number of people on welfare. One of the contract's drafters was Newt Gingrich, a Republican congressman from Georgia, who was then elected Speaker of the House.

> **midterm elections:** congressional elections that happen halfway through a presidential term.

FOREIGN RELATIONS UNDER CLINTON

Clinton also guided the United States into two heavily criticized military conflicts. Let's take a look at those and what they did—and didn't—have in common.

THE BOSNIAN WAR

After World War II, the anti-Nazi hero and Soviet ally Josip Tito united six Slavic republics, including Bosnia, Serbia, and Croatia, into a single state: Yugoslavia. The majority of the population belonged to one of three ethnic groups. The biggest, the Bosnians, were mostly Muslim. The other two groups were Serbs, mostly Orthodox Christian, and Croats, mostly Roman Catholic.

Tito died in 1980, and the communist government crumbled in 1992. Now the Muslims and Bosnian Croats wanted Bosnia to be independent from Yugoslavia. But the Serbs did not want that to happen.

THE BOSNIAN WAR (1992–1995)

The former Yugoslav republics in the Bosnian War

WHAT HAPPENED?

The Serbs began an **ethnic cleansing** of the Muslim population. Some Serbs assaulted, murdered, and imprisoned hundreds of thousands to take control of Bosnia. Serbs drove out the surviving Muslims from their homes.

HOW DID THE UNITED STATES INTERVENE?

At first, the United States only sent peacekeeping forces. These forces are armed but do not use their weapons except in self-defense.

Other countries criticized the inaction by the United States. Why was one of the most powerful countries in the world standing by and watching as thousands of innocent people were being murdered?

With the next presidential election a year away, Clinton finally authorized military force. U.S. aircraft attacked Serbian forces in August 1995.

HOW DID THE WAR END?

The warring parties signed a peace agreement in Dayton, Ohio, on December 14, 1995. The agreement divided Bosnia into the Bosnian Croat Federation and the Bosnian Serb Federation.

ethic cleansing: the forcible relocation of one group by another because of their ethnicity or religion.

refugee: a person who has been forced to leave his or her home because of war, religion, or ethnicity.

THE RWANDAN GENOCIDE (APRIL 7–JULY 15, 1994)

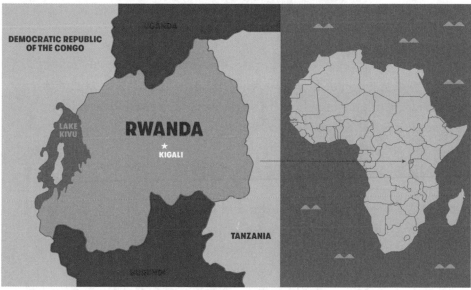

Rwanda

This African country was made up of two ethnic groups: the Tutsi and the Hutu. The Hutu were the majority. When the country became independent from Belgium in 1962, the two groups began to fight.

Many of the Tutsi had helped the Belgian colonizers, who had treated the Tutsi as an elite group. So the new Hutu-dominated government chose policies that discriminated against Tutsi people.

WHAT HAPPENED?

The Rwandan Armed Forces wanted a Hutu government. In April 1994, the armed forces began massacring the Tutsi. They killed 800,000 people in three months. More than two million people, both Hutu and Tutsi, fled the country to refugee camps.

Very reluctantly. Not until June did the United States recognize that what was happening was genocide. Even then, Clinton didn't order military action. Instead, the United States joined an international community that provided aid. The international group also put the leaders of groups that had tortured and killed on trial as war criminals.

The Rwandan Patriotic Front, made up largely of Tutsi, was able to gain control of the country. A cease-fire took effect July 31, 1994.

AN ATTACK ON IRAQ

In June 1993, Clinton ordered a missile strike on Iraq. This was punishment because Iraqi agents may have tried to assassinate former President George H. W. Bush in Kuwait that spring.

VIETNAM IS FINALLY RECOGNIZED

In July 1995, the United States extended full diplomatic recognition to Vietnam. This happened twenty-two years after the United States withdrew military forces from that country.

NAFTA: A STEP TOWARD GLOBALIZATION

In the 1990s, Mexico, Canada, and the United States traded huge amounts of goods with each other. They realized they could all benefit if they stopped taxing each other's imports. It was an important step in the globalization of the economy. The idea was that by removing trade barriers, the world's economy would become more efficient. Big corporations would manufacture wherever it was cheapest, poor countries would get more jobs, and everyone would benefit from less expensive goods.

On January 1, 1994, Clinton signed the North Atlantic Free Trade Agreement (NAFTA), along with Mexican president Carlos Salinas de Gortari and Canadian prime minister Brian Mulroney. To ease Americans' fears that they would lose manufacturing jobs to Mexico, where labor was less expensive, Clinton also passed laws to protect labor standards.

The plan didn't completely work. Business owners profited from more trade, and consumers enjoyed lower prices because of the extra competition between countries. But 700,000 U.S. workers lost their jobs when production moved to Mexico. And all a U.S. factory owner had to do was threaten workers with moving to Mexico to keep them from joining a union or refusing a pay cut.

> **genocide:** the attempt by one group to destroy another group because of its ethnicity or religion. A form of mass murder.
>
> **diplomatic recognition:** the official statement by one country that the government of another country has the right to run its economy and act internationally.
>
> **globalization:** the removal of barriers that slow the easy movement of products and services between countries.

WOMEN RISE TO KEY POSITIONS

Ruth Bader Ginsburg

A SUPREME COURT JUSTICE

In 1993, President Clinton appointed Ruth Bader Ginsburg to the Supreme Court. As an attorney, Ginsburg dedicated her career to fighting for gender equality. She continued championing these causes as a Supreme Court justice, defending Roe v. Wade, same-sex marriage, and equal pay for women. She served on the Court until her death in 2020.

AN ATTORNEY GENERAL

Also in 1993, Clinton appointed the first woman to become U.S. attorney general, Janet Reno. She served until 2001, the second-longest serving attorney general in U.S. history.

A SECRETARY OF STATE

In 1997, Clinton appointed Madeleine Albright to be his secretary of state. She was the first woman to serve in that position. Albright, whose family had come to the United States from Czechoslovakia when she was a child, was championed for the job by First Lady Hillary Clinton.

TECHNOLOGICAL BREAKTHROUGHS

THE WORLD WIDE WEB IS BORN

A British computer scientist named Tim Berners-Lee invented the World Wide Web in 1990. (Today many of us consider the World Wide Web to be "the internet.") The first text message was sent in 1992, and Amazon opened for online business in 1995. In 1998, Apple sold its first iMac computer. Because of these advances, individuals and businesses could communicate in words and images as never before—twenty-four hours a day, seven days a week.

SEND IN THE CLONES

In 1996, Scottish scientists introduced a sheep named Dolly, who was the first cloned mammal.

clone: a plant or animal that scientists have grown from one cell of its parent. The clone is an exact copy of the parent.

Dolly the sheep

A WAR AGAINST CRIME, ON U.S. SOIL

THE CRIME RATE SOARS

In 1991, the United States reached its highest reported crime rate since the government began keeping records. Around one out of seventeen people was found guilty of breaking the law. In response, Congress signed the Violent Crime Control and Law Enforcement Act in 1994.

The act set aside $6.1 billion to hire one hundred thousand more police officers and build more prisons and jails. It also cracked down on illegal immigration, limited the sale of automatic weapons, and extended the death penalty. It said anyone charged with a crime who was thirteen or older could be tried as an adult.

THE RESULTS OF PUTTING LOTS OF PEOPLE IN PRISON

These laws came at the expense of Black and Latinx Americans.

In 1993, the incarceration rate of Black people in state and federal prisons was seven times that of white people. By 1995, the incarceration of Black men had increased to ten times the rate of white men.

POLICE BRUTALITY GETS ATTENTION

Police brutality against Black people was a well-known fact of life among people of color. However, it had not gained much attention in the white media.

incarceration: putting someone in a jail or prison.

police brutality: the phrase used to describe unnecessary police violence that can include beatings, abuse, and even murder.

In 1991, a group of Los Angeles police officers severely beat a Black man named Rodney King after a high-speed car chase. A neighbor captured the beating on video and released it to a local television station. The shocking footage appeared on television around the world.

Nonetheless, three of the four officers who were charged with use of excessive force were found not guilty.

Within hours, people outraged by the verdict started protesting. In some areas, the anger soon spilled over into rioting. The 1992 Los Angeles riots, which lasted five days, killed sixty-three people and injured more than two thousand.

During the riots, protesters filled the streets and even shut down Interstate 80, a major highway.

 The Los Angeles riots have been called protests, riots, and an uprising. Why do you think these different terms might be used? Who do you think used each one?

_____

_____

_____

_____

SCANDAL AND IMPEACHMENT

In 1994, a woman named Paula Jones filed a lawsuit against Clinton. She said he had sexually harassed her when he was governor of Arkansas and then tried to make her seem untrustworthy when she told the public what he had done.

Clinton claimed presidential immunity. A judge ruled that the case wouldn't go to trial until Clinton was out of office. But an investigation into his past behavior began.

MONICA LEWINSKY

Led by prosecutor Kenneth Starr, the investigation uncovered that Clinton had conducted a romantic affair with a White House intern, Monica Lewinsky. At first Clinton denied it. But when one of Lewinsky's coworkers secretly taped her admitting to the affair, Clinton was charged with perjury and obstruction of justice.

Congress began the impeachment process in 1998. The Senate found Clinton not guilty after a five-week trial. Clinton served the rest of his three years in office.

presidential immunity: the principle that a president should be protected from private lawsuits while he or she is in office.

perjury: lying to a jury.

obstruction of justice: trying to interfere with the investigation or prosecution of a crime.

Do you think that a president's private life should be grounds for impeachment? What if the behavior is criminal?

_____

_____

_____

_____

_____

_____

The World Trade Center in Manhattan, 1990s

TERRORISM ON U.S. SOIL

Terrorism is the illegal use of force or violence to scare a country or its people to try to reach political or social goals. Beginning in 1993, the United States endured terror attacks on its own soil from some foreigners and some Americans.

terrorism: the deliberate and illegal use of force or violence to scare a country or its people to try to reach political or social goals.

radical: a person who has extreme views about politics or society that most other people don't share.

TERROR ATTACKS IN THE 1990S

THE WORLD TRADE CENTER BOMBING

ACT OF REVENGE

On February 26, 1993, a 1,200-pound bomb hidden in a truck exploded in a parking garage of the World Trade Center in downtown Manhattan. The bomb killed six people and injured more than 1,000 others. The government found out that a group of Southwest Asian radicals led by Ramzi Ahmed Yousef were behind the attack. A court convicted four of the terrorists involved.

FOR WHAT?

Ramzi Ahmed Yousef planned the bombing. He said he did it to pay back the United States for supporting Israel. Yousef disagreed with the way Israel treated the Palestinians, a group living in and around the land that became Israel in 1948. Now Palestinians live as a minority population in Israel.

OKLAHOMA CITY FEDERAL BUILDING BOMBING

ACT OF REVENGE

On April 19, 1995, a white army veteran named Timothy McVeigh blew up a truck filled with explosives in front of the Federal Building. This caused the deaths of 168 people, 19 of them children. It also injured nearly seven hundred more. Authorities executed McVeigh in 2001 for the crime. A court sent Terry Nichols, who helped plan the bombing, to prison for life. Another accomplice, Michael J. Fortier, was sentenced to 12 years in prison.

FOR WHAT?

McVeigh said he was paying back the United States for killing civilians (non-soldiers) in standoffs with the FBI. He specifically mentioned standoffs in 1992 in Ruby Ridge, Idaho, and 1993 in Waco, Texas.

ATLANTA OLYMPIC GAMES BOMBING

ACT OF REVENGE	FOR WHAT?
At 1:25 a.m. on July 27, 1996, a 40-pound pipe bomb filled with nails and screws exploded at Centennial Olympic Park during the summer Olympics. It killed two people and injured more than 100. A white man named Eric Robert Rudolph, who was also a suspect in a bombing at an abortion clinic in Alabama, was arrested. He confessed to the bombings and went to prison for life.	Rudolph said he was angry that abortion is legal.

THE GEORGE W. BUSH ERA

THE SUPREME COURT INTERVENES IN AN ELECTION

George W. Bush is the son of President George W. H. Bush and was the former Republican governor of Texas. He was elected president in 2000. He defeated Clinton's vice president, Al Gore, in a tense showdown.

Gore won the popular vote. But the winner depended on Florida's electoral college vote. The electoral college is the system by which Americans choose a president (see page 140 for more on the electoral college). Electors from each state cast votes based on how people in their state voted.

Bush and Gore face off in the 2000 election

FLORIDA DECIDES THE ELECTION

Florida was extremely close—Bush led by only 1,784 votes. That meant the rules required a recount. This time, Bush came out ahead by only 327 votes. The two candidates then argued in court over doing *another* fair and accurate recount. During the recount process, investigators realized that there were serious problems with the design of the **ballots** themselves. Therefore, it was unclear who some voters had intended to vote for.

Bush didn't want a recount, but Gore did. The Supreme Court ruled in favor of Bush. Gore formally accepted Bush's victory on December 13.

When Bush appealed to the Supreme Court, it ruled in his favor 5 to 4. The five votes came from conservative justices who got their jobs from Republican presidents. The four votes against Bush came from liberal justices who got their jobs from Democratic presidents.

Many voters in Florida used voting machines that punched holes to indicate who they intended to vote for. But some of the machines did not fully punch through the ballot paper, leading election officials to question if the votes could be counted.

VOTER SUPPRESSION IN FLORIDA

Before the election, Florida had released a list of 58,000 alleged felons who would no longer be allowed to vote. A felon is someone who has been found guilty in court of a serious crime. This decision disproportionately hurt Black voters, who were arrested and imprisoned at a higher rate than whites.

The National Association for the Advancement of Colored People (NAACP) sued Florida for violating the Voting Rights Act. Then the company that had put together the list checked it again. It found 12,000 names of people who had *never* been felons. Florida officials had wrongfully denied thousands of people the right to vote.

ALL IN THE FAMILY

George W. Bush was not just the son of a former president who shared his name. His brother, Jeb Bush, was the governor of Florida from 1999 until 2007. Jeb ran for president in 2016 but was unsuccessful.

Al Gore's father, Albert Gore, Sr., was a Tennessee senator. The elder Gore supported civil rights and opposed the Vietnam War. These liberal views got him voted out of office in 1970.

ballot: a piece of paper or electronic record that people mark their votes on.

9/11

On September 11, 2001, members of a group called al-Qaeda hijacked two large passenger jets and crashed them into the twin towers of the World Trade Center in New York City. This killed more than 2,600 people in the buildings and all 265 people who were on the planes. The terrorists hijacked a third plane and crashed it into the Pentagon, the headquarters for the U.S. Department of Defense located near Washington, D.C. They also took control of a fourth aircraft, but on that plane a group of passengers overpowered the terrorists. That plane ended up crashing in a field in Pennsylvania.

Al-Qaeda is a terrorist group that was mostly run and financed by the royal family of Saudi Arabia. Its leader was Osama bin Laden. Statements from the group said al-Qaeda was striking back at the United States for its support of Israel, its military presence in Saudi Arabia, and its direct or indirect support of the persecution of Muslims in various parts of the world.

After the twin towers of the World Trade Center collapsed, people began to call the site **Ground Zero**. This term originally described where a nuclear explosion has taken place.

One World Trade Center

In 2014, property developers built the Freedom Tower on the site. Its official name is One World Trade Center. At 1,776 feet, it is the tallest building in the Western Hemisphere. The neighboring National 9/11 Memorial has panels with the names of the 2,983 people killed in both the 1993 and 2001 World Trade Center attacks.

Ground Zero: originally used to describe the site of a nuclear blast, now also refers to the site of the terrorist attacks in New York City on 9/11.

THE WAR ON TERROR

BUSH LEADS A WAR ON TERROR AT HOME

After 9/11, the U.S. government made changes to try to prevent any possible surprise terrorist attack. These included the Patriot Act, which made it easier for the government to search and spy on both citizens and noncitizens. It also allowed for the indefinite detention of any noncitizen suspected of terrorism without charging them with a crime. Indefinite detention means being locked up without knowing when you may be released.

Many groups said the Patriot Act was too damaging to the rights of citizens and noncitizens. In 2015, Congress voted to change the Patriot Act and limit some of the powers it gave the government.

 Was Congress right to allow more spying to try to stop possible terrorist attacks? Was it fair for the government to keep noncitizens in jail for long periods without charges?

_____

_____

_____

_____

_____

_____

A PRISON AT GUANTÁNAMO

The government sent many of the people it thought were potential terrorists to Guantánamo Bay, a U.S. military prison in Cuba. There, CIA agents tortured some of them. Government officials called this torture "enhanced interrogation"—in other words, improved questioning. The

United States chose to place the prison in Cuba, where neither U.S. law nor international laws applied. This program was widely debated in the United States, as many political leaders, activists, and lawyers argued that torture was inconsistent with the values of the United States.

The government also created the Department of Homeland Security. This government agency oversees agents who are in charge of monitoring people and goods at the country's borders. The department also does anti-terrorism work.

A SURGE OF ISLAMOPHOBIA

Since the 9/11 attacks, Islamophobia has increased in the United States. In 2001, the FBI reported 481 hate crimes against Muslims and Arab Americans, compared with 28 the year before. It's important to remember that Muslims follow the teachings of a holy book called the Quran, which does *not* support violence or terrorism.

> **Islamophobia:** fear of or prejudice against Muslims, who follow the religion of Islam.

THE WAR ON TERROR ABROAD: AFGHANISTAN

The month following 9/11, the United States invaded Afghanistan. The goal was to destroy al-Qaeda and the Taliban, a fundamentalist group that was responsible for many crimes.

WHERE IS AFGHANISTAN?

AFGHANISTAN

The United States supported Afghans who were fighting the leaders of al-Qaeda and the Taliban. This part of the war lasted until 2004. That's when the first democratically elected president of Afghanistan, Hamid Karzai, took office. But the fighting between the Afghan groups continues.

As many as 2.7 million Afghans fled the country, which the war all but destroyed. Some 100,000 civilians were killed. By 2018, there were more than two thousand U.S. military deaths and more than twenty thousand injured.

A DISASTER IN SPACE

On February 1, 2003, the seven-person crew of the space shuttle *Columbia* died when the shuttle exploded as it reentered the atmosphere over Texas. This was the second major setback for the U.S. space program. In 1986, the space shuttle *Challenger* had exploded 73 seconds after takeoff, killing all seven members of its crew. Among those killed was Christa McAuliffe, a high school teacher from New Hampshire, who had been selected from more than 11,000 candidates to be the first teacher in space.

THE IRAQ WAR

In 2003, the United States went to war in Iraq. President George W. Bush said he believed that the country, under the rule of Saddam Hussein, was building up an arsenal of weapons of mass destruction.

After one month, U.S. troops had taken over the capital city of Baghdad. They did so after a bombing campaign that killed thousands of Iraqis, mostly civilians, and toppled Hussein's government. Bush posed on a U.S. aircraft carrier behind a banner that read "Mission Accomplished."

But the war would go on for seven more years and kill hundreds of thousands of people. The exact number is unclear, as the U.S. military did not keep a count of Iraqi deaths. The U.S. Department of Justice lists 4,424 deaths of U.S. soldiers and more than thirty thousand additional wounded.

DOUBTS ABOUT U.S. MOTIVATIONS

Secretary of State Condoleezza Rice was the first Black woman to hold the role. She said that the fact that Hussein had used weapons of mass destruction on his own citizens in the 1980s was proof of the weapons' existence. The United Nations was less confident and did not support the war.

Many people believed that the United States had invaded Iraq to protect its interests in the country's oil. One poll released by the Pew Research Center in 2019 reported that 64 percent of the veterans it interviewed said the Iraq war was not worth fighting. Another 58 percent felt the same about the war in Afghanistan.

weapons of mass destruction: implements of war (weapons) that can cause large numbers of deaths, such as a nuclear bomb or chemical weapons.

THE SECOND TERM OF THE BUSH PRESIDENCY

A NATURAL DISASTER: HURRICANE KATRINA

On August 29, 2005, Hurricane Katrina struck the Gulf Coast, hitting the city of New Orleans especially hard. The city gets protection from levees, which control flooding from the Mississippi River. But the hurricane broke the levees. The city was underwater.

Hurricane Katrina flooded the streets of New Orleans. Rescue boats like this one had to collect survivors from the top floors and roofs of their houses.

The state ordered residents to leave immediately. But more than 30 percent of New Orleans residents were so poor that they had no way out. As the waters rose, they had no way to get to food, water, or medicine.

Dr. Jullette Saussy, an emergency doctor and director of New Orleans Emergency Medical Services at the time, told *U.S. News,* "Imagine hearing, 'I'm in an attic with my kids. I can't swim and the water's rising. . .' and having to say things like, 'Put your baby in a shoebox and put it up high.'"

THE RESULTS OF KATRINA

The country's racial and economic divides showed in the fallout of Katrina. Of the 1,400 New Orleans residents who died, 62 percent were Black. Thousands of Black Americans were permanently displaced when the disaster destroyed their homes.

In 2020, the population of New Orleans was growing, but it was still about 100,000 people lower than it had been in 2005.

levee: a man-made wall that controls flooding from a river or other body of water.

THE END OF GEORGE W. BUSH'S TERM: HOW DID HE DO?

The second term of Bush's presidency saw rising crises that would affect the outcome of the 2008 election. These included:

- Higher oil prices caused by the ongoing war in the Middle East

- Growing concerns about the environment. These included the U.S. decision not to support the Kyoto Protocol. The

United States was one of only six countries that didn't sign it, including Afghanistan, Andorra, Southern Sudan, and Taiwan. This was a United Nations treaty designed to protect the environment. One hundred eighty other countries signed it.

• Worries about the great cost of the wars in Afghanistan and Iraq, as well as the tax cuts Bush gave to the wealthy. All of these increased the country's debts.

• A housing crisis as people signed up for mortgages they couldn't pay for.

• The worst economic collapse since the Great Depression.

How would this play out politically? Read on!

CHAPTER 11 VOCABULARY

ballot: a piece of paper or electronic record that people mark their votes on.

clone: a plant or animal that scientists have grown from one cell of its parent. The clone is an exact copy of the parent.

diplomatic recognition: the official statement by one country that the government of another country has the right to make and enforce its own laws and act internationally.

ethnic cleansing: the forcible relocation of one group by another because of their ethnicity or religion.

genocide: the attempt by one group to destroy another group because of its ethnicity or religion. A form of mass murder.

globalization: the removal of barriers that slow the easy movement of products and services between countries.

Ground Zero: originally used to describe the site of a nuclear blast, now also refers to the site of the terrorist attacks in New York City on 9/11.

incarceration: putting someone in a jail or prison.

Islamophobia: fear of or prejudice against Muslims, who follow the religion of Islam.

levee: a man-made wall that controls flooding from a river or other body of water.

midterm elections: congressional elections that happen halfway through a presidential term.

obstruction of justice: trying to interfere with the investigation or prosecution of a crime.

perjury: lying to a jury.

police brutality: the phrase used to describe unnecessary police violence that can include beatings, abuse, and even murder.

presidential immunity: the principle that a president should be protected from private lawsuits while he or she is in office.

radical: a person who has extreme views about politics or society that most other people don't share.

refugee: a person who has been forced to leave his or her home because of war, religion, or ethnicity.

terrorism: the illegal use of force or violence to scare a country or its people to try to reach political or social goals.

weapons of mass destruction: implements of war (weapons) that can cause large numbers of deaths, such as a nuclear bomb or chemical weapons.

NOTES

12 A FIRST DRAFT OF THE HISTORY OF TODAY

In 2020, Ibram X. Kendi, an American author and antiracist activist, wrote, "Americans are deeply divided—and we're deeply divided over why we're deeply divided." What led to his statement, and what does it mean for the country? Let's unpack the issues.

CHAPTER CONTENTS

THE 2008 PRESIDENTIAL ELECTION

THE OBAMA ERA

THE 2016 PRESIDENTIAL ELECTION

THE TRUMP PRESIDENCY

PANDEMIC

GUN CONTROL

THE #METOO MOVEMENT

CLIMATE CHANGE

A RACIAL DIVIDE CONTINUES

NEW LEADERS PROMISE "A TIME OF HEALING"

THE 2008 PRESIDENTIAL ELECTION

Two issues were vital to this election:

- People were tired of the ongoing, unpopular war in Iraq

- They found themselves in the midst of the worst economic crisis since the Great Depression (called the Great Recession)

The presidential candidates Barack Obama (1961–), a Democratic senator from Illinois, and Republican senator John McCain of Arizona (1936–2018), debated how to fix this mess and others.

A 2008 presidential debate between John McCain (left) and Barack Obama.

The Great Recession ended in 2009. The main reason was a federal government **bailout** of banks that had made bad business decisions. This particular bailout cost $700 billion.

The recession had severe effects. A total of 8.7 million Americans lost their jobs, and some were unemployed for long periods. Four million people lost their homes because they couldn't pay their mortgages back to the bank. And 2.5 million businesses went bust.

Obama's 2008 campaign was the first to rely heavily on the internet to gather support. (McCain used it to a lesser degree.) Four years later, when Obama won the 2012 election against Republican Mitt Romney, he was the first candidate to use social media sites, including Twitter and Facebook.

RACIST ATTACKS

Obama faced racist attacks during his campaign. People claimed he was born in Kenya and not the United States. If that had been true, it would have meant he could not serve as president, according to the Constitution. (Future President Donald Trump was one of the loudest voices spreading this conspiracy theory.) Others falsely claimed he was a practicing Muslim and stoked racist fears of Muslims. Obama's opponent, John McCain, steered clear of such attacks.

bailout: a payment to save a person or organization that's in financial trouble.

THE OBAMA ERA

In January 2009, Obama became the first Black president of the United States. He served for eight years. Here are some of the changes he made during his presidency:

- He introduced and got Congress to pass the Affordable Care Act. This law created a government program to make health insurance easier to afford for more people. Many people with preexisting health conditions (such as diabetes or asthma) and people in low-income communities were able to get health insurance for the first time. The act quickly earned the nickname Obamacare.

- The Deferred Action for Childhood Arrivals (or DACA) Act ensured that children who accompanied undocumented immigrants who entered the United States illegally were not at risk of being deported. People protected under DACA could have jobs and go to college.

- Obama signed the Dodd-Frank Wall Street Reform and Consumer Protection Act into law in 2010. This put more government controls on banks.

- Obama allowed gay and lesbian members of the U.S. military to serve openly. Since the 1990s, the official policy in the military had been "Don't Ask, Don't Tell."

undocumented immigrant: a person who is without the official papers that allow him or her to stay in the country legally.

deport: to force someone to leave a country, usually to return to the country they came from.

A couple celebrates the repeal of "Don't Ask, Don't Tell."

- He stopped allowing the torture of prisoners at Guantánamo. (See Chapter 11 if you don't remember what Guantánamo is.)

- He made rules requiring higher fuel efficiency ratings for cars and trucks, and closed toxic power plants. This meant less pollution.

- He signed the Omnibus Public Lands Management Act. This law protected two million acres of land as wilderness. It also provided billions of dollars to develop renewable energy and technology. Renewable energy comes from wind, solar power, and other power sources that don't run out.

- He created the "Race to the Top" program for schools. It let states apply for billions of dollars in competitive grants aimed at improving public education.

- He increased support of veterans. This included a $78 billion G.I. bill for tuition and tax cuts for employers who hired veterans. (You learned about an earlier G.I. bill in Chapter 9.)

Supreme Court Justices Elena Kagan (left), and Sonia Sotomayor (right).

- He chose two women, Sonia Sotomayor and Elena Kagan, for the Supreme Court. Sotomayor become the first Hispanic woman to serve on the country's highest court.

- He signed the Claims Resolution Act. This law provided $4.6 billion for a legal settlement with Black and Native American farmers whom the government had cheated out of payments for natural resources.

SAME-SEX MARRIAGE BECOMES LEGAL

Same-sex couples earned the legal right to marry in 2015 thanks to the Supreme Court decision *Obergefell v. Hodges*. The court ruled that not allowing same-sex couples to marry violated the Fourteenth Amendment. That grants citizens "equal protection under the law."

CONTINUING WARS ABROAD

Obama withdrew troops from Iraq in 2011. But the military situation in Afghanistan worsened. The Taliban's continued attacks on Afghan civilians and U.S. forces led him to send troops back to Afghanistan that same year.

In May 2011, U.S. military forces executed Osama bin Laden. He was the terrorist behind 9/11. While many Americans considered this a huge victory, al-Qaeda continued without him.

KILLED FOR BEING BLACK

There was a Black president in the White House. Many people thought it might be a time of new opportunity and achievement for Americans of color. But systemic racism continued to play out in all areas of American life. Some of the most serious examples were in interactions between Black people and law enforcement.

> systemic racism: policies and practices that exist in institutions (like laws, or the government) that result in disadvantages for certain groups—historically in the United States, people of color. Unlike overt discrimination, no individual intent is necessary.

TRAYVON MARTIN

On February 26, 2012, high school student Trayvon Martin was shot and killed by George Zimmerman in Sanford, Florida. Zimmerman, who was part of a neighborhood watch group, decided Martin was a threat. Zimmerman followed Martin and then got into a physical fight with him that ended in the 17-year-old's death.

911 recordings later showed that Zimmerman had followed and interacted with Martin even though police officers told him not to. Nonetheless, at his trial, Zimmerman claimed he acted in self-defense. A jury found him not guilty.

OBAMA JOINS THE CAUSE

Obama spoke out after the ruling. He said he identified with Martin. Obama added, "I think it's important to recognize that the African American community is looking at this issue through a set of experiences and a history that doesn't go away."

He went on to talk about his own experiences and the experiences of other Black boys and men. Others had followed them while they shopped in department stores, expecting them to steal. Some people locked their car doors when Black people walked by. And some women held their purses more tightly when Black men got onto their elevators. "Those sets of experiences inform how the African American community interprets what happened one night in Florida," he continued.

 What do you think Obama meant about Black people's experiences informing their feelings about the shooting?

_____

_____

_____

_____

_____

_____

THE BLACK LIVES MATTER MOVEMENT

Moved to action by the Martin murder, three activists named Alicia Garza, Patrisse Cullors, and Opal Tometi created the Black Lives Matter Movement (BLM). Cullors described it as "our call to action. It is a tool to reimagine a world where black people are free to exist, free to live. It is a tool for our allies to show up differently for us. . . It offers a new vision for young black girls around the world that we deserve to be fought for, that we deserve to call on local governments to show up for us."

While the Black Lives Matter Movement (BLM) has united many, some white Americans have tried to dismiss and misrepresent the movement. These Americans insist, "All lives matter." Some police unions have responded with "Blue Lives Matter." Blue refers to the color of most law enforcement officers' uniforms.

The point of BLM, its supporters argue, is not that Black lives matter *more* than others. It is that Black lives deserve to be singled out as important because of the racism and violence that Black people have suffered through history and that continue today.

#SAYHERNAME

#SayHerName is a movement intended to give voice to the Black women who have suffered brutality at the hands of the police. Activists began it after the death of Sandra Bland in July 13, 2015.

Bland was a 28-year-old Black activist from Naperville, Illinois. A police officer stopped her for failing to signal while changing lanes in Waller County, Texas. The officer then arrested her. Video evidence showed that he had used excessive force. Three days later, jail officials found her dead in her jail cell.

Between 2015 and 2020, of the 247 women shot and killed by police, 20 percent were Black, according to *The Washington Post*. Only 13 percent of the female population is Black.

THE 2016 PRESIDENTIAL ELECTION

The 2016 election pitted Donald J. Trump (1946–), a real estate developer, against former senator Hillary Rodham Clinton (1947–). After serving as First Lady in the 1990s, Clinton won election as a U.S. senator from New York. Later, Obama made her his secretary of state.

It was an ugly campaign. Trump harshly criticized Clinton for using a private email address for part of her time in office (a no-no for conducting official government business). Trump promised to "make America great again." During the campaign, he insulted women, Mexican Americans, the Muslim family of a slain American soldier, and a journalist with a physical disability.

Clinton won the popular vote, but Trump won the electoral vote. He took the oath of office on January 20, 2017.

When President Trump read something in the media he didn't like, he called it "fake news," even if the reports were true. This led more people to distrust the media and dismiss news they didn't agree with as "fake." For many Americans, Trump's message of distrust of big media companies and career politicians rang true.

THE TRUMP PRESIDENCY

Donald Trump

Once elected, President Trump focused on stopping illegal immigration, eliminating government regulations and safeguards, and cutting taxes for the wealthy. Some of the things he did in office include:

- The new president signed an executive order reversing parts of the Affordable Care Act.

- He reversed a ban on Arctic leasing in order to allow more offshore oil and gas exploration in previously protected areas.

- He signed a law that allowed some power suppliers to ignore some energy conservation standards.

- He stripped federal funding from "sanctuary cities," including New York, Seattle, and San Francisco. These were places where many undocumented immigrants could live without fear of being detained or deported.

- Trump allowed officials to separate families caught at the U.S.-Mexico border. Authorities sent undocumented immigrants seeking **asylum** in the United States to prison. Officials separated nearly 4,000 children from their parents between April 19 and May 31, 2018. As of April 2021, 445 children had not yet been reunited with their parents.

asylum: protection given to a person who is fleeing another country to escape harm.

- He ordered the creation of a task force to reduce crime, with a focus on drug trafficking, illegal immigration, and violent crime.

- He signed a bill that would provide more than $250 million a year to historically Black colleges and universities in the United States. The bill also benefits dozens of institutions that have high enrollment of Latinx and Native American students.

- Trump signed the Tax Cut and Jobs Act. This cut corporations' taxes from 35 percent to 21 percent and nearly doubled tax deductions for wealthy individuals.

- He signed the First Step Act, which supported prison reform and helping formerly imprisoned people return to society.

ANOTHER IMPEACHMENT

In December 2019, the U.S. House of Representatives impeached Trump. He became the third president in U.S. history to be impeached, after Andrew Johnson (Chapter 5) and Bill Clinton (Chapter 11).

Trump was impeached for asking Ukraine's president, Volodymyr Zelensky, to investigate Joe Biden and his family in exchange for aid money for Ukraine. Biden had recently secured the Democratic nomination to oppose Trump in the 2020 presidential election. Trump said the Bidens might have been involved in illegal deals in Ukraine for cash. Then the president delayed aid payments that were supposed to go to Ukraine until Zelensky promised to start a Biden investigation.

Trump was found not guilty by the Senate. The vote was split along party lines.

Looking for dirt on a political opponent is nothing new in politics. What made it different in this case?

_____

_____

_____

_____

_____

_____

_____

PANDEMIC

In January 2020, the first case of the novel coronavirus, or COVID-19, was diagnosed in the United States. It was a flu-like illness that doctors and scientists had never seen before. Also, it had no treatment or vaccine.

In little more than a year, more than 100 million people in the world were diagnosed with it. Some 3.8 million died, with more than 820,000 deaths in the United States as of December 2021.

A disproportionate number of Black people, Native Americans, other people of color, and poor people died from the disease. By the fall of 2020, the death rate of Black Americans from COVID-19 was two or more times higher than for whites or Asians.

COVID-19 HITS HARD

In March 2020, COVID-19 was declared a pandemic. In the United States, many schools and businesses closed.

Businesses and schools across the country shut down in-person work, but essential workers, like those who worked in supermarkets, had to continue to work in person.

At first, only "essential workers," such as bus drivers, supermarket employees, and hospital workers went to their jobs. Since these jobs put people at risk for exposure, they were hit the hardest. Restaurant workers lost jobs by the millions, as many restaurants either stopped indoor dining or shut down altogether.

> **pandemic:** occurs when a disease spreads rapidly over the entire world.
>
> **epidemic:** occurs when a disease spreads rapidly in just one part of the world.

GOVERNMENT CONFUSION

The pandemic in the United States was made much worse by the Trump administration's refusal to believe in the deadliness of the virus and to recommend that people wear masks and socially distance. Instead, the governors of each state had to decide how that state would react. In states that left restaurants open or didn't recommend certain safety precautions, the virus continued to spread quickly.

The economy went into a free fall. Millions of people lost their jobs. The unemployment rate reached 14.7 percent, the highest it had been since the Great Depression. More Americans fell into poverty than at any time since the 1930s.

DENIED A SECOND TERM

The sinking economy and the administration's mismanagement of the COVID-19 pandemic doomed the Trump campaign. In a bitterly contested election, former vice president Joe Biden (1942–) came out on top.

Biden won the popular vote by more than 7 million votes and the electoral college by a count of 306 to 232. Yet Trump refused to concede defeat, insisting, with no evidence, that the election had been "stolen" due to fraudulent voting.

A VIOLENT AND CHAOTIC ENDING

On January 6, 2021, thousands of people stormed the United States Capitol in Washington, D.C. They were supporters of Donald Trump who believed his claims that the presidency had been "stolen" from him. Trump had been encouraging supporters to "fight like hell," and the rioters wanted to stop Congress from counting the electoral votes that would officially declare Biden president. Many of them carried weapons. Shouting, "Fight for Trump!" some people attacked the security guards with steel pipes and baseball bats and sprayed them in the face with chemicals.

Rioters vandalized the building and posed for selfies. The building was eventually locked down and members of Congress evacuated, but Trump at first refused to send in the National Guard. Four citizens died, one of whom was shot by Capitol police. About 140 police officers were injured, and one was killed. It took four hours to secure the building, and only in the late afternoon did Trump tell the mob to go home, still claiming the election had been stolen from him. The next morning, Congress met to count the electoral votes and proclaimed Biden the new president.

Four of the officers who were caught in the attacks died by suicide over the next seven months. More than 600 people were charged in the insurrection.

It was the first time in the history of the United States that the transfer of power from one president to the next was not peaceful. Investigation after investigation into claims that the results of election had been altered by fraud showed these claims to be false.

In Trump's last days in office, the House of Representatives voted to impeach him a second time for incitement of insurrection. Trump was acquitted again. But this time, seven Republican senators voted to convict him. Trump is the only president to have been impeached twice.

On the following pages, you'll find a look at some of the issues that are likely to shape the history of today.

GUN CONTROL

The Second Amendment of the Constitution guarantees Americans the right to bear arms. This has become an ever-growing argument between those who want to protect the amendment and those who point out that when the Founding Fathers wrote the amendment, weapons were far less powerful.

After a 2018 mass shooting in Parkland High School, students across the country walked out of school and staged protests to advocate for stricter gun control laws.

A growing number of mass shootings continue to fuel the argument.
Here are some of them:

DECEMBER 14, 2012	After murdering his mother at their home, in Newtown, Connecticut, a twenty-year-old former student forced his way into Sandy Hook Elementary School. He opened fire, killing twenty children and six adults.
JUNE 17, 2015:	A white supremacist entered Emanuel African Methodist Episcopal Church in Charleston, South Carolina, killing nine Black worshipers. He said he targeted the church because of its history of supporting civil rights.
JUNE 12, 2016	A shooter entered Pulse, a gay nightclub in Orlando, Florida, and killed forty-nine people. He pledged allegiance to the radical Islamist terrorist group ISIS, which opposes homosexuality.
OCTOBER 1, 2017	A man opened fire at a music festival in Las Vegas, Nevada. He killed sixty people before killing himself.
FEBRUARY 14, 2018	A former student entered his old high school in Parkland, Florida, and opened fire, killing seventeen people and injuring another seventeen.

THE #METOO MOVEMENT

Activist Tarana Burke founded #MeToo in 2006. Its goal is to bring attention to the survivors of sexual assault and harassment and interrupt sexual violence.

The movement became more widespread in 2017. It became a hashtag on social media when female actors began speaking up about the sexual harassment and violence they had experienced in the entertainment industry.

Many spoke about the abuse they had suffered at the hands of a movie producer named Harvey Weinstein. Weinstein went to prison for his crimes. As many more women began speaking up and saying "#MeToo," companies fired many more predators.

SEXUAL VIOLENCE STATISTICS

Sexual violence has affected millions of Americans. Members of the LGBTQ+ community are sexually harassed more than their straight peers, and 47 percent of transgender people report being sexually assaulted. 65 percent of transgender Native Americans have survived sexual assault.

> transgender: a person whose gender identity doesn't match the gender they were assigned at birth.

According to the National Women's Law Center, Black women experience sexual harassment in their workplace at nearly three times the rate of white women. Sexual crimes are crimes of power. For this reason, the people committing them often target people who they think are powerless and unable to defend themselves.

A SUPREME COURT NOMINEE'S ME-TOO MOMENT

In 2018, President Trump nominated Brett Kavanaugh to replace Justice Anthony Kennedy, who was retiring from the Supreme Court. Professor of psychology Christine Blasey Ford wrote to the Senate Judiciary Committee. She said that Kavanaugh had sexually assaulted her when they were teenagers.

Blasey Ford testified at the Senate Confirmation hearing, along with another woman who did not publicly reveal her name but who said Kavanaugh had assaulted her, too.

The Senate still voted to confirm Kavanaugh, and he became a Supreme Court justice. But Ford's story became another important part of the #MeToo movement, which continues to support girls and women who face similar situations in public and personal spaces today. As more survivors say, "#MeToo," they gain more power.

CLIMATE CHANGE

Scientists have been concerned for decades that human activity is contributing to the gradual warming of the planet. Study after study has shown the negative effects human activities are having on the planet. For example: When people drive cars or fly in airplanes, the energy that powers those vehicles goes into the air as a gas called carbon dioxide. Carbon dioxide then gets trapped in Earth's atmosphere and heats it up.

GLOBAL WARMING

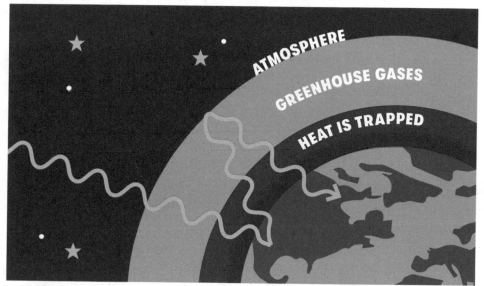

Earth's atmosphere traps what are called greenhouse gases inside. This leads to global warming and climate change.

GLOBAL WARMING

Some other things that contribute to global warming: drilling for oil and raising cattle. Believe it or not, large-scale cattle production worsens global warming because their burps and farts release methane. Methane is about 25% more powerful than carbon dioxide at trapping heat. Also, to produce a pound of steak, factory farmers have to use 2,500 gallons of water and destroy 35 pounds of topsoil due to erosion.

The atmosphere gets so hot that it melts the polar ice caps. This causes widespread flooding from rising water levels, more intense heat waves, and more instances of extreme weather, such as hurricanes. The six warmest years on record have taken place since 2014.

CLIMATE CHANGE DENIERS

Scientists have published overwhelming evidence that climate change is real. But a lot of people insist it's a hoax.

President Trump was one such climate-change denier. He wanted to supercharge the economy, and thought that helping the American fossil fuel industry was the best way to do that. So during his presidency, he reversed hundreds of regulations that had protected the environment. He also opened up millions of acres of protected lands to mining, oil exploration, and cattle farming.

In 2015, the United States and nearly 200 other countries came together to fight climate change with the Paris Agreement. Each country pledged to cut greenhouse emissions.

During Trump's presidency, the United States became the first country to withdraw from the agreement. On his first day in office, President Biden signed the document that brought the United States back into the agreement.

A RACIAL DIVIDE CONTINUES

THE MURDER OF GEORGE FLOYD

On May 25, 2020, a video surfaced of a Black man named George Floyd being forced to the ground by three police officers as they tried to arrest him for allegedly trying to pass off a fake $20 bill.

A white police officer named Derek Chauvin kneeled on Floyd's neck. He kept his knee there for more than nine minutes. Floyd continued to plead, "I can't breathe." Other officers stopped bystanders from intervening. The bystanders watched in horror as Chauvin killed Floyd by suffocating him.

Many Americans reacted with outrage to Floyd's death. People grew increasingly vocal during the summer about Black people being victims of police brutality.

BREONNA TAYLOR

These victims included Breonna Taylor, who was a 26-year-old paramedic in Kentucky. In March 2020, police broke into her house while she was sleeping, shot her, and killed her.

As a result of the case, local officials banned the use of no-knock warrants, which police were allowed to use at the time. They also fired some of the law enforcement officers involved and paid Taylor's family $12 million to settle a lawsuit. As of July 2021, no one had been charged in her death.

The Black Lives Matter street mural in Washington, D.C., painted in June 2020. Letters are so big that the mural can be seen from space.

A GROWING PROTEST MOVEMENT

The United States became the setting for a movement with numbers that had never been seen before. Across the country, hundreds of thousands of people from all different racial and ethnic backgrounds marched in support of Black Lives Matter. In Washington, D.C., Mayor Muriel Bowser authorized the painting of "Black Lives Matter" on a street leading to the White House in June 2020.

> During the ongoing protests, many held signs that said, "Defund the Police." This reflects the belief that some of the $100 billion spent each year on law enforcement would be better served going to job training, social services, and violence prevention programs.

 Do you think there are situations that might end more positively if authorities sent a social worker to respond to a distress call rather than a police officer?

_____

_____

_____

_____

_____

_____

WHITE NATIONALISTS FIGHT BACK

While masses of Americans stood up against racism, another movement was growing louder as well: white nationalism. People who believe in the supremacy of the white race shared many of President Trump's attitudes toward undocumented immigrants and Muslims.

These groups had tended to exist on the fringe, with little attention from the media. But they moved into the mainstream when the president refused to criticize their actions.

At a 2017 white supremacist rally in Charlottesville, Virginia, a white nationalist drove his car into a crowd of counter-protesters. He killed a woman named Heather Heyer and injured 35 others. President Trump responded to the act by saying there were "very fine people, on both sides."

WHITE SUPREMACIST VIOLENCE

Acts of violence by white nationalists continue to become more common—and public.

- In the summer of 2020, right-wing militia groups stormed the state capital in Michigan. Similar groups threatened to do the same in Virginia and Oregon. They protested COVID-19 restrictions and proclaimed their right to bear arms.

- In October 2020, the FBI announced that they had discovered a plot to kidnap Gretchen Whitmer, the Democratic governor of Michigan who enacted a lockdown in response to the spread of COVID-19.

- QAnon is a catchall name for a group of loosely related pro-Trump, anti-Democratic Party conspiracy theories that first appeared in 2017. QAnon promotes the view that the U.S. government is controlled by a secret group of liberals that wants to bring down Trump and his supporters.

- In December 2020, with Trump refusing to admit he had lost the election, members of the white nationalist group the Proud Boys protested Biden's victory in the nation's capital. They encouraged violence and tore down Black Lives Matter signs in front of churches.

Police responded to Black Lives Matter protestors with military force, while the white militia members in Michigan, Virginia, and Oregon were treated respectfully. After the January 6 insurrection (page 414), President-elect Biden tweeted, "No one can tell me that if it had been a group of Black Lives Matter protestors yesterday that they wouldn't have been treated very differently than the mob that stormed the Capitol."

NEW LEADERS PROMISE A "TIME OF HEALING"

Joe Biden was sworn in as the forty-sixth president of the United States on January 20, 2021. Addressing a nation dealing with a continuing pandemic, Biden described a vision of a unified country, better-paying jobs, and a fight against climate change.

Joe Biden and Kamala Harris

VICE PRESIDENT HARRIS

Biden's vice president is Kamala Harris, whose mother is Indian and whose father is Jamaican. She became not only the first female vice president but also the first vice president of South Asian descent and the first Black vice president.

During her acceptance speech, she addressed the importance of rooting out systemic racism, combating climate crisis, and unifying the country. She said: "Protecting our democracy takes struggle. It takes sacrifice. There is joy in it and there is progress. Because 'We the People' have the power to build a better future. And when our very democracy was on the ballot in this election, with the very soul of America at stake, and the world watching, you ushered in a new day for America."

 What do you think about what Harris said about democracy requiring struggle? Can you name some ways U.S. history has reflected that struggle?

_____

_____

_____

_____

_____

_____

_____

_____

LOOKING AHEAD

That's where we're going to leave off with our brief first draft of the history of today. You've learned a lot about our country's past, positive and negative. You've learned about the important truth-finding role of a historian—how history can shape people's opinions about our country and our world.

You've learned about the tools a historian uses: researching using primary and secondary sources, and keeping a sharp eye out for possible bias. Practice using these tools. They will serve you well, whatever you choose to do.

Above all, we hope you've learned that the United States was founded on ideals that are worth aiming for and protecting, even if we don't always live up to them. Learning our history will help you make this a better country!

CHAPTER 12 VOCABULARY

asylum: protection given to a person who is fleeing another country to escape harm.

bailout: a payment to save a person or organization that's in financial trouble.

deport: to force someone to leave a country, usually to return to the country they came from.

epidemic: occurs when a disease spreads rapidly in just one part of the world.

pandemic: occurs when a disease spreads rapidly over the entire world.

systemic racism: policies and practices that exist in institutions (like laws, or the government) that result in disadvantages for certain groups—historically in the United States, people of color. Unlike overt discrimination, no individual intent is necessary.

transgender: a person whose gender identity doesn't match the gender they were assigned at birth.

undocumented immigrant: a person who is without the official papers that allow him or her to stay in the country legally.

NOTES

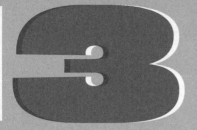

13

HOW TO THINK LIKE A HISTORIAN OUT IN THE REAL WORLD OF RESEARCH, NEWS, AND SOCIAL MEDIA

Out in the real world of research, news, and social media, information flies around at lightning speed. What's true? What's important? What's fair? Answering questions like these takes clear thinking. Read on for some lessons from historians on the art of critical thinking. It's more challenging than you'd thought!

CHAPTER CONTENTS

IMPORTANT THINGS TO KNOW (AND EMULATE) ABOUT HISTORIANS

DETECTING BIAS

EVALUATING INTERNET SOURCES

FAKE NEWS

PRIMARY SOURCES
SECONDARY SOURCES
BIAS

As you move through middle school, you're going to have the fun of working more independently. Soon, all your papers, projects, podcasts, and slideshows will be based on your own research.

The internet is a huge help. You can find out almost anything you need to know simply by typing the right words into a search engine. As of early 2021, there are about 1.8 billion websites on the internet, and more are being added by the minute.

But there are downsides to the internet, and you need to be smart about figuring out what's helpful and what's harmful. When it comes to learning the facts, you need to know how to tell the difference between what's true and what's made up.

You're not alone on the journey: one study found 70 percent of seventh graders didn't know how to tell whether they were reading a trustworthy source, or how to check if a claim was true.

> **claim:** a statement that can be proved or disproved.

GETTING SMARTER ABOUT SOURCES

Adults aren't always good at telling whether what they're reading is accurate, either. It's clear we all need to get smarter about sources. But guess who has been figuring out which sources to trust, and which ones to second-guess, even before the internet? The same people who have mastered thinking critically while they dig for the truth: historians. It's not a talent reserved for geniuses. It just takes some practice and some detective skills. You're already ahead of the game, because you've got the tools to learn to think the way they do.

IMPORTANT THINGS TO KNOW (AND EMULATE) ABOUT HISTORIANS

1. HISTORIANS ARE PERSISTENT

Historians have an extremely important job. They piece together what happened in the past and try to understand why things happened the way they did. To do this, they have to sort through many versions of events. But before they put anything out into the world about what they've discovered about the past, they need to be as sure as they can be.

You could say that historians are in the "truth profession," because they need to be as accurate and fair as they can be. It pays to care about the truth, even if you're still a student. Finding the truth can be more work, and it requires more questioning and digging. But what's the point of learning "might be true" history?

2. HISTORIANS ARE SKEPTICS

Historians don't believe everything they read, and neither should you. They know the internet is powerful but also riddled with misleading information and even lies. They check and recheck their facts. They are suspicious of one-sided accounts. They look for real stories, and they trust the words of scholars they respect. They always consider whose story might be missing and which accounts could be understated or overstated.

> **skeptic:** a person who questions the things that they read or hear.

3. HISTORIANS USE MANY KINDS OF SOURCES

Historians use lots of different sources, some of them primary and some secondary.

PRIMARY SOURCES

If you turn back to the introduction, you'll recall that primary sources are firsthand accounts of events, written by people who actually lived during the time period. Primary sources can also be images— artwork, photographs, ads, posters, films, anything made or written during a certain time period. Historians mainly use primary sources because if someone was actually there, chances are they can describe events accurately. (Or at least their version of events at the time.)

SECONDARY SOURCES

You could think of secondary sources as secondhand information, but they're still important. Just remember that some secondary sources are better than others, and that's where your thinking comes in.

Most often, historians and other experts create the best secondary sources, based on primary sources. In secondary sources (such as books, articles, and video sources), historians analyze cause and effect. They also find meaning in patterns and form theories about why things happened the way they happened.

A historian might also consult a secondary source to find out how other scholars have interpreted a time period, person, or event.

So the first step toward researching like a historian is to use multiple sources, both primary and secondary. There's just no other way to get a full picture. You know that saying, "There are always two sides to a story?" Well, when it comes to history, there can be even more than two.

ARE ALL TEXTBOOKS CREATED EQUAL?

Textbooks can be useful for an overview—the view from 30,000 feet. They cover a lot of ground and offer a big picture of history. But when you cram the whole history of the world or a country into one book, lots has to be left out.

Historically, the stories of Black people, Indigenous people, women, and poor people have been left out of textbooks. Instead, the textbook writers give space to, say, a king's marriage.

You should also know that U.S. textbooks can vary in their telling of history, depending on the publisher and the state in which the textbook is used. After a textbook is written, a panel of people from the state reviews it and might ask for certain changes. The textbook company then makes those changes to the books that students will use within that state. That's why a textbook from California, for example, might contain some details that are different from a textbook in Texas.

panel: a group of people brought together to discuss, investigate, or decide a specific issue or subject.

Vocabulary Focus: Objective vs. Subjective

We can define these words as follows:

- Something that is **objective** presents or deals with facts as they actually are, without distortion from personal feelings, prejudices, or interpretations.

- Something that is **subjective** presents facts that are colored or skewed by personal views, experiences, or beliefs.

We've already said that one big objective truth is not really a thing because a person (with a personal view) is always telling the story. That's why you consult a few different sources. But there are degrees of subjectivity, and there are also facts.

Let's use a soccer game as an example. Different people are observing different parts of the game, and they're probably rooting for one team or the other. Still, there are certain objective facts—for example, the score! Some people might not like the score, or they might want to disagree with it. But there's still a score by the end of the game. What other examples of soccer game facts can you think of?

The subjective part comes in with people's personal viewpoints—in other words, what they identify with, their background, and their beliefs. For example, if the grandfather of a midfielder on one team explained the game to you, he might carry on about his granddaughter's incredible footwork (which someone else might consider average). There's nothing wrong with the grandfather's loving viewpoint. But you shouldn't expect him to give you an objective picture of the whole game. For a more complete view, you would need to talk to lots of people, including those from the other team.

objective: an account or story that presents or deals with facts as they actually are, without distortion from personal feelings, prejudices, or interpretations.

subjective: an account or story that presents facts that are colored or skewed by personal views, experiences, or beliefs.

DETECTING BIAS

We've established that all accounts of history (or current events) will have a perspective depending on who wrote them. And this will be true for both primary and secondary sources. So you'll also need to be alert to bias, which is related to perspective, but different.

> **bias:** prejudice or slant in favor of one side of an issue over another, usually in a way considered to be unfair.

Sometimes people write biased accounts on purpose, to persuade their readers to see the subject from a certain point of view. Sometimes people have what's called unconscious bias. When someone is unconscious, they're asleep or knocked out, right? So unconscious bias means the writer might believe they are telling the full story, but they're really telling only part of it, or they are telling it through a point of view they themselves are unaware of. In a way, these writers or speakers are asleep to their own perspective!

Readers can be asleep to bias, too. They might read something and take it in as true, not realizing they are getting a slanted version of things. For example, on social media, opinions fly around, and we know they're opinions. But in some news stories, or other sources that are supposed to be unbiased, subjectivity can be harder to detect.

There are many reasons to avoid sleepy reading, writing, or speaking. Most importantly, you can get foggy about what's fact and what's opinion. Historians certainly don't settle for this type of communication, so you'll want to keep your eyes wide open. You'll need to be alert to clues that reveal bias. And your tools are here to help!

BECOMING A BIAS DETECTIVE

 Slow down and read carefully. Reread often. Be on the lookout for words that carry an opinion, express an emotion, or make a judgment.

BIAS BUZZ WORDS

best	*weak*	*radical*
worst	*sadly*	*smart*
amazing	*surprising*	*coward*
unbelievable	*shocking*	*hero*
better than	*brave*	*unfair*
terrible	*angry*	
dangerous	*fanatical*	

 As you read, ask yourself: Is this author trying to get me to feel a certain way about the topic, a person, or a group of people? Is the message trying to make me feel angry at someone? To feel sorry for someone? To admire someone?

 Is only one side being presented here? Whose perspective is missing?

CASE STUDY: CHRISTOPHER COLUMBUS

Let's try this out with a common topic in world history: Christopher Columbus.

SAMPLE 1

Read this excerpt from *The Life of Christopher Columbus*, written by John S. C. Abbott in 1875:

[Columbus] was thoughtful, studious, pensive; of a deeply religious nature; ever pondering the mystery of this our sublime earthly being... He was modest, sensitive and magnanimous. He was a natural gentleman, exceedingly courteous in his bearing, without a shade of vanity.

How do you feel about Columbus after reading this excerpt? Do you find yourself admiring him?

_____

_____

_____

_____

_____

_____

_____

Let's notice which words and phrases create these feelings:

thoughtful	sensitive
studious	magnanimous (generous)
deeply religious	natural gentleman
sublime (beautiful or excellent)	courteous (polite or respectful)
modest	

We can tell from this positive language that the author wants to present a positive image of Columbus.

Now try it with two more paragraphs about Columbus from other authors.

SAMPLE 2

Now check out this excerpt from *A Young People's History of the United States*, by Howard Zinn (2007):

Columbus's men searched Haiti for gold, with no success. They had to fill up the ships returning to Spain with something, so in 1495 they went on a great slave raid. Afterward, they picked five hundred captives to send to Spain. Two hundred of the Indians died on the voyage. The rest arrived alive in Spain and were put up for sale by a local church official. Columbus, who was full of religious talk, later wrote, "Let us in the name of the Holy Trinity go on sending all the slaves that can be sold."

Now how do you feel about Columbus? Which words contributed to those feelings?

_____

_____

_____

_____

_____

_____

SAMPLE 3

Okay, now a third excerpt, this one from a 1913 textbook by Henry Eldridge Bourne and Elbert Jay Benton:

> *As he failed to gain great riches for himself and others, [Columbus] became unpopular. Once he was taken back to Spain in chains like a common prisoner. Though his last days were saddened by misfortune, everyone now regards him as the greatest of discoverers.*

How do the authors of this passage want you to feel toward Columbus? How do you know?

_____

_____

_____

_____

_____

Let's work on separating facts from opinions in all three excerpts.

Which sentences are only facts?

_____

_____

_____

_____

_____

_____

_____

Which sentences are biased?

_____

_____

_____

_____

_____

_____

_____

_____

Do you have any theories about how the different times in which these texts were written (1875, 2007, and 1913) might affect the different biases?

_____

_____

_____

_____

_____

_____

_____

_____

_____

_____

Did you notice Abbott's and Zinn's very different perspectives on religion?

ABBOTT	ZINN
"[Columbus was] of a deeply religious nature, ever pondering the mystery of this our sublime earthly being…"	"Columbus, who was full of religious talk, later wrote, 'Let us in the name of the Holy Trinity go on sending all the slaves that can be sold.'"

Can you name the two attitudes at play here? Which words and phrases are key?

_____

_____

_____

_____

_____

_____

_____

_____

Great work! You're getting good at being a bias detective! When you can notice authors' opinions within a text, you have the power to form your own opinion.

EVALUATING INTERNET SOURCES

With more than a billion websites online and bias lurking everywhere, you can see why serious historians are careful about which sources they use. Before they even *think* about using a source, they check into it to make sure it's reliable.

What do we mean by "reliable"?

Another word for reliable is trustworthy. You probably know people who are trustworthy. Those are the people you choose as true friends, right? They're the ones who tell the truth and have your back. They are also responsible and keep their word. It's the same with sources, especially on the internet. Some you can trust, and some you can't. The challenge is to figure out which is which.

LOOK BEFORE YOU CLICK

 As soon as you type a search into your browser and press Enter, you can start deciding which links to check out and which ones to pass by. Follow these tips to avoid unreliable websites:

- **Beware of ads.** When you do an internet search, sometimes the links at the top of the search results are there because the organization paid the search engine to give them a spot at the top. Most of the time, the word "Ad" will appear in boldface before the link. The sites could be selling something or promoting an opinion, so it's best to scroll past them.

- **Examine the name of the website or URL.** When you are looking for facts, it's important to rely on experts. Usually, experts work at universities, colleges, government agencies, and major news organizations. Let's face it—not everyone is an expert.

- **Take a close look at the ending of the URL.** This ending, or suffix, can give you clues to the site's reliability. There used to be restrictions on what kind of suffixes different groups could use, but now there are only two with restrictions. Only approved universities can use .edu. Only U.S. government agencies can use .gov.

- **If you see two letters, it means it's a site from another country.** For example, .uk tells you the organization is based in the United Kingdom.

COMMON URL SUFFIXES AND WHAT THEY MEAN

URL SUFFIX	WHAT IT MEANS	EXAMPLE	WHICH GROUPS CAN USE THIS SUFFIX?	RELIABILITY FACTOR
.edu	University or college	columbia.edu	Only higher education institutions	Probably reliable
.gov	U.S. governmental agency	nasa.gov	Only U.S. governmental agencies	Probably reliable. Might have a pro-government bias.
.org	Nonprofit organization	PBS.org (public broadcasting system)	any	Usually reliable, but could be political
.com	Company	natgeo.com	any	Widely used by schools as well as companies. Use caution.

.net	member of a network (like an internet service provider)	historyforkids.net	any	Like ".com"—widely used. May or may not be reliable.

Also look carefully at the main URL name (the part before the dot). The words in the URL can sometimes give you clues. Does the name seem emotional, one-sided, or out to prove something? If so, chances are you won't find objective information there. For example, a site called www.attackallsystems.com might be coming from one side of an issue, right?

Try it out now. Which of these URLs seem to be reliable, and which would you have doubts about?

- www.factcheck.org
- www.redalertpolitics.com
- www.history.com
- www.100percentfedup.com
- www.nasa.gov/stem/forstudents

Names can be tricky. Some names might sound objective, but in fact they promote one side of politics or the interests of a certain group. For example, Aim.org (Accuracy in Media) sounds objective, but the organization describes its sites as conservative. Since they lean to one side of politics, they might be promoting a particular point of view.

Once you click on a site, check to see if there are links within it to other sources. If not, that may be a sign that the site is not reliable. Good sources usually connect to other good sources, which help you verify the information.

verify: to make sure that something is accurate or true.

WHAT IS WIKIPEDIA?

 Let's look closely at the word:

WIKI   PEDIA

A **wiki** is an internet space where people can share their knowledge on something. Sometimes wiki spaces are private to one organization. Other times they are public, meaning anyone can add to the wiki and edit it. The wiki can be updated as people discover things. One person can correct another. (The word *wiki* is Hawaiian and means "fast.")

It comes from the word **"encyclopedia,"** a collection of information about many topics. Back in the day, an encyclopedia was a collection of hardcover volumes. The topics were arranged alphabetically. So there would be a book with all the "A" topics and a "B" book and so on, filling up a bookshelf with 26 or more volumes.

Wikipedia is a public wiki that gathers information from anyone about millions of topics. Over the years, Wikipedia has sometimes gotten a bad rap. You may have been cautioned against using it. The main thing to remember, as with any source, is not to use Wikipedia *only*. The nice thing about Wikipedia is it provides many links you can follow. So it can be a good place to start—especially the Simple English version, which is easier for students to understand.

wiki: an internet space where people can share their knowledge on a given subject.

encyclopedia: an exhaustive collection of information on a wide variety of topics.

PROS AND CONS OF WIKIPEDIA

PROS	CONS
Covers millions of topics	Dense and very detailed—can be overwhelming
Contains many links you can follow for further info and that verify the information	Can contain difficult vocabulary (even the Simple English version)
Bots (automated computer programs—computer "robots") continually comb through and delete entries with suspicious features, such as all caps or dramatic punctuation.	Entries are not necessarily from scholars or experts. That's why you shouldn't cite Wikipedia as a source, but you can get sources from the links and at the end of entries.
People are constantly updating the information and monitoring the site for false information.	
Available in many languages	
The Simple English version is easier for kids and learners of English to use.	

cite: to use something as evidence for your claim.

SHORTCUTS TO RELIABLE, READABLE SOURCES

WEBSITE	DESCRIPTION
www.kidzsearch.com	Google created a search engine called **Kidzsearch** just for kids. It uses safety filters to screen the sites, and it moves educational sites up on search results. It has a Kidztube tab, a wiki tab, games, cool facts—and ads.
www.commonsense.org/education /top-picks/most-reliable-and -credible-sources-for-students	**Common Sense** was created by parents for parents, but you can use it too to find good sources.
mediabiasfactcheck.com	On **Media Bias/Fact Check**, you can enter the name of a source and find out how reliable it is based on the site runners' measures of objectivity.
simple.wikipedia.org	**Simple English Wikipedia** was created especially for students and for adults learning English. In this version of Wikipedia, the articles are easier to read.

CLICKBAIT

If you've been on the internet or social media even a little bit, you've seen clickbait. It's there to distract you, to lure you in, to make you so urgently curious that you just have to click the link. That way, the site (supported by advertisers) gets more views, which means more people see their ads. The more people click, the more money they make.

TAKING CHARGE OF YOUR ATTENTION

The creators of these links and sites are banking on your attention, so that's why they will do almost anything to get it. Justin Rosenstein, a former engineer at Facebook and Google, thinks it's gotten out of hand. He says these sites and their links are controlling people. "We're the product," he says. "Our attention is the product being sold to advertisers."

So, you need to decide: Do you want other people controlling your attention, or do you want to be in charge of it? We hope you choose the second option. To be in charge of your own attention, you need to know clickbait when you see it. Here are some common signs:

- Big, bold lettering

- Bright colors

- Over-the-top punctuation, such as !!!! and ??

- Attention-grabbing photos and GIFs that you wouldn't see in a newspaper or on the local news.

Clickbait intends to be obvious. It screams out at you, offering some secret or some amazing thing that will change your life. Does the site actually deliver what it promises? Almost never.

Common kinds of clickbait:

- Promises of money or moneymaking schemes

HERE IS THE MONEYMAKING SECRET THAT
BANKS DON'T WANT YOU TO KNOW!

- Miracle products or cures for illness

THIS PRODUCT WILL CURE A HEADACHE IN SECONDS!

- Hyped-up headlines

GIRL RESCUES MOM FROM LION ATTACK! YOU WON'T BELIEVE WHAT HAPPENS NEXT!

- How-to's that play on people's desires and emotions

FIVE EASY STEPS TO BEING THE MOST POPULAR KID IN YOUR SCHOOL—#3 WILL SHOCK YOU!

Notice how these phrases are asking you to get emotional, crave the information, and then click? When you see lures like this, think: Do I really want to take this bait?

FAKE NEWS

We hear a lot about fake news. We're going to divide fake news into two categories: Funny Fake News and Not Funny Fake News.

FUNNY FAKE NEWS

Funny fake news has been around for many years. A newspaper called *The Onion*, founded in 1988, is one example. The headlines were beyond ridiculous—and on purpose! Often, they were making fun of the real news to give people a laugh or just creating bizarre stories to entertain people. A few people did believe the stories because the newspapers looked real, and the articles were always written as though they were true. But the publisher didn't intend to fool people. The idea was to publish wild stories for the fun of it. The writers also wanted to make a point through satire, by making fun of things they observed in society. Here's an example of a headline from *The Onion* from December 2020:

> "CDC Announces Children Will Be Last to Receive Covid Vaccine because What Are Those Little Twerps Going to Do about It"

You can see how the topic is real. The vaccine was actually being rolled out at the time, and in fact children were going to be the last to get vaccinated. But the last part is meant to make people laugh. People still subscribe to *The Onion* online and enjoy its twist on current events.

> **satire:** a kind of comedy that uses irony—saying the opposite of what is really meant in order to be funny—and exaggeration to poke fun at something.

NOT-FUNNY FAKE NEWS

In recent years, people have begun to create fake news that is not intended to be funny at all, and it's a serious threat to our society. All fake news is nonsense, but it can be disguised as real news. It even sometimes contains a kernel of truth.

Fake news goes out onto the internet and tries to grab people's attention, just like clickbait. When fake news plays on people's beliefs, prejudices, or fears, they can start to believe untrue stories about political figures, events in the world, health cures, diseases, and other hot issues. Some people even believe in conspiracy theories, which tell them that individuals or groups (usually the government) are carrying out secret schemes that are dangerous to them. Sometimes the claims are outrageous, like the government is making fake snow to trick people. But it's hard to argue with someone who thinks they have discovered a secret truth. A secret truth can make the real truth seem false. In this way, conspiracy theories can turn the world upside down for those who believe in them.

Let's consider the consequences of people not knowing how to tell true information from made-up information. How will they make choices in their lives? How will they treat other people who believe something different? How will they vote?

> **conspiracy theories:** beliefs that individuals or groups (usually the government) are carrying out secret schemes that are dangerous to people.

HOW DOES A FAKE NEWS STORY SNOWBALL?

Have you ever made a snowman? You start by packing a little snow in your hands. Then you make a ball and pat on more snow. Then your friends might add more. Once the snowball is big enough, you can roll it on the ground. As it picks up more layers of snow, rolling along the ground, the snowball gets bigger and bigger and bigger.

Think about how rumors grow at your school. One friend tells another friend something, and suddenly everyone is whispering about it. Even worse, sometimes someone makes something up about someone else and then begins to spread the lie. The more people believe it, the more power the story has, even though it's not true. And if it's a gripping enough story, sometimes people don't even *care* if it's true or not—it's too good not to spread.

Fake news stories can grow on the internet like a snowball. People embrace them with the same enthusiasm as a rumor at your school, and it happens in minutes. Over the course of hours, a phony story can travel worldwide, picking up hundreds of thousands of views. This is where some people's reasoning goes wonky: They think the story is true because it's all over the place. They figure it's real because so many people know about it. Does that sound like the way historians think? Pretty much the opposite!

FAKE NEWS CASE STUDY: THE 5G HOAX

Let's look at how a false claim started out in a local newspaper article, snowballed into a big story on the internet, and resulted in people setting more than twenty cell towers on fire. (This is not fake news—the fires really happened. Go ahead and fact-check it!)

In 2019, 5G cell towers started going up around the world to provide faster mobile connections. 5G is the latest and fastest technology for mobile networks, and it's gradually replacing WiFi. Some people don't trust new technology, so there were people who didn't like 5G. (There were also people who didn't like towers and antennae going up when cell phones came into widespread use in the 1990s.)

Around the same time that 5G towers were being built near Wuhan, China, the first coronavirus cases occurred in Wuhan. Diseases don't spread through radio waves. Coronavirus and other viruses are spread only through droplets that come from human noses and mouths. However, some people decided to believe that radio waves and a virus were connected— and many, many people fell for it.

Scientists say, "Correlation is not causation." That's a fancy way of saying that just because two things happen around the same time, it doesn't mean that one caused the other.

HOW A FAKE NEWS STORY WENT VIRAL

JANUARY 22, 2020:

A doctor in Belgium told a reporter from a small local newspaper that new 5G cell towers built in Wuhan, China, could be related to the coronavirus outbreak.

HOURS LATER:

The newspaper took down the article because the claim was false and embarrassing.

But it was too late. Anti-5G groups and individuals had already quoted the article and made links to it on Facebook in Belgium and the Netherlands.

DAYS LATER:

Quotes from the article appeared on English-speaking Facebook.

Talk show hosts on YouTube started discussing the theory and got tens of thousands of views.

A FEW WEEKS LATER:

Bots (internet robots) picked up on the trend and automatically sent the theory to an even wider audience.

MARCH 2020:

Celebrities—some with more than a million followers—started to post on social media about the 5G-coronavirus conspiracy theory.

APRIL 2020:

Believers in the theory tried to destroy more than 20 cell towers in the United Kingdom, setting them on fire and posting videos on the internet. Videos of the fires went viral and spread the fake news even farther.

Many fake stories that go viral follow this pattern: from **hearsay** to websites to YouTube to bots to targets with many connections. The result is a "news" sensation that happens to be completely false.

> **hearsay:** information that you hear secondhand, which means it comes from someone who didn't directly witness an event and can't positively confirm if it's true or not.

WHY DO PEOPLE CREATE FAKE NEWS?

- To make money. The more people visit a website, the more money it brings in.

- To promote a certain idea, political party, or opinion. But often the fake news is targeted at the people who already share those beliefs. Why? Because it will spread faster.

- To turn one group of people against another group.

- To harm the reputations of people they don't like or they disagree with. If you harm someone's reputation, you make that person seem bad or untrustworthy.

- To sell products.

WHY DO PEOPLE BELIEVE FAKE NEWS?

- It confirms what they already believed.

- They are afraid of something they can't control (such as coronavirus) and they like the certainty the fake news provides (even if it's unproven).

- It's exciting! They feel like they're in on a secret.

- They feel part of a group that believes it.

- Their friends or relatives send it to them, and they trust those people.

- They don't trust the government.

- They don't know how to fact-check.

> **fact-check:** A fact-check is just what it sounds like; it means investigating and checking to make sure your facts or the facts that someone else is presenting are accurate.

GETTING REAL ABOUT FAKE NEWS

Anyone can fall for a fake news story. Usually, it's for one of two reasons. One, it fools people whose own biases make them too eager to agree with or believe a story. Second, fake news fools people who read it without thinking critically. The good news is that anyone can get better at spotting and avoiding fake news. You can start now!

TIPS FOR SPOTTING FAKE NEWS

If something makes you suspicious—whether it's big lettering or a claim that doesn't sound right—slow down and think.

Let your own knowledge ground you. Trust your common sense. If something seems outrageous, silly, exaggerated, or impossible, it probably is!

Do some digging to see if it's true.

- Check out the author of the story or post. Is the person knowledgeable on the subject? Do they work for an organization that studies the subject in an objective or fair way, like a university, research group, or government agency? (If the story or post doesn't name the author, that could be a clue, too.)

- Consult reliable sources (review pages 444–449) to see if those sources give the same information. This is called cross-checking, and it's vital if you have any doubts.

- Consult one of these fact-checking sites. They may have already checked the facts for you.

  - apnews.com/hub/not-real-news

  - mediabiasfactcheck.com

  - www.politifact.com/

  - www.factcheck.org/

  - www.washingtonpost.com/blogs/fact-checker/

  - www.snopes.com/

  - truthbetold.news/category/fact-checks

 Look for signs of bias or one perspective (look back at the definition of *bias* on page 436 if you need to).

WHAT'S AHEAD?

Some experts warn that the fake news problem will get worse before it gets better. Around the world, people are growing more stubborn in their opinions and more untrusting of those who disagree with them. Technology continues to evolve, which will always bring new challenges.

You may have seen some deepfake videos. The term "deepfake" is used for clips where it looks like someone is saying or doing something they never said or did. This is possible because of new apps that can imitate the appearance of a person and then literally put words in their mouth—as well as place them where they've never been, acting in ways they never have. It's easy to believe what you're seeing, even though it's not real. You'll need to be on the lookout from here on. Use our tools to evaluate sources, detect bias, and filter out fake news.

CHAPTER VOCABULARY

bias: prejudice or slant in favor of one side of an issue over another, usually in a way considered to be unfair.

cite: to use something as evidence for your claim.

claim: a statement that can be proved or disproved.

conspiracy theories: beliefs that individuals or groups (usually the government) are carrying out secret schemes that are dangerous to people.

deepfake: video that is digitally altered so that someone appears to be doing something they didn't say or do. Often used to spread false information.

encyclopedia: a collection of authoritative information about many topics.

fact-check: just what it sounds like: investigating and checking to make sure your facts or the facts that someone else is presenting are accurate.

hearsay: information that you hear secondhand, which means it comes from someone who didn't directly witness an event and can't positively confirm if it's true or not.

objective: an account or story that presents or deals with facts as they actually are, without distortion from personal feelings, prejudices, or interpretations.

panel: a group of people brought together to discuss, investigate, or decide a specific issue or subject.

satire: a kind of comedy that uses irony and exaggeration to poke fun at something.

skeptic: a person who questions the things that they read or hear.

subjective: an account or story that presents facts that are colored or skewed by personal views, experiences, or beliefs.

verify: to make sure that something is accurate or true. You might already recognize this word from Instagram or TikTok, where accounts can request to be verified, or proven authentic.

wiki: an internet space where people can share their knowledge on a given subject.

★★ BONUS SECTION ★★

THE DECLARATION OF INDEPENDENCE
TRANSLATED INTO PLAIN ENGLISH

THE WORLD'S MOST FAMOUS BREAKUP LETTER

The Declaration of Independence was a breakup letter. In the old days, it was common for a man to use a letter to let a woman know that he no longer wanted to "court" her. Nowadays, a man or a woman might do this in person or over the phone or by text message (though breaking up by text is not recommended!). But in the Declaration of Independence, the Founding Fathers made it clear to King George III of Britain that they were no longer interested in his, uh, attention—let alone his taxes and his laws.

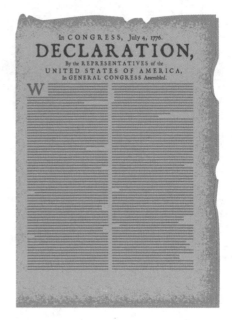

Of course, the document served multiple purposes. In addition to "breaking up" with Great Britain, the colonies also announced themselves to the world as the independent United States of America and declared for themselves all the "powers of the earth" that all established nations possessed.

THE FOUR PARTS OF THE DECLARATION

The Declaration has four sections.

THE PREAMBLE

The preamble identifies why the Founders created the Declaration. Mainly, they wanted to let the world know that thirteen North American colonies had become one united nation, with all the rights and powers of nations. Basically, this means that the American Revolution was not a civil war within Britain. Instead, it was a war between two nations. This was important because it would allow the United States to receive aid and make alliances with other countries.

THE DECLARATION OF RIGHTS

The declaration of rights provides the document's most enduring statements. Here is where the Founders declared that "all men are created equal" and that "they are endowed by their Creator with certain unalienable Rights, that among these are Life, Liberty and the pursuit of Happiness." These words have influenced and inspired generations of thinkers, activists, and politicians across the globe.

THE LIST OF GRIEVANCES

The list of grievances outlines colonial complaints against King George III. Although the document is biased, since it provides only one group's point of view, the grievances have their roots in the colonial complaints of the previous decade.

Two of the biggest complaints were "no taxation without representation," which is no doubt pretty familiar to you at this point. The other, to put an end to the "quartering of soldiers," may be less so.

Before the revolution, the British military made colonists open their homes to provide shelter for British soldiers—to "quarter" them. The colonists, understandably, wanted no part of that. That's why quartering is a major complaint on the list of grievances.

A PLEDGE OF UNITY

Lastly, the colonists "mutually pledge to each other our Lives, our Fortunes, and our sacred Honor" in declaring their independence from Britain.

THE TRANSLATION

Let's go through the Declaration of Independence phrase by phrase. That way, you'll be able to read the original language while also understanding what the document means in the plain English of today.

In Congress, July 4, 1776

TRANSLATION	NOTES
In Congress, July 4, 1776	As you read, remember that this is a breakup letter.

The unanimous Declaration of the thirteen united States of America.

TRANSLATION	NOTES
All thirteen united States of America agree with the ideas in this document.	The words "unanimous" and "united" are important because the colonists didn't have a history of working together for a common cause. They had tried to work together during the French and Indian War. But leaders rejected a plan Benjamin Franklin put forward to do this.

When in the Course of human events it becomes necessary for one people to dissolve the political bands which have connected them with another,

TRANSLATION

When it is necessary to break up with your nation

and to assume among the powers of the earth, the separate and equal station to which the Laws of Nature and of Nature's God entitle them,

TRANSLATION

and create a new nation,

a decent respect to the opinions of mankind requires that they should declare the causes which impel them to the separation.

TRANSLATION

You need to explain why you want to break up.

We hold these truths to be self-evident, that all men are created equal, that they are endowed by their Creator with certain unalienable Rights, that among these are Life, Liberty and the pursuit of Happiness.

TRANSLATION

It's obvious that all men are created equal, and that God has given them the rights to life, freedom, and the chance to look for happiness.

NOTES

For the Founders, "all men" meant all white men. They (and the British government) understood the hypocrisy of a nation of slaveowners stating that "all men are created equal." Importantly, though, this phrase allowed for all men and women to later claim political equality in the United States.

That to secure these rights, Governments are instituted among Men, deriving their just powers from the consent of the governed, That whenever any Form of Government becomes destructive of these ends, it is the Right of the People to alter or to abolish it, and to institute new Government, laying its foundation on such principles and organizing its powers in such form, as to them shall seem most likely to effect their Safety and Happiness.

To guarantee the rights of life, liberty, and the pursuit of happiness, men create a government. But that government has to have the permission of the people to govern. When the government ignores peoples' rights, the people have the right to put an end to that government and create a new one that will guarantee those rights.

The government has to have the consent of the governed? What's next, carriages that can drive without horses?

Prudence, indeed, will dictate that Governments long established should not be changed for light and transient causes; and accordingly all experience hath shewn, that mankind are more disposed to suffer, while evils are sufferable, than to right themselves by abolishing the forms to which they are accustomed.

People should think carefully before changing their government. Historically, we know that people generally prefer to suffer rather than take the revolutionary step of rebellion.

But when a long train of abuses and usurpations, pursuing invariably the same Object evinces a design to reduce them under absolute Despotism, it is their right, it is their duty, to throw off such Government, and to provide new Guards for their future security.

When, time after time, the government continues to abuse and oppress the people, it is the right and duty of the people to overthrow the government and create a new one that will protect their rights.

Are you starting to see a theme here? Creating a new government is difficult but sometimes necessary.

Such has been the patient sufferance of these Colonies; and such is now the necessity which constrains them to alter their former Systems of Government.

We, the American colonies, now find ourselves in this sad condition. Things are so bad, we're going to change the way we govern ourselves.

The history of the present King of Great Britain is a history of repeated injuries and usurpations, all having in direct object the establishment of an absolute Tyranny over these States.

TRANSLATION	NOTES
King George III has repeatedly injured us and has become an absolute tyrant. (A *tyrant* is a harsh ruler with total power.)	The authors of the Declaration of Independence blame the king for certain actions taken by Parliament, not by the king himself. It is easier to get people to see one person (the king) as being evil than it is to get people to believe an entire group of people (Parliament) are evil.

To prove this, let Facts be submitted to a candid world.

TRANSLATION	NOTES
Following are the facts that prove this history of abuse.	Some of these "facts" are really opinions. The Declaration of Independence itself is a piece of persuasive writing, designed to create support for the cause of independence.

He has refused his Assent to Laws, the most wholesome and necessary for the public good. He has forbidden his Governors to pass Laws of immediate and pressing importance, unless suspended in their operation till his Assent should be obtained; and when so suspended, he has utterly neglected to attend to them. He has refused to pass other Laws for the accommodation of large districts of people, unless those people would relinquish the right of Representation in the Legislature, a right inestimable to them and formidable to tyrants only.

TRANSLATION

The king has refused to allow our local legislatures to pass laws that are necessary for our peace, happiness, and wealth without his personal agreement. These actions prove that he is a tyrant.

He has called together legislative bodies at places unusual, uncomfortable, and distant from the depository of their public Records, for the sole purpose of fatiguing them into compliance with his measures.

TRANSLATION

The king has forced our lawmakers to meet at inconvenient places in the hopes that they won't be able to attend. This has limited our ability to govern our local affairs.

He has dissolved Representative Houses repeatedly, for opposing with manly firmness his invasions on the rights of the people.

TRANSLATION

The king has ended our legislative meetings when we complained about the violations of our natural rights.

He has refused for a long time, after such dissolutions, to cause others to be elected; whereby the Legislative powers, incapable of Annihilation, have returned to the People at large for their exercise; the State remaining in the mean time exposed to all the dangers of invasion from without, and convulsions within.

TRANSLATION

By refusing local self-government in which we can freely elect our leaders, the king has planted opportunities for conflict both from inside the colonies and from outside powers.

He has endeavoured to prevent the population of these States; for that purpose obstructing the Laws for Naturalization of Foreigners; refusing to pass others to encourage their migrations hither, and raising the conditions of new Appropriations of Lands.

TRANSLATION	NOTES
The king has tried to control our population through immigration laws as well as laws that stop us from expanding into new territory.	Here, the document most likely refers to colonial objections concerning the Proclamation of 1763 and the Quebec Act of 1774.

He has obstructed the Administration of Justice, by refusing his Assent to Laws for establishing Judiciary powers. He has made Judges dependent on his Will alone, for the tenure of their offices, and the amount and payment of their salaries.

TRANSLATION	NOTES
The king completely controls the judges.	If the king controls the judges, then the colonists can't really govern themselves.

He has erected a multitude of New Offices, and sent hither swarms of Officers to harass our people, and eat out their substance.

The king has created new governmental positions. The officers in these positions harass us, politically and economically.

He has kept among us, in times of peace, Standing Armies without the Consent of our legislatures. He has affected to render the Military independent of and superior to the Civil power.

Against our wishes, the king has sent soldiers to America to watch over us. He is making his military stronger than our officials.	A standing army is one that the government pays and maintains in peacetime. Historically, English-speaking peoples like the colonists had feared having standing armies during "times of peace." They saw them as the instruments of a dictator.

He has combined with others to subject us to a jurisdiction foreign to our constitution, and unacknowledged by our laws; giving his Assent to their Acts of pretended Legislation:

The king has refused our local laws in favor of the arbitrary laws of people in Parliament who have never visited the United States.	Take *that*, people in the British Parliament!

For Quartering large bodies of armed troops among us: For protecting them, by a mock Trial, from punishment for any Murders which they should commit on the Inhabitants of these States:

TRANSLATION	NOTES
The king has forced us to provide housing for soldiers whose presence in America we do not approve. Also, the king protects them when they break the law—even if they commit murder.	Imagine having a soldier from another country staying in your home whether you like it or not!

For cutting off our Trade with all parts of the world:
For imposing Taxes on us without our Consent:

TRANSLATION	NOTES
The king has limited our trading rights. He has also taxed us without providing us the required representation.	The English people demanded and got the right of "no taxation without representation" in 1215, with the signing of the Magna Carta (Great Charter).

For depriving us in many cases, of the benefits of Trial by Jury:
For transporting us beyond Seas to be tried
for pretended offences

TRANSLATION	NOTES
The king has at times deprived the colonists of trial by jury. Instead, sometimes accused colonists get shipped to Britain to be tried by British courts.	It's hard to have a fair trial when you're thousands of miles from where the "crime" supposedly happened!

For abolishing the free System of English Laws in a neighbouring Province, establishing therein an Arbitrary government, and enlarging its Boundaries so as to render it at once an example and fit instrument for introducing the same absolute rule into these Colonies: For taking away our Charters, abolishing our most valuable Laws, and altering fundamentally the Forms of our Governments: For suspending our own Legislatures, and declaring themselves invested with power to legislate for us in all cases whatsoever.

The king has removed local leaders and assemblies and replaced them with men loyal only to Britain. Moreover, the laws they pass do not represent our best interests. Lastly, the king has destroyed our charters (local constitutions).

Some of these complaints relate to the Quebec Act of 1774; others to the Intolerable (or Coercive) Acts of 1774, which were England's response to the Boston Tea Party of 1773. These punishments only applied to Massachusetts, but others thought: if the English could strip away the rights of those in Massachusetts, what's to prevent them from doing the same to us?

He has abdicated Government here, by declaring us out of his Protection and waging War against us.

He has plundered our seas, ravaged our Coasts, burnt our towns, and destroyed the lives of our people. He is at this time transporting large Armies of foreign Mercenaries to compleat the works of death, desolation and tyranny, already begun with circumstances of Cruelty & perfidy scarcely paralleled in the most barbarous ages, and totally unworthy the Head of a civilized nation.

The king has ended government in the colonies and started a war against us. He has attacked our coastal cities and burned our towns and now he is bringing foreign mercenaries (hired soldiers) to complete our ruin. Such behaviors are unworthy of a civilized leader.

The authors discuss the king's official reaction to the fighting at Lexington and Concord in April 1775. Also, the authors refer to British attacks on merchant vessels in the waters off of Rhode Island and Massachusetts.

He has constrained our fellow Citizens taken Captive on the high Seas to bear Arms against their Country, to become the executioners of their friends and Brethren, or to fall themselves by their Hands.

The king has kidnapped American sailors and forced them to wage war against us.

He has excited domestic insurrections amongst us, and has endeavoured to bring on the inhabitants of our frontiers, the merciless Indian Savages, whose known rule of warfare, is an undistinguished destruction of all ages, sexes and conditions.

TRANSLATION	NOTES
He has encouraged loyalists, Native Americans, and enslaved people to rise in arms against us in an uncivilized manner.	Notice anything about the Founders' attitude toward Native Americans here?

In every stage of these Oppressions We have Petitioned for Redress in the most humble terms: Our repeated Petitions have been answered only by repeated injury.

TRANSLATION	NOTES
For years, we have humbly asked the king to reconsider his actions, but he responds with more injuries.	In truth, the colonial reactions to the Stamp Act and Tea Act were anything but humble. The colonists destroyed public and private buildings, tarred and feathered government officials, and destroyed tea.

A Prince whose character is thus marked by every act which may define a Tyrant, is unfit to be the ruler of a free people.

TRANSLATION	NOTES
Simply put, the king is not worthy of us.	Take that, King!

Nor have We been wanting in attentions to our British brethren. We have warned them from time to time of attempts by their legislature to extend an unwarrantable jurisdiction over us. We have reminded them of the circumstances of our emigration and settlement here. We have appealed to their native justice and magnanimity, and we have conjured them by the ties of our common kindred to disavow these usurpations, which, would inevitably interrupt our connections and correspondence.

TRANSLATION

In addition to our asking the king to reconsider his actions, we have asked our brothers in Great Britain to help. We have reminded them that we are brothers and that the king's behavior can hurt our relationship as well.

They too have been deaf to the voice of justice and of consanguinity. We must, therefore, acquiesce in the necessity, which denounces our Separation, and hold them, as we hold the rest of mankind, Enemies in War, in Peace Friends.

TRANSLATION

Their refusal to help convinces us of our need to declare our independence even though feelings of affection remain.

We, therefore, the Representatives of the united States of America, in General Congress, Assembled, appealing to the Supreme Judge of the world for the rectitude of our intentions, do, in the Name, and by Authority of the good People of these Colonies, solemnly publish and declare, That these United Colonies are, and of Right ought to be Free and Independent States; that they are Absolved from all Allegiance to the British Crown, and that all political connection between them and the State of Great Britain, is and ought to be totally dissolved;

TRANSLATION	NOTES
Accordingly, with the approval of the people, we, the representatives of the United States, declare our independence from Great Britain.	This statement was mostly wishful thinking. The majority of Americans opposed independence at this time.

and that as Free and Independent States, they have full Power to levy War, conclude Peace, contract Alliances, establish Commerce, and to do all other Acts and Things which Independent States may of right do. And for the support of this Declaration, with a firm reliance on the protection of divine Providence, we mutually pledge to each other our Lives, our Fortunes and our sacred Honor.

TRANSLATION	NOTES
As independent states, we have the powers that all free countries possess, including the right to wage war and trade with other nations. Lastly, we—the representatives signing this document—pledge our lives to each other.	Note that they do not call themselves one independent nation but rather a collection of independent states. The United States really became united thanks to the Constitution rather than this Declaration. But the tension between individual states' rights and centralized federal power continues to play out today.

SOME BACKGROUND

THOMAS JEFFERSON, COPYCAT

Jefferson's masterpiece was no original text. In fact, if it had been a term paper, Jefferson would likely have been accused of cheating. More than anything, Jefferson just restated colonial thoughts and attitudes. These had been strongly influenced by the English philosopher John Locke's theory that all men were entitled to "life, liberty, and property." Do you see how Jefferson borrowed that phrase?

But that's how Jefferson wanted it. He said it was meant "to be an expression of the American mind." Of course, the document wasn't his alone. Benjamin Franklin helped, as did John Adams. And before its publishing, much of the Continental Congress took a stab at editing it. These edits, led by Adams, Franklin, and others, greatly improved Jefferson's original draft.

This group—the Founders—were all white men. Of the fifty-six, most were plantation owners, lawyers, and merchants. Two of them would become presidents of the United States—John Adams (number 2) and Thomas Jefferson (number 3). In fact, Adams and Jefferson died on the same day in 1826—on the fiftieth anniversary of the Declaration.

By the time the Declaration was written and signed, the American Revolution had already been underway for more than a year. Yet the Founders still had not declared their independence. They debated for months before they reluctantly took that fateful step. Ultimately, they realized that they were already actually at war and that King George III refused to negotiate with those "rebels."

But the document was really just one of three documents that made the United States. . . well, the United States. As part of the debate over independence, the Founders realized that they needed to do two more things. First, they needed a system for making alliances with other nations. This would allow them to trade freely with nations like France. This alliance system would also allow nations to come to their defense in the war against Great Britain. They also understood the need to create a system of government with which to govern their newly unified thirteen states.

Those two other primary founding documents—the Articles of Confederation and the Constitution—are discussed in Chapter 2. We're digging into the specifics of the Declaration of Independence because it so effectively expresses the ideals on which the United States was founded.

INSPIRATION AND OPPORTUNITY

The Declaration of Independence was mainly a particularly nasty breakup letter. But along the way, Jefferson and the rest of the founding crew managed to express what were then new ideas about individual freedom and natural rights. Although these ideas only applied to white men at the time, the very inclusion of the phrase "all men are created equal" created an opportunity for future generations of Americans to redefine their government. Black Americans used it to help bring about the abolition of slavery, the rights of citizenship, and the right to vote. Women used it to achieve the right to vote. The LGBTQ+ community has used it to begin the process of achieving equal rights. And that's just to name a few. Moreover, it is this part of the Declaration that endures, and the part that the United States, and the world, aspires to achieve.

U.S. PRESIDENTS

#	PRESIDENT	DATE
1.	George Washington	(1789–1797)
2.	John Adams	(1797–1801)
3.	Thomas Jefferson	(1801–1809)
4.	James Madison	(1809–1817)
5.	James Monroe	(1817–1825)
6.	John Quincy Adams	(1825–1829)
7.	Andrew Jackson	(1829–1837)
8.	Martin Van Buren	(1837–1841)
9.	William Henry Harrison	(1841–1841)*
10.	John Tyler	(1841–1845)
11.	James K. Polk	(1845–1849)
12.	Zachary Taylor	(1849–1850)*
13.	Millard Fillmore	(1850–1853)
14.	Franklin Pierce	(1853–1857)
15.	James Buchanan	(1857–1861)
16.	Abraham Lincoln	(1861–1865)*

17.	Andrew Johnson	(1865–1869)^
18.	Ulysses S. Grant	(1869–1877)
19.	Rutherford B. Hayes	(1877–1881)
20.	James A. Garfield	(1881–1881)*
21.	Chester A. Arthur	(1881–1885)
22.	Grover Cleveland	(1885–1889)
23.	Benjamin Harrison	(1889–1893)
24.	Grover Cleveland	(1893–1897)
25.	William McKinley	(1897–1901)*
26.	Theodore Roosevelt	(1901–1909)
27.	William Howard Taft	(1909–1913)
28.	Woodrow Wilson	(1913–1921)
29.	Warren G. Harding	(1921–1923)*
30.	Calvin Coolidge	(1923–1929)
31.	Herbert Hoover	(1929–1933)
32.	Franklin D. Roosevelt	(1933–1945)*
33.	Harry S. Truman	(1945–1953)
34.	Dwight D. Eisenhower	(1953–1961)
35.	John F. Kennedy	(1961–1963)*

36.	Lyndon B. Johnson	(1963–1969)
37.	Richard Nixon	(1969–1974)
38.	Gerald Ford	(1974–1977)
39.	Jimmy Carter	(1977–1981)
40.	Ronald Reagan	(1981–1989)
41.	George H. W. Bush	(1989–1993)
42.	Bill Clinton	(1993–2001)^
43.	George W. Bush	(2001–2009)
44.	Barack Obama	(2009–2017)
45.	Donald Trump	(2017–2021)^
46.	Joe Biden	(2021–)

*died in office
^impeached (but not convicted)

IT'S A FAMILY MATTER!

There have been three pairs of presidents who are direct relations to each other:

- John Adams is the father of John Quincy Adams.
- William Henry Harrison is the grandfather of Benjamin Harrison.
- George H. W. Bush is the father of George W. Bush.

TEXT CREDITS

Page 289: Shigeko Matsumoto, as told to Haruka Sakaguchi for the documentary project "1945," by Haruka Sakaguchi.

Page 314: Pauli Murray, "The Liberation of Black Women," published in *Voices of the New Feminism*, 1970, Beacon Press.

Page 399: Copyright © 2022 by Ibram X. Kendi.

Page 439: Howard Zinn, excerpt from A Young People's History of the United States: Columbus to the War on Terror, adapted by Rebecca Stefoff. Copyright © 2007, 2009 by Howard Zinn. Reprinted with the permission of The Permissions Company, LLC on behalf of Seven Stories Press, sevenstories.com.

ABOUT THE CREATORS

Rebecca Ascher-Walsh has written for media outlets including *The L.A. Times, Entertainment Weekly, The Wall Street Journal, and Travel & Leisure*, and is the author of four books for National Geographic, including *Devoted: 38 Extraordinary Tales of Love, Loyalty, and Life with Dogs*. She lives in New York City with her husband and twin seventh-grade daughters.

Annie Scavelli is the Humanities Department chair and a history teacher at the Institute for Collaborative Education in Manhattan. She earned a master's degree in education from Teachers College of Columbia University and a bachelor's degree in anthropology from Johns Hopkins University. She currently lives in New York City.

Sideshow Media is a print and digital book developer specializing in illustrated publications with compelling content and visual flair. Since 2000, Sideshow has collaborated with trade publishers, institutions, magazines, and private clients to deliver well-crafted books on a wide variety of subjects. Sideshow excels at making complicated subjects accessible and interesting to young readers and adults alike. Visit www.sideshowbooks.com.

Carpenter Collective is a graphic design and branding studio led by partners Jessica and Tad Carpenter. They focus on bringing powerful messages to life through branding, packaging, illustration, and design. They have worked with clients ranging from Target, Coca-Cola, and Macy's, to Warby Parker, Adobe, and MTV, among many others. They've earned a national reputation for creating powerful brand experiences and unique visual storytelling with a whimsical wink. See more of their work at carpentercollective.com.